24 (11-91) 55

WITHDRAWN

RIPON COLLEGE
A HISTORY

Robert Ashley
George H. Miller

RIPON COLLEGE PRESS
RIPON, WISCONSIN
MCMXC

Printed in the United States of America by

RIPON COMMUNITY PRINTERS
RIPON, WISCONSIN

TABLE OF CONTENTS

FOREWORD

Shortly after his early retirement in 1981, George Miller began a detailed, scholarly, fully documented history of Ripon College set in the context of American higher education. Miller's intent was to provide a background study for faculty, administrators, and trustees. Subsequently, the administration decided that the College also needed a shorter, less detailed, less scholarly, and more "popular" history. Unlike the "archives" version, this "history" would be available for purchase by all segments of the college community; it could also be used as a gift for donors.

The task of producing the revision was assigned to Miller and his fellow Emeritus Professor Robert Ashley. Miller is primarily responsible for the years 1851-54 (when President Kuebler resigned); Ashley, for 1955-85 (the Pinkham and Adams administrations). However, the end product is very definitely a collaboration. In the short version, notes and other scholarly apparatus, as well as national historical references, have been kept to a minimum. Similarly, no attempt has been made to provide an exhaustive index. Anyone wanting the complete story, fully annotated, should consult the Ripon College Archives.

Strictly speaking, this history ends with President Adams' departure from the campus in the winter of 1985, but occasionally goes beyond that date in order to complete narrative sequences. For obvious reasons, no attempt is made to evaluate the Stott administration, but a brief progress report is appended.

Thanks are due to Loren J. Boone, Director of College Relations; Kenneth Cartier, Vice President for Finance; Joan Eick, Secretary to the Vice President and Dean of Faculty; Valerie Krueger, Secretary to the Vice President for Finance; Douglas Northrop, Vice President and Dean of Faculty; and Bonnie J. Wolff, Secretary in the Office of College Relations.

CHAPTER I

IN THE BEGINNING:
THE LYCEUM OF RIPON

Whatever motives there may have been, one great one inspired them all—the pioneers were bound to show their respect for education.

Jehdeiah Bowen

During a gentle snowstorm in the early spring of 1851, "two grim, determined men"[1] climbed the hill overlooking the village of Ripon. Into the possibly still half-frozen ground, they pounded some stakes outlining the first building of what was eventually to become Ripon College. So says Tradition, although Tradition is not certain how hard it was snowing (or even if it was snowing at all) and whether there were two or three men present. Nevertheless, by the time of this alleged incident, plans were well under way for establishing an educational institution in Ripon. On November 23, 1850, at least 15 citizens attended a meeting at the American House on the site of the present city hall to form "a corporation for mental improvement and the promotion of education" to be known as the Lyceum of Ripon.[2] Normally, a lyceum is not a school or college but an organization which sponsors lectures, discussions, and debates on public issues of interest to the community. However, the Lyceum elected nine directors and authorized them "to contract for the erection of a building . . . to be used for the purpose of education." Furthermore, within two months the directors had obtained a charter for a "college," so it seems reasonably clear that from the start the intent had been to establish a school of some sort.[3]

The nine elected directors were David P. Mapes

(president), Alvan E. Bovay (secretary), E. L. Northrup (treasurer), Warren Chase, Jehdeiah Bowen, John Scott Horner, Asa Kinney, Almon Osborn, and Edwin Lockwood. Some of these names still echo on the campus: Bovay, Mapes, and Scott are *residence halls* (although Scott Hall was named after a later personage); Northrup and Bowen have remote descendants on the faculty (Douglas Northrop, Professor of English and Dean of Faculty, and John Bowen, Professor of Economics); and Bowen's Woods is located between Scott and Johnson Halls. Mapes and Bovay were the principle "stakers"; they were not the only remarkable men among the nine directors. Nor was the village itself then and in the near future just an ordinary midwestern pioneer community. The earliest settlers had established an experimental communistic society, however short-lived. The village has a valid claim to be called the birthplace of the Republican Party. Both the College and the community played crucial roles in the famed Booth War (see Chapter Two). The First Wisconsin Cavalry was organized on the campus and occupied East Hall; a squad of First Wisconsin cavalrymen, including at least one Ripon citizen, later helped capture Jefferson Davis, the fleeing President of the defeated Confederate States of America.

Among the nine directors, John Horner was considered the first citizen of the village. A Virginian, a graduate of Washington (now Washington and Jefferson) College in western Pennsylvania, and a southern Democrat, he served under appointment from Andrew Jackson as secretary and acting territorial governor of Michigan and subsequently of Wisconsin when it was separated from Michigan. Later, en route to Green Bay to head the federal land office there, he spotted and later bought a promising piece of land that straddled Silver Creek. Twelve years later (1849), he collaborated with David Mapes in developing this land, which became the heart of Ripon. However, his role in the evolution of the College was relatively minor.

The next to arrive in the Ripon area was New Englander Warren Chase, the most colorful of the directors. In the summer of 1844, he led a small party of pioneers from Southport (now Kenosha) into the valley just west of Horner's promising piece of land. He named the valley Ceresco (after Ceres, the Roman goddess of agriculture) and established the Wisconsin Phalanx, an experiment in communal living inspired by the theories of the French social philosopher Charles Fourier. "Ceresco" still survives as the name of a Ripon elementary school and of the park on the west side of Union Street just before it joins Highway 23; the row of connected apartments at the far end of the park is a relic of the communal "long house." For five years the Fourierites prospered to an extent greater than those in most utopian socialist experiments until they were surrounded and swallowed by the more conventional settlers in Ripon proper (in both senses of the word). In 1850, Chase and his followers began liquidating their commune, reorganizing it as the Village of Ceresco, and merging it with Ripon.

Despite his radical beliefs in utopian socialism, abolition, spiritualism, women's rights, and free love, Chase remained an acknowledged local leader. He had been elected as a delegate to both the 1846 and 1847-48 Wisconsin constitutional conventions, served a two-year term in the first state legislature, ran for governor as the Free Soil Party's candidate in 1849, and was briefly one of the first trustees of the College. But the Lone One, as he called himself in his autobiography, *The Life Line of the Lone One; or an Autobiography of the World's Child,* soon left Wisconsin to seek his Eden elsewhere. His radical ideas and his distrust of ministers, doctors, and lawyers, the training of whom was the main purpose of undergraduate institutions throughout most of the 19th century, would have carried little weight with his less radical fellow trustees.

David Mapes, the third of the village's founding fathers to arrive on the scene, was undoubtedly the most important of the three. Born in the tiny village of Coxsackie on the Hudson River 20 miles below Albany, he received a good grammar-school education, though he liked to claim that much of his learning "was picked up from guide boards and sign posts."[4] As this quotation implies, he had a restless temperament and never stayed in one place or in one job (including school teaching) for very long. Also, he had an abiding interest in public and community service; was constantly "reinvesting" his earnings in churches, schools, and other public works; and served two terms in the New York State Legislature. In 1844, he was operating a steamboat between New York City and Kingston (just north of the U. S. Military Academy on the Hudson River) and a line of stagecoaches running west from the latter city. This promising venture foundered on a reef in the East River, putting an end to both his boat and his business. At this point, Captain Mapes, as he was thenceforth called, headed west "where all go to mend or make a fortune,"[5] settled briefly in Racine, and then with his son began roaming the Wisconsin territory looking for a promising town site. He found it in 1845 just east of Ceresco, but this was the land already purchased by Governor Horner. When Horner would not sell at Mapes' price, the captain bought other land adjoining Horner's and began to farm it. Four years later the two men reached an agreement, whereby Mapes would become the town boomer, booster, and promoter (today he would probably be called a developer) in return for half of Horner's lots. Horner would have the right to name the village (Ripon, after his ancestral home in Yorkshire, England) and the streets (Blackburn, Scott, and Watson, after relatives; Houston, Jackson, and Jefferson, after admired statesmen) and could expect to receive enhanced profits from the sale of his remaining lots.

For more than a decade, Mapes labored to develop his community: building a flour mill and a public house, donating lots to prospective settlers who would agree to establish places of business on the square, obtaining railroad trackage south to Milwaukee and north to the Wolf River, and persuading the Federal Government to move the post office from Ceresco to Ripon. In the meantime, he became the dominant force in propagating the idea of a college: he was the first president of the Lyceum and, later, of the College's Board of Trustees; if Ripon College had a single founder, it was David Mapes. Yet, for Mapes, the promise of a college was mainly one way of promoting a town, and under his guidance the College never became much more than a promise. As wagons filled with pioneer families rolled into town, stopping for a meal or a night's lodging at his public house on the square, he would engage his customers in conversation to measure their potential as citizens. If he was sufficiently impressed— if he thought they were "big fish"—he would offer them inducements to stay, one of them being the prospect of a college. "Our object," he wrote, "was to draw around us a class of inhabitants who would have the pride to educate their children."[6] In this object, he was notably successful.

One of the biggest fish Mapes caught was Alvan Earl Bovay. Another New Yorker, he was born in Adams, where Mapes was living at the time. He graduated from Norwich University in Vermont and then took a teaching job in New York City. There,he joined the National Reform Party, which was advocating a homestead law (free land) for the benefit of the American worker and was also supporting the occasionally violent efforts of the tenant farmers on the great landed estates of the Hudson Valley to change the state laws for the benefit of the tenants. These so-called "rent wars," in which Bovay played an important role as speaker and propagandist, occurred in the same area where Mapes was operating his steamboat-stagecoach business, so the two men may have heard of each other, though neither ever said so in their books. But Bovay had read about Warren Chase and his Ceresco commune in the *New York Tribune*, published by Bovay's political associate Horace Greeley, one of the great maverick editors of the day. Since the rent wars were winding down, Bovay decided to emigrate to Ceresco and start a law practice. He arrived just as the Phalanx was disbanding, but Mapes persuaded Bovay to cast his lot with the emerging Village of Ripon. So he purchased land near the current site of the Valley Bank and began developing "Bovay's Addition" to the village. As one of the town's first lawyers, Bovay played an important role in Ripon's growth into a city. As a political reformer with strong Whig Party connections in the East, he took a leading part in the famous 1854 meeting in the Little White School House (now located on Blackburn Street between the M & I Bank and the Republican House), where the new Republican Party was formed. As a onetime professor of languages and mathematics in several now defunct eastern colleges and academies, he played a relatively brief but dominant role in the making of a college. Virtually all the surviving records of the Lyceum and the early years of the College are in his hand, and he was both a trustee and a faculty member. It is quite possible that he was the driving force behind Mapes' plan for a school.

Two other Lyceum directors deserve mention: Ezra Northrup and Jehdeiah Bowen. Northrup, still another New Yorker, was the first merchant to build a store on the square and, as one of the few villagers with ready cash, became a major contributor to the new educational institution. He served as Lyceum treasurer and later became a college trustee. Bowen was a Welshman who had come to the United States in 1830, clerked in an eastern Pennsylvania store owned by Mapes, and later decided to follow his former employer to Wisconsin, arriving in Ripon in 1850. Among his successful business ventures was a knitting works that survived until the late 1960's, occupying the corner of Watson and Seward Streets, where Ripon Drug now stands. He was active in politics as Bovay's chief ally in forming the Republican Party in Ripon, as mayor of the city, and as a member of the state legislature. Of the original Lyceum directors, he served on the college board longest, until 1882, during which time he twice served as treasurer, 1855-61 and 1865-82.

In Bovay's minutes of the November 23 meeting, there is a hint of uncertainty and possibly open disagreement about what kind of institution would best suit the interests of the village, there being, apparently, some feeling that colleges tended to be elitist and sectarian.   But Bovay recorded no summary of the discussion; he merely noted the election of the Lyceum directors and the receipt of notes totaling $345 for stock in the new corporation. The four December meetings seem to have been concerned with plans for the construction of a building; then suddenly on January 1, 1851, without any explanation of their action in the minutes, the directors voted to apply for a charter "to found, establish and maintain at Ripon in the County of Fond du Lac, an institution of learning of the highest order, embracing also a department of preparatory instruction."[7]

This motion created a problem: the corporation needed a new name since "Lyceum" did not even remotely suggest what the board had in mind. On the motion of Ezra Northrup the directors agreed to sell the honor of naming the school to the highest bidder. Although seemingly crass, this was a fairly common technique. After what Bovay described as a "spirited" bidding, a local merchant named William S. Brockway, who was attending his first board meeting, won the auction for $250; in a sense Mr. Brockway bought an entire college for a sum that would hardly pay the incidental expenses of many Ripon students today. The upshot of the matter was that on January 29, 1851 (now accepted as the official date of the founding of Ripon College), the State of Wisconsin granted a charter to Brockway College.

Thus a small group of remarkable men in a far from ordinary community planned what was eventually to become a nationally known and respected institution of higher education. Today one has to be impressed by the vision of these men and the quickness with which they took the first step. They were genuinely concerned about the quality of life in their new settlement and chose its location for its beauty as well as the availability of water power and other practical considerations. It seemed then and seems now quite appropriate to crown the hill with a small liberal arts college. Of course, Brockway was also a "booster" college. Like hundreds of other communities on the expanding frontier, Ripon believed that a college would attract settlers, increase land values, and help develop a prosperous permanent settlement. Brockway College was distinctive mainly in that it prospered: the survival rate among frontier colleges, whether merely planned or actually constructed, was about one in five.

Many years later, Jehdeiah Bowen neatly summarized the community's motivation:

> If the question were asked, what was intended to be done with that building [East Hall], the replies of those who contributed might have differed widely. While some would have said that it was designed for a high school, others would have replied that it was built on purpose to entice settlers, that the proprietors might sell village lots. But whatever motives there may have been, one great one inspired all—the pioneers were bound to show their respect for education.[8]

NOTES TO CHAPTER I
THE LYCEUM OF RIPON

[1]Pedrick and Miller, 222.

[2]Ripon College *Trustees' Minutes,* I, 2.

[3]*Ibid.*

[4]Mapes, 12.

[5]*Ibid.,* 52.

[6]*Ibid.,* 138.

[7]*Trustees' Minutes,* 4.

[8]E.H. Merrell, "Ripon College," 156-57.

CHAPTER II

ROUGH SLEDDING
BROCKWAY COLLEGE
1851-1863

If we would save the college from per-version, it is indispensible [sic] that it should be made a college for both sexes.

Executive Committee, Board of Trustees

From the outset, Brockway College experienced rough sledding, and the board meetings were not all sweetness and light. At the second annual meeting on July 28, 1852, President Mapes had to call for an apology from Mr. Runals (a New York lawyer who later became Superintendent of the Ripon Public Schools, a member of the state legislature, and a municipal judge) "for indecorous language toward one of the members . . ., whereupon E. L. Runals refused to make the apology but used the most furious and insulting language toward the president."[1] Secretary Bovay did not mention the cause of the dispute, but it must have centered around the serious problems which faced the new institution: a still uncompleted building; a lack of money, students, and faculty; and disagreement over the type of school desired, most probably the latter. It seems clear that the trustees, no doubt strongly influenced in this direction by Bovay, Chase, and Mapes, wanted a college and a preparatory department free of any church affiliation or control.

At first, they tried to rely on local public support to construct their building: selling stock in the corporation; accepting donations in the form of lumber, stone, and lime; and holding fundraising drives, such as a Fourth of July picnic and a Christmas festival. Still short of money, they appealed to the state, hoping to secure help from the so-called University Fund established through a grant of land from the federal government. Failing in this attempt, they turned, reluctantly no doubt, to a church.

There were a number of Episcopalians—Bovay, the Brockways, Horner, Mapes, and Northrup—on the board, but the Episcopal Church was not particularly active in supporting western colleges. The Methodists were already backing Lawrence, and Lawrence, a rival even in those days, was even actively selling "scholarships" in the Ripon area. So the trustees appealed to the Congregationalists: they had established the first church in the Ripon area, and its minister, the Reverend F. G. Sherrill, was associated with the Winnebago District Convention of Presbyterian and Congregational Churches. Through Sherrill, the Brockway board proposed that the convention adopt the College, assume half of its $800 debt, complete the building on the hill, and open a preparatory department in the spring of 1853; in return, the board would cede the entire property of the College to the convention. The convention appointed a committee of ministers—Sherrill of Ceresco, Freeman of Oshkosh, and Walcott of Menasha—to study the feasibility of the proposal. Although the three ministers were favorably inclined, they found that the churches in the Winnebago District, all of them relatively new, were reluctant to shoulder any added financial burdens. All seemed lost, when Brockway found an "angel," the Reverend Jeremiah W. Walcott.

Reverend Walcott was another of those New Englanders who loom so largely in Ripon's history, a graduate of Dartmouth and Auburn Theological Seminary in New York, and principal of two preparatory schools before moving to Wisconsin. He had the education, the experience, and, most importantly, the money to take over a school, which is exactly what he did—he made a "takeover bid": he would pay off Brockway's debt and run the College at his own expense. Both the College and the convention accepted Walcott's proposal, the convention noting with satisfaction Walcott's "design of nourishing a literary institution under proper religious influences."[2] However, a touch of wistful sadness tinges Bovay's minutes:

> Session was a short one; no valedictory from the president [Mapes]; no speech making from anybody, although the occasion would have justified it; there being before and around us the visible fruits of our long, disinterested, unaided and much suspected labors. Adjourned sine die [i.e., without setting a date for the next meeting].[3]

It was the final meeting for Mapes and other founding fathers; like old soldiers, they were fading away, watching the enterprise slip from their grasp.

Walcott kept his bargain: he paid the debts and furnished enough rooms for academy classes to begin in the spring of 1853. At that time, Martha J. Adams became the school's first instructor, inaugurating a Ladies Department with six students. The Men's Department opened in the fall, with W. M. Martin, Walcott, and Bovay (part-time) serving as additional faculty. Henceforth, men and women were taught together. Courses were offered for students wishing to prepare for college (the Classical Course), for those intending to become school teachers, and for those contemplating business careers (the Higher English Course). There was also a Common English Branch, which apparently included work normally taught in the upper grades. Incredibly, quarterly fees were as follows: Common English Branches, $4; Higher English Branches, $5; Languages (Latin and Greek), $6; French (Extra), $4; Music on Melodion, $8; Pianoforte, $10; Drawing, $2; Painting (in water colors), $3; Oil Painting, $10; Vocal Music, free; boarding "in good families," $1.50 per week. Advertisements listing these prices were preceded by the following bit of puffery:

The institution is in a flourishing condition, and
affords superior advantages for acquiring a thorough
knowledge of all the Common, Higher English and
Ornamental Branches and Languages. Particular
attention will be given to those preparing to teach.[4]

By 1855, 72 men and 72 women, many part-time,
were being taught by a faculty of four; nearly all students
came from within 20 miles of the campus; apparently, more
would have enrolled if there had been a dormitory or more
housing in town. For this reason, it was decided in 1855 that
a second building should be constructed west of East Hall
and used primarily as a women's dormitory.

In the fall of 1854, Walcott asked the Winnebago Convention to assume full responsibility for operating the school,
feeling, justifiably, that he had done his job; the institution
was "in a flourishing condition" and much respected in the
region. But he lacked funds for a second building as well as
for the establishment of a Collegiate Department. He also
sensed the need for haste, since rival academies at Fox Lake
(Downer College, subsequently Milwaukee Downer) and at
Beaver Dam (Wayland University, now Wayland Academy)
might also have collegiate ambitions. So once again, the
district polled its membership and this time received a
positive response. At their January, 1855, meeting, the
ministers and churches agreed to undertake a fund-raising
campaign and to hold a special meeting at Ripon in March.
The delegates at this meeting called for a new charter with a
board of trustees nominated or approved by the Winnebago
Convention, instructed the board to purchase the property
owned by Walcott (the area now occupied by East, Middle,
West, Bartlett, Todd Wehr, and Farr Halls; the Library; and
the Union), and agreed to undertake "the endowment and
organization of the Collegiate Department of the Institution
as contemplated in the [original] College charter."[5] The new
charter, differing significantly from the original one only in
that it named the new trustees, still governs the operation of

Ripon College. The requirement that the trustees be approved by the convention was incorporated in the by-laws rather than the charter. The only other mention of religion was a provision that "no religious tenets or opinions shall be required to entitle any person to be admitted as a student."[6] The new trustees included Walcott, Northrup, and Bowen from the previous board, plus 11 others, including seven ministers of nearby Congregational churches. Though local interests were somewhat protected, control was firmly centered in the Winnebago District Convention.

Without question, Brockway College was now in a stronger position to raise money. It now had, theoretically at least, the financial support of every Congregational and Presbyterian church in the district. By 1861, these churches had raised an estimated $25,000. Furthermore, the convention appointed "agents," usually ministers of affiliated churches and often members of the board, to help with fund raising not only in the district, but in the East as well. Today, these men would be called development officers. But, for a number of reasons, Brockway still had severe financial problems. In the late 1850s, the country as a whole was suffering from a depression; Mapes' railroad projects were draining the local supply of capital. Also, conservative churches were possibly a little leery of an institution which was located so close to Ceresco, the center of a much publicized, but considerably exaggerated, free-love controversy. In addition, the school was strongly identified with radical abolitionism, particularly after the Booth War, an episode that sometimes resembled a Mark Twain parody of an Alexander Dumas narrative.

In 1854, Edward Daniels, the College Librarian, and Oscar Hugh La Grange, a Brockway student, had helped Milwaukee newspaper editor Sherman Booth "rescue" a fugitive slave from a Milwaukee jail. For this violation of the Fugitive Slave Act and other laws, Booth had been thrown in the same jail, released on legal technicalities, then six years later imprisoned again. On July 4, 1860, Booth attempted to read a previously announced statement from his jail window, but was prevented. Thereupon, La Grange, who was present for the occasion, asked Booth to throw down the manuscript attached to a string, which Booth did. But La Grange couldn't decipher the writing and asked Mrs. Booth to translate it for him so he could copy it. This being accomplished, the Brockway student requested a Wisconsin supreme court justice in the assembled crowd to read it aloud. "Read it yourself," said the judge. La Grange, obviously having the time of his life, mounted a stone wall beneath Booth's window, nominated the judge for president of the assemblage, declared him elected, and then read Booth's Fourth of July oration. All this, La Grange later maintained, was "a farcical demonstration to mislead the guards and thus prepare for the success of a future attempt to release their prisoner."

Nearly a month elapsed before the future attempt was made. On August 1, La Grange and Daniels led a rescue party of 10 men, who hoodwinked the jailer, stole his keys, released Booth, and locked the jailer in Booth's cell. Booth and his rescuers then took a train to Waupun, where, ironically, they spent the night as the guests of the warden of the state prison. On August 4, Booth arrived in Ripon and began to address an overflow crowd at the City Hall, but was interrupted by the arrival of Federal Deputy Marshal Frank McCarty and two assistants from Fond du Lac. When McCarty attempted to seize Booth, he was "thrust aside by stalwart young men" (Brockway students?) and hustled off the stage "in a manner unceremonious," while the angry crowd shouted, "Hang him, shoot him, kill him." As Booth was being driven away to Green Lake in a carriage, Bovay offered a resolution that Booth "shall not be arrested by United States marshals in Ripon," and Professor Daniels proposed a "league of freedom" pledged to resist the enforcement of the Fugitive Slave Law; 120 people joined the league. For several weeks, Ripon became the center of open resistance to federal authority, frustrating repeated attempts by United

States marshals to recapture Booth. Finally, after many citizens, including La Grange, began to have second thoughts about defying federal authority, Booth was seized in Berlin on October 8, with no resistance offered, "Booth being accompanied by ladies only." Booth's subsequent fine was remitted by President Buchanan in one of his last acts before turning the presidency over to Abraham Lincoln. Bovay, Daniels, and La Grange were all indicted, but later pardoned by Lincoln.[7]

To return to more mundane matters, the Winnebago Convention became convinced that it could not raise enough money to run the school within its own district so they decided to appeal to the Milwaukee and Madison Districts, largely Congregationalist, and to the Milwaukee and Fox River Presbyteries. At a special Educational Convention at Ripon in July, 1855, the Winnebagans requested statewide support for the completion of the new dormitory. What they got was a sometimes acrimonious debate over the future of Brockway College. Brockway's local backers were strong believers in co-education and saw the opening of a female collegiate department as a first step toward the creation of a men's department also. But, because the southern delegates were already supporting a men's college at Beloit, they balked at creating a northern competitor. Leading spokesmen for the opposing views were two men with the same name: the Reverend Henry L. Chapin, pastor of the Ripon Congregational Church, and the Reverend Aaron L. Chapin, President of Beloit College. The Brockway trustees and the Winnebago Convention were forced to compromise, and even then they did not get full statewide support. In return for a promise of Milwaukee backing, they agreed to allow Milwaukee representation on the board and to postpone the opening of the Men's Collegiate Department "until such time as God in his Providence shall indicate its necessity";[8] the trustees, to be sure, reserved the right to interpret God's wishes. Actually, the College received very little money from Milwaukee and, of course, none from Madison, while at the same time surrendering a bit of local autonomy. In fact, the opening of either collegiate department did not occur for eight years.

This surrender caused local resentment, as did a protracted financial controversy towards the end of 1857. Three local businessmen—our old friend Ezra Northrup, T. B. Robbins, and E. P. Brockway, brother of the late William Brockway, who had purchased the right to name the College in 1851—pledged a total of $2,000 to the Reverend J. J. Miter, an "agent" of the College; both Northrup and Robbins were brothers-in-law of the two Brockways and had interests in the Ripon banking firm of Catlin and Brockway, where the pledges were kept. Suddenly, without any warning, the pledges (no actual money had yet been deposited) were physically removed from the bank. The brothers-in-law stoutly maintained that their subscriptions were subject to certain conditions and that these conditions had not been met. Foremost among these was an understanding that Reverend Walcott would resign from the board; the Brockway clan publicly stated their conviction that Walcott, the College's chief creditor, should not also be its principal and a trustee. With equal stoutness, Miter denied any knowledge of this particular condition and demanded the return of the pledges. But neither his efforts, nor those of the trustees, the Winnebago Convention, and concerned citizens like Mapes and Bovay, brought fruit. At this point, the College was in the direst straits of its history: finances were in complete disarray, the community was deeply divided, and much local support had been lost.

Faced with imminent disaster, the Executive Committee of the Board—Bertine Pinkney, a Rosendale farmer, an Episcopalian, and President of the Board; John P. Taggart, a Ripon merchant and also an Episcopalian; the Reverend Calvin Bayley, a Congregational minister from Waupun who had been appointed principal of the Preparatory Department (Walcott had resigned in 1858); and the ever reliable Jehdeiah Bowen—on May 25, 1861, reached a series of decisions that rescued the College. They began their report to the board with a preamble: "Resolved, That in the judgement of the committee, the 'indications of Providence' plainly show that if we would save the college from perversion . . . it is indispensible [sic] that it should be made a college for both sexes, of high order and worthy of the aims and wishes of its founders and benefactors. . . ." They then recommended that the board adopt certain principles as "the settled policy of the Institution," as follows:

1.   A course of study not inferior to that pursued in the better class of colleges in our country shall be prescribed. . . .

2.   A preparatory department shall be organized. . . . In this department a normal class shall be instituted annually for the special instruction of those who are preparing to become teachers. . . .

4.   The two sexes shall have equal advantages in the College. . . .

5.   The greatest care shall be taken to secure teachers of the highest attainments and skill and to offer inducements to the public to avail themselves of the advantages of this College.

6.   An earnest and efficient effort shall be put forth to free the College from debt. An agent shall be employed and placed in the field at once, who shall have charge of the financial affairs of the College. . . .

9.   The country for 50 miles around shall be canvassed for pupils. . . .

The committee also recommended an immediate search for a president, the establishment of an endowment, and the appointment of Reverend Chapin as financial agent.   In addition, they urged the ministers of the convention "to preach as soon as may be, on the subject of Education in connection with this College, not only to secure pupils, and facilitate the collection of funds, but especially to create an atmosphere of congenial influences to aid the proper work of the financial agent."[9]

With its blend of idealism and pragmatism, this statement of principles is an impressive document even today. One cannot help being struck by mid-19th-century Ripon's commitment to excellence and especially to coeducation. Except for its florid style and its emphasis on the role of ministers, the document has a decidedly modern tone and even today would serve as a more than acceptable guide for Ripon College.

The choice of Chapin as Brockway's financial agent was a fortunate one, and he seems to have been the dominant force at Brockway in the late 1850s. A native of Vermont and, like Walcott, a graduate of Dartmouth, he interrupted his studies at Andover Theological Seminary in Massachusetts to become Ripon's Congregational pastor in 1855. He and his wife had originally intended to do missionary work abroad, but his health was not robust (he knew little about Wisconsin winters) and, anyway, to Mrs. Chapin, Ripon "seemed almost like going to a foreign land."[10] He was soon appointed to the Board of Trustees, and his wife became an instructor in the Preparatory Department. Also a leader in the Winnebago Convention, he was assigned the task of writing the 1861 Narrative on the State of Religion in the district. In his narrative, Chapin noted with obvious satisfaction that his own church had experienced "a general revival of religion," that this revival had begun in Brockway College, and that "the increase of religious interest is directly traceable to the day of prayer for colleges." He went on to say:

The importance of that institution, not only as a place for literary culture, but as a means of Grace, is felt more and more each year and it is earnestly hoped

that means now put in operation may place that
Institution free from embarrassment and enable it to
prosecute vigorously and successfully the good work
which we believe God has ordained.[11]

Chapin obviously knew how to make a sales pitch.

Unfortunately, the Civil War put a crimp in the plans
to open the Collegiate Department. For financial reasons, the
trustees decided to severely limit academic instruction and to
rent the campus to the Army for $5 a day; Brockway College
for three months became Camp Fremont, the rendezvous of
the First Wisconsin Cavalry. Colonel Edward Daniels, the
doughty veteran of the Booth War who had organized the
regiment, established his headquarters in East Hall, where
the soldiers also had their dormitory. La Grange, that other
famed Booth War veteran, later joined the unit, eventually
served as its colonel, and became a hero for swimming across
"the deep, swift L'Anguille River [in Arkansas] 13 times,
towing behind him a little skiff loaded with disabled
comrades . . . an athletic feat of heroism rarely equaled."[12]

Despite the distractions of the war, Brockway College
got its financial house in order and, in the fall of 1862,
reopened the Preparatory Department with a large comple-
ment of students under the direction of Clarissa Tucker
Tracy and Edward Huntington Merrell, heads of the Ladies'
and Men's Departments. Variously known as the institution's mother or grandmother, Tracy had been hired by the
Board of Trustees in 1859 on the recommendation of Bowen.
Like Bowen, she had come to Wisconsin from eastern Pennsylvania, where they had mutual friends. Her career in
teaching had begun at the tender age of 14, but was interrupted from time to time so that she could finish her own
education. After completing her studies at Troy Female
Seminary in upstate New York, she taught at a number of
academies for young women in Pennsylvania and New York;
but, following the death of her husband and the youngest of
her two children, she accepted Bowen's invitation to become

teacher and matron of the new dormitory (Middle Hall) in October of 1859 at the age of 40. Although her specialty was botany, she taught English and mathematics, ran the dining room, and served as housekeeper, counselor, and nurse to both men and women, all at a beginning salary of $300 a year. Tracy House, a college-owned building torn down to make way for the Valley Bank, was named after her. More will be said of her later.

Merrell, a New Yorker and a graduate of Oberlin College and Seminary, became principal of the Preparatory Department while still in his 20s. A firm believer in the evangelical mission of the small, church-related liberal arts College and a respected teacher of classics, he became a much sought after public speaker all over the country, thus incidentally making the name of both Brockway and Ripon widely known. He served the College until 1901, held the institution's first professorship, and, in 1876, became its second president. Legitimately, he could be considered Ripon's godfather.

But the father was unquestionably William Edward Merriman. Following the recommendation in the 1861 master plan proposed by the Executive Committee, the trustees had begun a widespread search for a president; they found him in Green Bay. Merriman came from Massachusetts, studied at Williams College under Mark Hopkins, one of America's great college teachers and administrators, and attended Union Theological Seminary in New York. As acting pastor of the Presbyterian Church in Green Bay, he became prominent in the affairs of the Winnebago District Convention and developed a strong interest in Brockway College. He served as moderator of a district meeting called in Ripon to hear a report on recent fund-raising efforts for Brockway. When it seemed that the College still needed $900, Merriman made an impassioned plea. According to a later report:

> His great soul was stirred to its depths. He seemed to
> see generations of students helped forward to splen-

did life work by keeping the doors of this college open, that otherwise would lead worthless lives. "We can save the College by becoming individually responsible for the $900 . . . deficit," he said. "I'll be responsible for the payment of $__, [sic]" naming a generous sum. Others followed, one after another until $500 remained, when the Reverend J. W. Walcott, who, almost from the beginning had carried the financial burdens of the College, said, "I'll stand for the balance." The College was saved! A shout of thanksgiving was heard and hymns of praise were sung.[13]

The trustees elected Merriman president and, at the same time, appointed Merrell Professor of Greek. Merriman accepted the board's offer "with the following express understanding":

1. That it is the aim of the trustees and friends of this institution to raise its grade so fast, and only so fast, as its own growth and the wants of the country will allow, till it becomes one of the highest order. 2. That meanwhile we will prosecute the work of preparatory and academical instruction as efficiently as possible; and that we will neither let our work at present limit our plans for the future, nor our hopes for the future interfere with the needed work of the present. 3. That we will on no account allow the Institution to incur any more debt. 4. That we will exert ourselves to the utmost to pay the present debt, and complete the buildings this year.[14]

After all the flights of evangelical rhetoric surrounding Merriman's appointment, this straightforward statement comes as a refreshing breath of common sense.

Merriman took office on July 21, 1863, and almost immediately was faced with another of Brockway's recurring financial crises. But once again the College was saved by the skin of its teeth. Several thousand dollars in pledges were accumulated, but the largest of them had one condition attached: the money would be given only after sufficient funds had been committed to pay off the entire debt. It was a case of all or nothing. Returning from an exhausting trip on horseback through the hinterland of the Winnebago District close to the end of his first year, the president stopped at the Dartford (Green Lake) home of the Reverend Sherlock Bristol, a long-time friend and trustee of Brockway College. Deeply despondent, Merriman reported that he had failed to reach his fund-raising goal and therefore would have to resign the presidency. Fortunately, Reverend Bristol was able to make a cash contribution sufficiently large to insure payment of all the pledges. Bristol later recalled that Merriman rode the remaining distance back to Ripon at a full gallop. The promised money was paid, the two buildings on the hill were completed, and the president was finally able to devote some attention to his students and faculty.

By this time, in fact, probably before Merriman assumed the presidency, the institution had been renamed Ripon College. Formal approval of the change was granted by the state in March, 1864, but the lack of fanfare accompanying this action suggests that the change was already an accepted fact. Following the dispute with E. P. Brockway and his brothers-in-law, the Winnebago District Convention, as early as 1859, had recommended the new name. Since local feeling against the Brockway clan was strong and since Ripon's booster spirit would obviously welcome the naming of the College after the community, the old name was doomed. So, with a new name, an able and respected president, and its financial crisis solved, Ripon College seemed poised for flight.

NOTES TO CHAPTER II
BROCKWAY COLLEGE 1851-1863

[1]*Trustees' Minutes*, I, 15.

[2]*Winnebago Convention Minutes*, 10-13.

[3]*Trustees' Minutes*, I, 16.

[4]See advertisements in the *Ripon Herald* throughout 1854.

[5]*Winnebago Minutes*, 43-46; *Trustees' Minutes*, 3-6.

[6]*College Charter*.

[7]Pedrick and Miller, 125-46.

[8]*Trustees' Minutes*, 24.

[9]*Trustees' Minutes*, II, 76-79; *Winnebago Minutes*, 162-64.

[10]"Henry L. Chapin," *Pedrick Genealogies*, Ripon College Archives.

[11]*Winnebago Minutes*, 176-77.

[12]Pedrick and Miller, 173.

[13]*Winnebago Minutes*, 215.

[14]*Trustees' Minutes*, II, 91-92.

CHAPTER III

NEAR TO THE POOR WILLIAM E. MERRIMAN 1863-1876

It is designed to keep this college near to the poor. The expense of education here is very low.

William Merriman

By any standard of measurement, William E. Merriman was an exceptional college president, one of the genuine "greats" in Ripon College history. Such was his reputation as a scholar and churchman that the College received the active support of churches in the central and northern part of the state, and relations with southern Wisconsin improved markedly. At the first meeting of the Winnebago Convention following Merriman's election as president, the entire body "most heartily" endorsed his appointment, and even President Chapin of Beloit, who had lobbied against statewide support of Brockway College, expressed his "Christian sympathy for the infant college and its newly chosen President."[1] At the same time, Merriman partially shifted the College's base of financial support and made it less dependent on the convention and its member churches. Slowly, but surely, central Wisconsin was losing ground to the prairie states further west as the wheat growing center of the country; lumbering and dairy farming were becoming the principal industries. Although the state made the transition successfully, the process absorbed much of the region's capital and did not lend itself to the creation of industrial centers; the region remained rural and sparsely settled. The new waves of settlers tended to be Welsh, German, Polish, and Scandinavian rather than Yankee, and the English-speaking Presbyterian and Congregational churches did not grow proportionately in numbers or in wealth with the general increase in population. Ripon's president seemed to be well aware of these demographic changes, since he attempted to attract students from diverse ethnic back-grounds.

In the 1860s, Merriman made a bold and nearly suc-cessful bid for Ripon to be designated the "land grant" institution of Wisconsin under the Morrill Act of 1862, by which Congress had given extensive land grants to the states to promote industrial and agricultural colleges. What he probably had in mind was an arrangement similar to that still in effect at Cornell University whereby the liberal arts college would retain private control, with the industrial and agricul-tural colleges funded by the state. Merriman's pitch was that Ripon could operate an agricultural college more efficiently than the state university—he presented figures to prove it—and that the community would provide a much more suitable moral environment for students than Madison. In 1866, the State Senate actually granted the land to Ripon, but Madison business interests killed the bill in the Assembly. Thus, both Ripon and Lawrence, which also made a bid, lost out to the University of Wisconsin; this was Ripon's second failure to receive state funds.

Consequently, Merriman, in 1868, turned once more to the churches or, more accurately, to a largely Congrega-tional-Presbyterian organization called the Society for the Promotion of Collegiate and Theological Education at the West, whose aim was to coordinate fund-raising activities of eastern churches on behalf of western schools. Organized in 1843, the society originally helped Illinois (the same institu-tion which joined the Midwest Collegiate Athletic Conference in the early 1980s), Western Reserve, Wabash, and Marietta Colleges as well as Lane Theological Seminary. Later addi-tions included Oberlin, Beloit, Knox, Iowa (now Grinnell), Carleton, and Colorado Colleges. But Ripon could not meet two membership requirements: 1) there must be no encumbrances on the College's title to its property, and 2) there must be no ecclesiastical control. Reverend Walcott still had reversionary rights to the college property, and the Winnebago Convention still had the power to nominate Ripon's trustees.

As it turned out, neither obstacle proved serious: Walcott, ever the institution's benefactor, waived his rights; so did the convention, with only two dissenting votes, at a June meeting in Rosendale. However, the Rosendale resolution made clear

> That this action is not intended to detach the College from the interest, influence, and sympathy of this convention, or our churches; but on the contrary, it is intended to remove obstacles in the way of its growth; to engage our churches more earnestly in building it up; and to secure the confidence and cooperation of our Brethren in other parts of the West, and also at the East.

Expressing complete faith in the College's trustees, the convention committed "the interests of the institution to their care, with the assurance that in the future, as in the past, they will maintain the integrity of their trust." The trustees, in turn, at a special October meeting, thanked the convention for its "fostering care" and gave assurance of their "earnest purpose to carry on the great work for which so much has been planned and given and to hand down to coming time, secured and enlarged, these early fruits of Christian Benevolence in Wisconsin."[2] Today, one is again impressed with the good sense, the spirit of harmony and cooperation, and the dedication to the best interest of the College displayed by all parties involved.

Armed with the approval of both the convention and the board, Merriman presented Ripon's application for membership to the Western College Society at its meeting in Marietta, Ohio, during November of 1868. Merriman's petition gives a very clear picture of the nature and character of the College and of its aims, goals, and philosophy. Concerning the school's relationship with the church, Merriman stated:

> It has been built up mainly by the Congregationalists. All but two of its trustees are ministers or members of Congregational churches, and the Board has the confidence of that denomination. It is a Christian College, under the influence of the Congregationalists. It looks to them for support, and will be consistent with their principles, but it is not designed to be sectarian; its privileges are open to all on the same terms, and it has no ecclesiastical connection or control. . . . Health, Christian character, and Christian usefulness are made prominent ends of instruction as conducted here. We seek to have the College pervaded with the Christian spirit, and characterized by Christian principles. As a result, we hope to secure a proper Christian morality in the students, and their devotion to useful service in Christian lives.[3]

Today, this sounds pretty sectarian: Ripon College was Christian, Protestant, and mainly Congregationalist. But it *was* free of church *control* and *was* open to students of any sect; hence it was nonsectarian as the word was then understood. Further, the reference to Christian morality was intended to assure the society that moral principles, not materialism, would undergird the institution. It was a very persuasive appeal. So was the rest of the petition.

Concerning coeducation, Merriman said: "This is no experiment here; experience has satisfied us that this is every way the best. We think it requires better conditions, and produces better results, than the education of the sexes separately." And on the role of the College in the community: "It is proposed to continue the Academical [Preparatory] Department in connection with the Collegiate. . . .The wants of the people demand this. . . ." Furthermore, "It is designed to keep this college near to the poor. The expense of education here is very low. Though there is no professorship endowed, the price of tuition is but $21 or $24 a year, and board in the College hall, where most of the teachers board with the students, has never been more than $2.50 a week, and generally less than that." The wants of the College were "a larger library and more apparatus and means of illustrating the Physical Sciences. But its great need is a productive capital sufficient for the proper support of the instructors."[4] The society was sufficiently impressed to recommend "that $50,000 be raised to endow Ripon College."[5]

The importance of support from the society can hardly be overstated. Its endorsement is somewhat comparable to accreditation today by a regional agency like the North Central Association. Its criteria were different, but the intent was much the same. Ripon had been placed on an approved list because it met certain predetermined standards; it would be subject to periodic visitation and review; if it continued to find favor with the society, it might claim a certain academic respectability, and it could also count on continuing eastern financial support. By securing the society's backing, Merriman may well have assured Ripon's survival.

Nonetheless, the College's relationship to and its dependence upon Wisconsin churches did not greatly change. Before leaving for Marietta, Merriman had asked the Wisconsin General Convention of Congregational and Presbyterian Churches at a meeting in Ripon to endorse an effort to raise $100,000, half of which might be raised in the East if the College were accepted by the Western College Society; the convention gave its unanimous approval. For many years, the Board of Trustees consisted largely of Congregationalists, many of them ministers, and the 20th century was nearly half gone before the College had a president who was not a clergyman. Membership in the society did not fundamentally alter the character of the College; it was still church related, only slightly less provincial, and, in some respects, more rather than less committed to the educational and religious values of the Congregationalists.

The dominant influence in the shaping of Ripon College, as it was in most colleges for better or worse in the latter half of the 19th century, was the college president. In Ripon's case, it was definitely for the better during Merriman's tenure. Fortunately for Ripon, he was a man of common sense, vision, and liberality of spirit who was able to raise the College above the narrow sectarianism of the time and whose reputation as a churchman, scholar, and teacher as well as his powers of persuasion, usually enabled him to get what he wanted from the Board of Trustees, the Winnebago Convention, and the Western College Society. Unfortunately, his health began to fail in the early 1870s, and he was not able to enjoy the long tenure the trustees had envisioned. Although they granted him leaves of absence in 1874 and 1875, he felt obligated to resign in 1876 and was succeeded by his friend and colleague Edward H. Merrell, who had served on the faculty since 1862.

NOTES TO CHAPTER III
WILLIAM E. MERRIMAN 1863-1876

[1]*Winnebago Minutes*, 240-41.

[2]*Trustees' Minutes*, II, 121-26, 128.

[3]Baldwin, 177-78.

[4]*Ibid.*, 177-80.

[5]*Ibid.*, 139.

CHAPTER IV

CONTROVERSY
EDWARD H. MERRELL
1876-1891

Instruction in the College shall recognize and be coincident with the principles of inspired truth, as revealed in the Christian Scriptures; the Bible shall be a textbook never to be displaced or neglected.

Executive Committee, Board of Trustees

Edward H. Merrell shared Merriman's commitment to "Christian education" and fully intended to follow the course laid down by his predecessor. But times were changing, and Merrell was ill-equipped to change with them. The two men were as different in personality and temperament as they could be. Portraits reveal a genial, approachable Merriman, but a dour, rather forbidding Merrell. The former was always the caring minister and father of his flock, remembered by students for his wise counsel both in and out of the classroom; the latter was the stern taskmaster, remembered for his reprimands from the chapel pulpit. While Merrell may well have been a more efficient administrator, he was certainly a less inspirational and flexible leader, and he was to have all kinds of trouble with his faculty. Merriman was willing and able to make modest changes in the curriculum, such as introducing a scientific course, but Merrell was reluctant to make any changes at all. Both were doing the Lord's work, Merriman in a way that brought people together, Merrell often in a way that divided them. Confronted with the rise of the new state university systems and the growing secularity of American higher education, Merrell was inclined to turn inward rather than face the realities of a changing world. Like many denominational college presidents towards the end of the century, he steered Ripon toward increasing sectarianism. Consequently, the College lost some of the momentum it had gained under Merriman.

Merrell faced many of the same problems as his predecessor, but they became exacerbated during his tenure. Chief among these was the problem of enrollment. Throughout most of the 19th century, the preparatory students greatly outnumbered the collegians; in fact, college enrollments were declining at an alarming rate. While the number of preparatory students averaged between 250 and 300, the collegians peaked at 75 in 1873-74, dropped to 55 in 1878, and reached a dangerous low of 19 in 1886-87. The College graduated four students, all women, in 1867, the first class; the largest class (1881) numbered 15 and the smallest (1886) only two; the average, up to 1896, was six.

While there are other causes for these low figures, the most significant was probably competition from state-supported institutions, not so much the university in Madison, which had fewer than 400 students, including preps, as the normal school at Oshkosh, which enrolled almost 500 students. In those days, teacher training was a very haphazard affair, and well into the 19th century individuals taught school while still in their teens and without any college education whatsoever. Normal schools like Oshkosh, so-called because they provided "norms" for teachers, were only junior colleges. The challenge of the state schools was the same as today: 1) they were cheaper (in fact, tuition-free in the 19th century); 2) they were more "practical" and "vocational"; and 3) they offered a much less rigid curriculum, hence a wider choice of courses. Obviously, prospective teachers would think twice before spending four relatively expensive years at Ripon when they could be certified after two tuition-free years at Oshkosh. Furthermore, the Central European immigrants, largely Roman Catholic and Lutheran, pouring into Wisconsin in great numbers were accustomed to inexpensive, state-subsidized education; the small, denominational, liberal arts college was entirely foreign to their experience. Since the population of the City of Ripon was increasingly German and Polish, the College was losing its appeal as a community institution. The steam was escaping from the evangelical movement, and its remaining energy was apt to be channeled into social crusades like the temperance movement and improvement in the lot of the laboring classes rather than education; hence it was becoming increasingly difficult to attract church support for colleges like Ripon, though paradoxically Roman Catholic and sectarian Protestant institutions began to flourish.

President Merrell's problems were compounded by the fact that he was out of tune even with his own church, both locally and nationally. The Congregationalists have always been among the more liberal Protestant denominations. They were willing to accommodate new scientific theories, like Darwin's; they were inclined to interpret the Bible somewhat less literally; they tended to see religion in "humanitarian"—we would probably say "humanistic" today—rather than supernatural terms. All of this was anathema—"logically, historically, and philosophically absurd"—to Merrell. In summary, Ripon College was being hit from all sides: competition from both state and sectarian schools and declining support from both the community and the church.

Today, it is difficult to reconstruct the events leading up to Merrell's resignation: the trustees' minutes and the College Days say nothing; the two local newspapers say a lot, but both were violently partisan, in opposite directions; Merrell's own account is necessarily one-sided. In any event, almost immediately after his appointment, Merrell seems to have had trouble with the faculty. Not surprisingly, salaries were one problem: they were often a month or two in arrears. For some faculty members, the school's difficulties stemmed from Merrell's conservative religious views. However, T. D. Stone, Editor of the Ripon Free Press and a staunch defender of Merrell, blamed the "Kenaston-Miter Clique," a "bunch of soreheads" who thought they knew better than the president how to run the College (Carlos Kenaston was Professor of Mathematics; the Reverend Henry Miter had served briefly as Principal of the Preparatory School). Anyhow, some faculty took their grievances to the trustees and received a hearing but no action. Professor Kenaston resigned from the faculty in 1881 but remained in Ripon, where he was an active member of the First Congregational Church and continued to express his views on the "college trouble." He was replaced as professor of mathematics and astronomy by the Reverend Stephen M. Newman, then serving as pastor of the Congregational Church, a fact that was to compound Merrell's problems. Newman, a New Englander, had come to Ripon in 1878. Educated at Bowdoin College and Andover Theological Seminary, he held decidedly liberal views, which seem to have pleased his congregation but not his president. He retained his post as minister of the church although relieved of some of his pastoral duties, and there is no doubt of his effectiveness, both as minister and as teacher. Merrell tried very hard to get along with him but couldn't. There simply was not room in the College for two such strong personalities with such antagonistic religious views.[1]

According to Editor Stone, Newman wanted to teach a course in natural history, which probably would have included some reference to Darwin, but was not permitted to do so. It was not long before Newman and Merrell became openly critical of one another and, although both denied it, may have taken their disagreements into their classrooms. In 1883, Newman resigned from the faculty and returned full time to his duties at the church, but the Merrell-Newman controversy continued. In July of the following year, Newman offered his resignation as pastor of the church, citing the "college trouble" as his reason. When a majority of his congregation, including a number of college faculty, former faculty, and trustees, asked him to withdraw his resignation, he suggested that a church council be called to give an advisory opinion. Newman's opponents, including Stone, saw the whole business as a conspiracy to force Merrell from office; they may have been right. A council made up of 18 ministers and delegates from Congregational Churches around the state, heard two days of testimony from members of the church, including college faculty and students. Although the moderator of the council had ruled that only those matters immediately germane to the minister's resignation could be received, the "college trouble" seems to have gotten a thorough airing. Merrell had decided to go east on a fundraising trip, but he was "represented" unofficially by some of his supporters. If Editor Stone is to be believed, Newman was allowed to give a four-hour attack on the president and his policies, attributing all the College's problems to Merrell's conservatism.

In the end, the council recommended that Newman withdraw his resignation. Although a small number of his parishioners chose to transfer their affiliation to other churches in the area, the majority of Ripon Congregationalists were pleased with the council's recommendation. It was clearly a rebuff for Merrell and an embarrassment for the College. Newman resumed his pastorate but remained in Ripon for only six months. In 1885, he accepted a call from the First Congregational Church in Washington, D. C., and subsequently became president of Howard University. He continued to hold the respect and affection of his many close friends in Ripon and returned to the city for short visits on a number of occasions.

Unfortunately, the church council had intensified rather than settled the "college trouble." Without question, the decline in enrollment, which hit bottom in 1886-87 shortly after the Merrell-Newman controversy, can be attributed at least in part to the unfavorable publicity the College received in the state press. The rift between the president and the local church, moreover, remained a source of tension in the community at large. That it upset the normal operations of the College is abundantly clear from the trustees' minutes.

The turnover in faculty, and in board members as well, was greater than usual during the 1880s; and there is evidence that faculty morale was at a very low ebb. Nonetheless, the board, in the midst of the Newman controversy, reaffirmed its confidence in "our present administration," though by a divided vote. Our old friend Jehdeiah Bowen, serving his last term on the board, supported the majority, but stipulated that his vote should not be taken to mean approval of the president's policies.

In 1888, Merrell sought a desperate solution to his estrangement from the local church by recommending that the board establish a separate college church. In January, 1889, the Executive Committee of the board, with Merrell absent, issued a statement wholeheartedly supporting his views and his suggestion for a new church:

While the College has not been and is not intended to be in any sense sectarian, it was the thought of the founders and is the purpose of the present Board, that it be distinctively and permanently Christian. By this it is intended, that instruction in the College shall recognize and be coincident with the principles of inspired truth, as revealed in the Christian Scriptures . . .; and that the Bible shall be a textbook never to be displaced or neglected. . . . In view of these facts and principles, and believing that the time in the history of the College has come for better provision for making these principles effective in our practical work, it is resolved: I. So soon as the funds of the College will allow, to appoint a Professor of Biblical Theology, whose duty shall be in general to teach the Scriptures, and supervise the Biblical instruction of other teachers in all departments, and assume the office of College Pastor and Preacher. . . .
III. For the successful promotion of these services and the best interests of the students, and the encour-

agement of good order . . ., we recommend the formation of a church, to membership in which officers
of the College, students and citizens of Ripon be
invited, and that the attendance on the part of all
students be required. . . .[2]

In its recommendation that all members of the faculty
should receive scriptural instruction from the pastor, this is
an alarming document, coming very close to thought control.
In fact, the hotter heads got cold feet, and it was decided,
before submitting the resolution to the full board, to select a
committee of five Congregational ministers from nearby
churches to consult with the leaders of the local church on
the whole question of church-college relations. This group
talked at some length with the new local pastor, the Reverend
Henry L. Richardson, and decided that he and Merrell could
come to substantial agreement and that the Ripon church
could once again become a source of strength for the College.
Consequently, the ministers recommended unanimously
that the establishment of a second church be postponed,
hoping that "Time with its sweet waters of forgetfulness must
be waited for . . . to obliterate all memory of the past."[3]
Merrell obviously had to be disappointed; it is very possible
he may have wished to resign as president, become college
pastor and preacher, and lead the faculty down a straight and
narrow path. But he offered no resistance to the board's
acceptance of the ministers' report.

Citing poor health, Merrell resigned as president two
years later in July, 1891, yet remained on the faculty for
another decade as professor of mental and moral philosophy,
a position that normally went with the presidency. Actually,
he had succeeded in what he called the "secularities" of his
office, tripling the small endowment, adding two new buildings, remodeling and enlarging a third, and acquiring Ingalls
Field. However, he had failed where his strongest interests
lay, the religious component of the educational process. As
a result, college enrollments had declined disastrously, and

"the work of the College" had suffered, as Merrell freely admitted, because of "doctrinal and other controversies."[4] Given the religious emphasis of his academic leadership, he was dependent finally on the backing of his church, and this he did not get. Two committees broadly representative of Wisconsin Congregationalism had refused to support him. Despite its earlier evangelical enthusiasms, the Congregational Church was liberal on most theological issues and had never had any serious quarrels with the academic community. It was prepared to accept the new scholarship of the post-Civil War era; Merrell was not. Like the church, the citizens of Ripon were ready for changes at the College—their college—and they were ready, willing, and able to bring them about.

NOTES TO CHAPTER IV
EDWARD H. MERRELL 1876-1891

[1]"Stephen Morrell Newman," *Pedrick Genealogies*.

[2]*Trustees' Minutes*, II, 301-02.

[3]*Ibid.*, 304-11.

[4]Merrell, Edward, "Ripon College," 174-79.

CHAPTER V

THE OFFER OF THE COLLEGE THE NINETEENTH-CENTURY FACULTY AND CURRICULUM

I would rather send my son to the most obscure college in the West, where he would have a few careful teachers instructing him from day to day, than the most distinguished college in the East, where he would seldom come into personal contact with his instructors. . . .

President James McCosh,
Princeton University[1]

Throughout the 19th century, American colleges and universities generally accepted a rationale eloquently expressed in the famous and influential Yale Report of 1828, written in response to a request from the Connecticut Legislature that Yale drop its entrance requirement for proficiency in Latin and Greek. To the legislators, as well as many educational reformers, the requirement was elitist, undemocratic, and irrelevant to careers in commerce and industry. These groups objected to a uniform curriculum and favored a broader range of courses, especially "practical" ones, and greater opportunity for "electives." The Yalies would have none of this heresy. Like those who today defend the liberal arts against vocationalism, they insisted that career training was best learned on the job or in the graduate schools: "Our object is not to teach that which is peculiar to any of the professions; but to lay the foundation which is common to all." Central to this task was the systematic study of mathematics and the great classics of antiquity. Mathematics developed the powers of reason; classical language and literature disciplined the mind but in addition formed the taste for "what is elevated, chaste, and simple." Other subjects were important, but to a lesser degree. The physical sciences familiarized the student "with facts, with the process of induction, and the varieties of probable evidence."

> By English reading, he [the student] learns the power of the language in which he is to speak and write; by logic and mental philosophy, he is taught the art of thinking; by rhetoric and oratory, the art of speaking. By frequent exercise on written composition, he acquires copiousness and accuracy of expression. By extemporaneous discussion, he becomes prompt, and fluent, and animated. It is a point of high importance, that eloquence and solid learning should go together. . . . To what purpose has a man become deeply learned, if he has no faculty of communicating his knowledge? Of what use is a display of rhetorical elegance, from one who knows little or nothing which is worth communicating?

Concerning the education of "merchants, manufacturers, and farmers," the report asks, as do present-day supporters of liberal versus business education:

> Is it not desirable that they should be men of superior education, of large and liberal views, of those solid and elegant attainments, which will raise them to higher distinction, than the mere possession of property; which will not allow them to hoard their treasures, or waste them in senseless extravagance; which will enable them to adorn society by their learning, to move in the more intelligent circles with dignity, and to make such an application of their wealth, as will be

most honorable to themselves, and most beneficial to their country?

In loco parentis, much maligned today, receives Yale's heartfelt blessing. Since students "are generally of an age which requires that a substitute be provided for *parental* superintendence . . . it is necessary that some faithful and affectionate guardian take them by the hand and guide their steps." In fact, Yale was one big, happy family or perhaps a series of small, happy families:

> As the students are gathered into one family, it is deemed an essential provision that some of the officers should constitute a portion of this family; being always present with them, not only at their meals, and during the business of the day; but in the hours allotted to rest. The arrangement is such that in our college buildings, there is no room occupied by students, which is not near to the chamber of one of the officers.[2]

The academic departments also were families with a revered patriarchal chairman to give the advanced courses and an older brother, a young instructor or tutor closer to the student's age, to handle the elementary courses.

Generally, Ripon College accepted the principles enunciated in the Yale Report, but with some important exceptions. Ripon has never been a school for the elite; time and again it stated its intent to educate "the poor." Also, it offered an alternative curriculum which did not require Greek and, from the beginning, stressed coeducation.

The Catalogue of the Officers and Students of Ripon College was the only official publication of the institution, hence the only official source of information from 1864 to 1900, serving as a catalog, a student handbook, an alumni directory, an admissions brochure, and an appeal for funds.

Throughout the century, the general information section changed very little; the calendar, the courses of instruction, student regulations, and even "Expenses" remained pretty much the same. The academic year was divided into three terms: the first from September 3 to November 25 (using the *1879-80 Catalogue* as a typical example); the second, after a week's vacation, from December 2 to March 9, with no time off for Christmas; the third, after a two-week vacation, from March 24 to June 23. Summer vacation lasted 10 weeks. Beginning in the fall of 1880-81, the calendar was altered to make the winter break include Christmas. Of course, most students lived close enough for occasional short trips home, but such trips were discouraged:

> Unless it is strictly necessary, students will not be allowed to make visits home or elsewhere, if their absence would include the time of any recitation. Even when no recitation is lost, such visits are highly detrimental to a student's progress. . . . Parents are requested to make their arrangements accordingly.

The modern luxury of "cuts" was unheard of. Classes ran Monday through Saturday, with Saturday afternoon and Monday morning reserved for study and recreation. Part of one day, usually Wednesday afternoon, was reserved for Bible study and "rhetoricals," that is, composition and speech. Sunday was not completely a day of rest since all students had to attend the church of their choice at least twice; they were also expected to engage in serious contemplation. Normally, each course met for one hour five days a week; laboratories consumed eight to 10 hours in two-hour blocks. The small size of the College made sectioning and registration unnecessary: 19th-century Riponites were spared the anguish of closed courses and full sections.

Coeducation prevailed. For a short time, the College offered a three-year "Ladies' Course," which eliminated some of the classical studies but had the same senior year as the "full Collegiate Course." However, the ladies preferred the longer program; in fact, the first four graduates (in 1867) had completed the full Collegiate Course, and all were women. Consequently, the Ladies' Course was dropped in 1867. In the following year, an alternative Scientific Course, leading to a B.S. rather than a B.A. degree, was added. The alternative curriculum substituted one year of German and an additional year of science for two years of Greek. Practical necessity rather than educational theory probably dictated the B.S. degree since many collegians simply had not studied Greek in their secondary schools. Of course, they could take Greek in the Preparatory School, but this would both complicate and lengthen their college careers. Even the classicists had a larger dose of natural science than do non-science majors today, and they studied as much mathematics, including surveying, as the scientists. All students also had to take Latin, elocution, logic, rhetoric, astronomy, philosophy, theology, political economy, speech, composition, Anglo-Saxon and Early English, Chaucer (in Middle English), Shakespere [sic], and "Milton, Dryden, Pope, etc." The senior year, a kind of capstone to the undergraduate program, was the same for all students. This curriculum suggests that Ripon's 19th-century students were more broadly educated than today's.

The course of study outlined in the *1879-80 Catalogue* and here reprinted was standard for most of the century. The second column is somewhat confusing: the capitalized words are course titles in the scientific curriculum; lower-case print designated authors studied or texts used in the courses listed under the classical curriculum, but actually taken by both groups of students.

COURSES OF INSTRUCTION.

COLLEGE.

CLASSICAL COURSE.   SCIENTIFIC COURSE.

FRESHMAN YEAR.

FIRST TERM.

CLASSICAL	SCIENTIFIC
GREEK. Xenophon's Memorabilia.	MODERN LANGUAGE. German.
LATIN. Livy.	LATIN. Virgil.
MATHEMATICS.	Geometry begun.
ELOCUTION.	Raymond.

SECOND TERM.

CLASSICAL	SCIENTIFIC
GREEK. Iliad.	MODERN LANGUAGE. German.
LATIN.	Horace.
MATHEMATICS.	Geometry finished.
ELOCUTION.	Raymond.

THIRD TERM.

CLASSICAL	SCIENTIFIC
GREEK. Thucydides.	MODERN LANGUAGE. German.
LATIN.	Tacitus.
NATURAL SCIENCE.	Botany. Wood.
ELOCUTION.	Raymond.

Essays and Declamations throughout the year: also Greek and Latin Prose Composition, and Smith's Greece with Lectures in the Classical Course.

SOPHOMORE YEAR.

FIRST TERM.

CLASSICAL	SCIENTIFIC
GREEK. Tragedy.	NATURAL SCIENCE. Chemistry.
LATIN.	Horace.
MATHEMATICS.	Trigonometry.

SECOND TERM.

CLASSICAL	SCIENTIFIC
GREEK. Plato.	NATURAL SCIENCE. Chemistry.
LATIN.	Cicero's Philosophical Works.
MATHEMATICS.	Analytical Geometry. Peck.

THIRD TERM.

CLASSICAL	SCIENTIFIC
GREEK. Demosthenes.	NATURAL SCIENCE. Chemistry.
LOGIC.	Jevon's Lessons: Fowler's
MATHEMATICS.	Inductive Logic.
	Surveying and Mensuration. Ray.

Declamations and Orations throughout the year.

JUNIOR YEAR.

FIRST TERM.

NATURAL SCIENCE. Chemistry.   NATURAL SCIENCE. Mineralogy.
RHETORIC.   Hepburn's Manual.
MATHEMATICS.   Mechanics. Peck.

SECOND TERM.

NATURAL SCIENCE.   {Geology.
                                             {Physics.
ENGLISH.   Anglo-Saxon and Early English.

THIRD TERM.

NATURAL SCIENCE. Chemistry.   NATURAL SCIENCE. Physics.
ENGLISH.   Chaucer and Shakespere [sic].
ASTRONOMY.   Snell's Olmsted.

Orations and Forensic Discussions throughout the year.

SENIOR YEAR.

FIRST TERM.

MENTAL PHILOSOPHY.   Porter.
NATURAL THEOLOGY.   Butler's Analogy.
EVIDENCES OF CHRISTIANITY.   Hopkins.
ENGLISH.   Milton, Dryden, Pope, etc.

Orations and Extempore Discussions.

SECOND TERM.

MENTAL PHILOSOPHY.   Porter.
POLITICAL PHILOSOPHY.   {Constitution of the United States.
                                                Pomeroy.
                                             {Political Economy. Mill.

Orations and Extempore Discussions.

THIRD TERM.

MORAL PHILOSOPHY.   Fairchild.
POLITICAL ECONOMY.
HISTORY OF PHILOSOPHY.

Nineteenth-century presidents always taught a full load, and the senior year was considered their year, their last chance to place their moral stamp on the students. In the *1880-81 Catalogue*, President Merrell described his course in Mental and Moral Philosophy as follows:

> The foundation of the work is given by a complete course in Psychology, which aims to put the student in possession of distinct knowledge of the powers of the soul. . . . Ethics or Moral Philosophy is studied under two divisions.   In the first the philosophical grounds of morality are discussed . . . and in the second the principles of morals settled in the first part are applied to problems of practice. . . . The general aim in this department is to reveal the student to himself and to put him in intelligent possession of his own powers. For this reason large freedom of opinion and discussion is encouraged, yet with the confident expectation that sound instruction will lead to a spiritual and intuitional psychology, and to theism as the only philosophy which can satisfy a fully enlightened reason.

Ripon's current Psychology Department must be at least mildly surprised to learn that their discipline once concerned itself with "the powers of the soul."

The extra requirements listed at the end of each year were the so-called "rhetoricals." They met only once a week, but were spread over four years and gave the student individualized practice in composition and speech. Topics were chosen by the instructor but could be varied to suit the needs and interests of the students. Modern history and politics often provided material, thus enriching a curriculum weak in what we now call the social sciences. Throughout the year, the president and the faculty gave regularly scheduled extra lectures, some on academic subjects of contemporary interest, others intended to impart "practical information"; attendance was required.

Throughout the 19th century, enrollment was about equally divided between the Classical and the Scientific Courses. Since it required no Greek, the latter could be considered the easier alternative, but apparently scientific students at Ripon were in no way regarded as inferior. Those planning on the ministry almost always elected the Classical Course; those planning on the law or teaching could take either. The amount of required reading seems not to have been great, but of course much of it was in Latin and, for the classicists, in Greek; also the students had to master both Old and Middle English. Consequently, much time was spent on the mechanics of translation. Most courses required only one book, presumably supplied by the College and re-used year after year, as in secondary schools today.

The "library" consisted of a general reading room, located at various times in each of the three main buildings; there were also small departmental libraries and separate reading rooms for each of the student literary societies. The *1879-80 Catalogue* stated that the College Library (presumably the General Reading Room) contained 4,000 volumes and was open 20 hours a week, with "ample facilities . . . for the consultation of books and the drawing of them." Over the years, the college catalogs always listed a larger library as one of Ripon's greatest needs. Likewise, the student newspaper frequently mentioned heavy use of the library and consequently the need for better accommodations and more books. The librarian was always a faculty member, who received no additional salary and no reduction in his teaching load.

Ripon's emphasis on the sciences required special facilities and equipment. Early in his term, Merriman encouraged the development of a "Cabinet of Natural History," and over the years the College assembled a respectable collection of mineral and botanical specimens. In 1877, a small one-story frame building known as the Observatory or the Laboratory was constructed just east of the present site of Lane Library. Although used by all the sciences for a time, it was designed principally for chemistry and astronomy. It included a chemistry lab, a chemistry lecture room with facilities for demonstrations, and "a considerable amount of apparatus from Germany."[3] For a time, astronomy had to get along with a transit telescope and a "slit in the roof," but it soon acquired "a fine astronomical clock" and a much larger telescope.[4] The cabinet apparently occupied a part of the observatory until the late 1880s, and somewhere there was a zoology lab where "most of the time is employed in a detailed dissection of the cat."[5]

Chemistry seems to have been the favored science in most liberal arts colleges in the 19th century, perhaps because it was theologically neutral. Hands-on laboratory work as a regular part of undergraduate instruction, as opposed to lecture-demonstrations or observation and classification of specimens, developed first and most fully in chemistry and then spread to the other sciences. This was true at Ripon, where adequate facilities for biology did not appear until space was made for them on the third floor of Middle College after the construction of a new women's dormitory (Bartlett Cottage) in the late 1880s. Physics had to wait for the completion of Ingram Hall in 1900. Ripon was trying very hard to keep "its methods of instruction in harmony with the most enlightened views of education,"[6] but clearly it was limited by the modesty of its resources.

Examinations, probably very much like today's, were given on the last two days of each term; they were written, two or three hours long, and of course much dreaded by the students. Degrees were conferred by the faculty with board approval. Early catalogs refer to an Examining Committee performing some function at Commencement time. Composed of regional Congregational ministers and probably representing the state Congregational Convention, they were examining the College, not the students. Much like the considerably more thorough periodic examiners from regional accrediting agencies and professional societies today, they visited classes, checked out the institution generally, and then reported to the board and presumably to the convention also.

During the Merriman years, the faculty, who taught both the preparatory and college students, averaged about 12, with a ratio of seven men to five women. The surprisingly high number of women was due to the need for "proctors" for lady students. In 1865, pay for men was $450 to $600 per year; for women, $300 to $375. The president earned $800. Although these figures were high enough to attract teachers, they were often not high enough to keep them. So the trustees occasionally granted across-the-board raises, mostly to the males; it was easier for men than women to find better-paying jobs elsewhere. By modern standards, faculty turnover was moderate. Among the men who stayed more than two years, only Presidents Merriman and Merrell were ministers. About half the men but none of the women had a master's degree (at that time an honorary rather than an earned degree); there was one M.D., but not a single Ph.D. Instructorships were apt to be filled by local people, many of them recent graduates of the College, with the professors recruited further afield through a network of personal and denominational contacts. Of course, the missionary spirit was still strong, the West was still the land of opportunity, many young men and women heeded Horace Greeley's advice to go west, and Ripon has always been an attractive place to teach. Consequently, despite lack of money and other resources, both Merriman and Merrell hired a number of very able teachers. Here are three examples.

Joseph Geery came to Ripon in 1868 as Professor of Rhetoric and English Literature. He was a native of New York City but received his preparatory and collegiate training at Oberlin College, where he may have made the acquaintance of Merrell. At this time, Oberlin's school year ran through the summer months so that students could earn money teaching school during the winter. As a young man, Geery spent his winters in southeastern Wisconsin teaching in the town of

Union, but returned to Oberlin each summer for eight consecutive years. Upon graduation, he took the position at Ripon, where he had the unenviable task of teaching the mysteries of grammar and syntax to the college students all four years; in other words, he was responsible for the rhetoricals. In addition, he taught the junior and senior courses in English literature, among them Chaucer in the original Middle English. Highly regarded by both students and faculty, he served as faculty secretary, a position comparable to that of dean but without any released time from his teaching duties; he represented the faculty on the Executive Committee of the Board of Trustees. He also served as member and chairman of the Fond du Lac County Board of Supervisors. Never in good health, he died of tuberculosis in 1884 while still a member of the faculty. A key figure in the pioneer period of the College's development, he typified the ideal 19th-century college professor. "He lived out before us," wrote William B. Shaw, one of his students, "the full embodiment of a cultured gentleman." This same student recalled a notice on the college bulletin board written in Geery's precise hand: "Those seniors who fail to hand in manuscripts of orations and essays on the dates specified will learn that there is indeed a God in Israel!"[7] An interesting sidelight on Geery: His son, William B. Geery, a graduate of the Academy but not the College, served as Chairman of the Federal Reserve Board and became a trustee of Ripon College in 1929.

C. Dwight Marsh, Professor of Biology from 1883 to 1903, was a summa cum laude, Phi Beta Kappa graduate of Amherst. At Ripon, he introduced the first biology course using modern laboratory techniques and was instrumental in the construction of Ingram Hall. Originally intended solely as a science facility, it actually became, much to Marsh's disappointment, an all-purpose classroom building. Ingram Hall and its laboratory equipment clearly enhanced Ripon's reputation. Actively involved in statewide organizations such as the Wisconsin Academy of Sciences, Arts, and

Letters, Marsh worked hard and successfully to cement Ripon's relations with the University of Wisconsin, an effort which paid off handsomely during Richard Hughes' presidency. Since some of Marsh's students considered him an atheist, Marsh probably accepted Darwin's theories of evolution and natural selection. Thus, it is surprising that he survived under the extremely conservative Merrell, but he did. He was the first person to become dean of the College, and he served as acting president during the interim between Presidents Flagg and Hughes. In 1903, he resigned to complete his Ph.D. in biology at the University of Chicago; perhaps he had hoped to be elected president; undoubtedly, he was disappointed in the fate of Ingram Hall. In any event, he enhanced his career as a research scientist by joining, in 1905, the Department of Agriculture in Washington, where he became a world-renowned authority on poisonous plants. Marsh represented the new breed of college faculty, a scholar-teacher rather than a minister-teacher, identified with a profession rather than a mission. He had much to do with the improved fortunes of Ripon College after the turn of the century, with the enhancement of its reputation, and with the reforming of its educational philosophy. Certainly, he was the father of modern science at the College.[8]

Cyrus Baldwin served as Professor of Latin from 1875 to 1884. A New Yorker and another graduate of Oberlin, he completed his studies at Andover Theological Seminary in Massachusetts, but was never ordained. After leaving Ripon, he held administrative positions in the YMCA in Iowa and California and, in 1890, became the first president of Pomona College in Claremont, California.[9] Three other Ripon College faculty members also became presidents of prestigious institutions: Stephen Newman, Professor of Mathematics and Astronomy (1881-83), Howard University in Washington, D. C.; William Ballantine, Professor of Chemistry and Natural Science (1873-76), Oberlin College; and James Eaton, Professor of Ancient Languages (1884-89), Whitman College in Walla Walla, Washington.

During the 19th century, the College was economically and efficiently run, as it always has been. In the modern
sense, there was virtually no administration. Even the
president carried a full teaching load, though he was away
from the campus frequently, making it necessary for some
other member of the faculty to fill in. But occasionally the
tables were turned, and he would substitute for an absent
instructor in both the Academy and the College. Other
"administrative" officers, such as the secretary of the faculty,
the registrar, the librarian, the assistant treasurer, and the
superintendent of the Ladies' Department, were regular
members of the faculty without released time. Proctors and
college matrons (at least until the 1890s) also had teaching
assignments, and all of the manual labor in the domestic
department and what would now be called buildings and
grounds was done by students in return for room and board.
The college payroll was as short as it was minimal, a reflection
of the size of the school and of its budget. This "exploitation"
of personnel was due both to the lack of national and local
professional organizations and to the missionary spirit that
had brought many of the faculty to a frontier college in the
first place. This attitude was beginning to change in the last
two decades of the century with the appointment of people
like Marsh, but it was still a significant force, and the College
clearly relied on it.

No one personified this missionary spirit more completely than Clarissa Tucker Tracy. She had come to Ripon
as superintendent of the Ladies' Department in 1859 and
was to maintain an uninterrupted association with the
College until her death at the age of 87 in 1905. She served
as a kind of dean of women, an instructor in biology, and head
of both the Food Service and Housekeeping Departments.
These duties included living in a dormitory as a proctor and
personally preparing the meals every day for more than a
hundred people. Most of her classes were in the Preparatory
Department, where she taught mathematics, English literature, and composition in addition to her specialty, botany.

She found time to research the wild flowers growing near Ripon and, in 1889, published a *Catalogue of Plants Growing Without Cultivation in the Ripon Area*. Her china was decorated with carefully painted reproductions of many of these plants done by her own hand. Students considered her an excellent teacher but were just a little afraid of her in the classroom, where she had the reputation of being "tough." But as counselor, preceptress, and friend she was remembered with love and respect by everyone in the college community.[10]

There was never any question that Ripon was a "Christian" college: "Instruction will be conducted on Christian principles, and it will be the aim of instructors to pervade it with a strong and healthful moral and religious influence."[11] Thirty years later, the *Catalogue* remained consistent: "The development of character is an essential part of the work of an educational institution and . . . there is no sound basis of character except in Christian principle."[12] Maintaining Christian principles was primarily the president's responsibility, and both Merriman and Merrell fulfilled it in a three-term required course in the senior year. Called Mental and Moral Philosophy, it was essentially a highly personalized course in Christian ethics.

This was supplemented by a one-term course, also taught by the president, called Evidences of Christianity, using a textbook of the same name written by one of Merriman's former teachers, President Mark Hopkins of Williams College. First published in 1846, it remained a bulwark of evangelical teaching for more than half a century, and it was still being used at Ripon in 1900. Both text and course attempted to demonstrate the unity of faith and reason, the perfect harmony between scripture and science, and the impossibility of establishing any true system of morality not based on Christianity, particularly evangelical Protestantism. The second textbook edition, published in 1879, included important new evidence on the compatibility of science and scripture but made no mention whatever of

Darwin's theory of evolution. Thus, the required curriculum of the College contained a solid core of orthodox evangelical instruction, untainted by any "modernist" ideas, through the end of the century.

Class work was reinforced by other required activities including attendance twice on Sunday at the church of one's choice, Sunday evening chapel at the College, and morning chapel on all other days. Chapel included prayers, hymns, and other devotional exercises, but it was not really a church service. It was a college assembly or convocation concerned with school business, announcements, and other administrative detail. Although there was always a short "talk" by some member of the faculty, or even a student, on an uplifting topic, it was not necessarily a sermon. Still, chapel was intended to set the tone for the day's work, and it constantly reminded the students of their religious obligations. It was one of the hallmarks of a Christian college.

The response of the college students to the religious requirements of the school is difficult to measure. They did cut chapel on occasion even though they received demerits for their boldness and might actually suffer loss of academic credit; and they did misbehave during chapel services in spite of the intimidating presence of the faculty and strict segregation of the sexes. Still, the overall impression that one gets from the *College Days* is one of willing acceptance. Many, quite possibly most, students participated in "extra-curricular" Bible study classes organized by students for students (with obvious faculty complicity since free time was reserved in the college calendar for just such activities). Informal gatherings in the Commons before Sunday evening chapel were sometimes used as occasions for hymn singing when recent performance indicated a need for more practice or simply to get everyone in the proper mood for the coming service. Very likely it was the students planning a career in the ministry who took the lead, but there were always plenty of willing followers. By background and training, most Ripon students of this era were prepared to accept the religious assumptions underlying much of their college experience. If not, they went somewhere else. Only rarely did a student or parent complain that religion might be interfering with education. Not surprisingly, the college YMCA, to be discussed in the next chapter, was one of the most popular undergraduate organizations.

NOTES TO CHAPTER V
THE NINETEENTH-CENTURY
FACULTY AND CURRICULUM

[1]*College Days*, March, 1873.

[2]Hofstadter and Smith, I, 279-89.

[3]*1977-78 Catalogue*, 29.

[4]*College Days*, May, 1886, 86.

[5]*1885-86 Catalogue*, 22.

[6]*1877-78 Catalogue*, 24.

[7]"Joseph Geery," Personnel File, Archives.

[8]"C. Dwight Marsh," Personnel Files, Archives.

[9]"Cyrus Baldwin," Personnel File, Archives.

[10]Ada Clark Merrell, *Life and Poems of Clarissa Tucker Tracy*;
Thomann, 14-18.

[11]*1866-67 Catalogue*, xix.

[12]*1899-1900 Catalogue*, 8.

CHAPTER VI

A CHRISTIAN COLLEGE
NINETEENTH-CENTURY
STUDENT LIFE

Ripon is situated in a region famed for beautiful summer resorts, the health-fulness of its climate, and absence of malarial diseases.

Ripon College Newsletter

Every student should be provided with table napkins, an umbrella, overshoes, and plenty of warm underclothing.

Ripon College Catalogue

Almost all students in both the Preparatory and Collegiate Divisions came from homes within 50 miles of Ripon, roughly half from the city itself. Of the first 120 graduates of the College, a third stayed in Wisconsin, another third went west, mostly to Minnesota and to the Dakota and Montana territories, and the final third scattered over the rest of the United States and a few foreign locales, the most exotic being Shanghai, China, Ceylon, and Burma. Thirty-one became teachers; 26, lawyers; and another 26, either ministers or missionaries. Among the more notable early graduates were James Armstrong Blanchard '71, Justice of the New York Supreme Court; Kossuth Kent Kennan '75, Tax Commissioner of Wisconsin; and Frank K. Sanders '82, Dean of the Yale Divinity School and later President of Washburn University in Topeka, Kansas.

In his appeal to the Western College Society, President Merriman had promised "to keep the College near to the poor," and the early catalogs echoed Merriman with a pledge "to make the expense of pursuing a course of liberal study as low as is consistent with a high degree of excellence in its results, and thus to keep a liberal education within reach of young men and women of limited means." The College certainly kept its promise.

To anyone paying the bills for a college education in the 1990s, the cost of a year at Ripon in the 1880s must seem fantastically minimal. Charges per term were $8 for tuition, $2-$5 for room rent, $4-$8 for fuel (kerosene lamps) and laundry, slightly less for books and stationery, $3.50-$6 per cord for firewood, $2.50 for chemistry lab, and $2 for incidentals; other expenses were $2.50 per week for board and 25 cents per week for tea and coffee. By living off campus, where "board in private families, with furnished room, varies from $2.50 to $3.50 per week" and by eating in a cooperative for $1.50 to $2.50 per week, a student could save a little money. Total cost for a full year (three terms) could be as low as $200.

Under the heading "self-help," the *Catalogue* encouraged students of "limited means" to work their way through school. For "young ladies," this meant assisting in "the Domestic Department," thus defraying part of their board. Young men, however, were left to their own devices; the College had some work for them, but did not guarantee it. Both sexes were told they might find teaching jobs in the Ripon area, but this almost certainly would lengthen their course of study. In fact, the College discouraged too much "self-help": no one was required to work, and no one was permitted more than two hours service per day. Furthermore, parents were urged to "consider that a good education is always worth more than it costs, and that money well expended in it is the wisest investment for their children." There is no way of telling how many students earned all their way, but certainly large numbers, like today, earned part of it.

The experience of Kent Kennan, class of 1875 and father of the famed George Kennan, who formulated the policy of containment during the cold war years and received a Ripon honorary degree in 1978, was probably typical. Before entering Ripon, he taught grade school for a year and managed to save most of his salary by living at his home near Milwaukee and walking the three miles to and from school. But he found teaching neither the easiest nor the safest way to earn a living:

> There were a few big boys who evidently cherished an ambition "to lick the teacher" but when they found out that I carried a revolver and usually kept my hand within reach of the large school bell (in itself a formidable weapon) they expressed their disgust with the school and the teacher and did not come any more.

At Ripon, Kennan lived part of the time with Professor Merrell's family, earning his keep by doing "chores."

> Professor Merrell kept a horse and a cow in the college barn, back of the middle building, and it was part of my duty to milk the cow night and morning, clean out the stables, feed and water the "critters" three times a day and curry the horse. My major duties, however, centered about the woodpile during the winter. It was no small task to saw and split cordwood into stove size and carry it up to seven stoves which had to be kept going.

Kennan spent most of his summers helping out on the family farm, but also earned money as a hod carrier. When it became necessary, he would drop out of school for a time and resume his career as a teacher. On one such occasion, he obtained a position at Lawrence University, where he taught calisthenics for a term. Then, with this experience behind him, he returned to Ripon as a sophomore and was able to persuade the faculty to give him "a large room in the basement of the 'West Building' for a gymnasium," which he "fitted up with parallel bars, trapeses, boxing gloves and other necessary paraphernalia." With this equipment, he taught a non-credit course in physical education for men. "I also organized a class of about a hundred young ladies," he continued, "who met at 7 a.m. each day [probably on the fourth floor of Middle College] and I drilled them in light gymnastics—especially in ring and wand exercises. For this I was allowed my room in West Building and my board in the commons."[1] Thus, Kennan helped put himself through school, an extracurricular program was organized, and the College got a free "coach."

In 1882, the College introduced a system of scholar-ships frequently used by other institutions. Its main pur-pose, however, was to raise money for the College, not to provide education for needy students. Scholarships were sold to anyone who would buy them for $50 apiece, the goal being to sell 1,000 and thereby raise $50,000 for endowment. Each scholarship could then be used by a student of the buyer's choice to pay for five years' tuition if used within 10 years. Although this may have been an effective recruiting device and may have helped worthy students, it was not an efficient system of college finance since a $50 scholarship bought more than $100 worth of tuition. Consequently, the system was abandoned in 1902. Meanwhile, no program of student aid based on academic merit had been established. The closest approach was a system of prizes offered each year to students already enrolled who had achieved distinction in a particular field of study. The first of these was the James Prize given annually to four students in the Collegiate De-partment judged by the faculty to have made the most progress in English composition. Established in 1870 through a gift of $1,000 from Mrs. John M. James of Boston, it is still presented today. A number of other similar cash awards were endowed before the end of the century as a way of recognizing academic excellence.

As Kennan's recollections suggest, the living was not easy during the 1870s, and it did not improve markedly before 1900, particularly for the men. Dormitory accommodations were spartan. Rooms furnished by the College included "a stove, bedstead, wash-stand, table and plain chairs"; students provided their mattress, bedding, lamp, curtains, a rug, a table spread, "and everything that contributes to the comfort and pleasantness of a room."[2] There was no central heating, no running water, and no indoor plumbing, luxuries, however, that most students did not enjoy in their own homes. The rooms must have been cold, and the winter-long necessity of fueling the stove by one's own labor and at one's own expense must have made them more so. According to H. S. Clapp, a student in the 1870s,

> Water for drinking and bathing was obtained at the college pump, and there being no bathrooms or other conveniences, the water was kept in pitchers and pails and heated on the stoves, student ablutions being performed in their own rooms whenever convenient. Each closet contained not only one's best clothes, but his supply of wood, water, and kerosene, and his broom, dustpan, extra bedding and other supplies. [3]

There were never enough rooms on campus for all preparatory and college students until the end of the century; either by choice or by necessity, many college students lived off campus. In the early years, East College provided a few rooms for men; but, after the construction of Middle as a women's residence hall and West for men, the original "college" (East Hall) ceased to house students. Middle and West were always multi-purpose buildings, West until the

1960s: Middle College contained classrooms, the dining hall, and a student lounge; West, the chapel, the "gymnasium," and more classrooms. Both had student clubrooms and, consequently, were the centers of student social life until the late 1880s. In 1883, the remodeling of East made it possible to relocate the chapel and the Athenian Society clubroom in that building; in 1888, with the completion of Bartlett Cottage for women, part of Middle College became available for men. A certain amount of reshuffling continued throughout the century, but Middle tended to be the residence hall for college men, West for the male preps.

In the well-established tradition of the Yale Report, a few young unmarried instructors lived in the dormitories as proctors in return for room and board; this practice was not given up entirely until the 1960s. In the late 1800s, the faculty enforced rules of social conduct as well as academic standards, and they met frequently to review regulations and to consider student petitions for changes. Yet, students were also encouraged to develop self-discipline:

> The regulations of the College are few and simple, and designed to cultivate manliness and self-respect by placing the student largely upon his honor and personal responsibility. [Presumably this applied to women as well as men.] Punctual attendance on all prescribed exercises and cheerful observation of the rules are required. Study hours must be spent in study. Students are expected to be exemplary in morals and manners. None but those who earnestly desire improvement are wanted here, and such as continue to be disorderly or idle cannot be allowed to remain. [4]

The *Catalogue* became more specific on three points only: as already mentioned, students were not to leave Ripon during a term unless "strictly necessary"; no student was permitted "to visit the room of a student of the opposite sex, except by special permission in case of severe illness"; and the use of tobacco in any form was "strictly prohibited." Although not mentioned in the *Catalogue*, the possession or use of alcoholic beverages on campus was also forbidden. Perhaps this could be taken for granted since it was proscribed by state law. But drinking on campus may not have been a problem in the 1870s, 1880s, or 1890s, since a poll of students eligible to vote showed that more of them supported the Prohibition Party than either of the major parties. Nevertheless, rules on this subject were posted in all dormitory rooms. Regulations concerning "hours," recreational activities, and general decorum were also enforced. Students were expected to be responsible, but it was thought best to keep them free of temptation; they were assumed to be earnest, but even more earnest proctors were provided to keep them in line.

On the other hand, there seem to have been plenty of high jinks by both preppies and collegians. Routine mischief included illegally ringing the college bell at odd hours of the night. The bell was legally used to summon students to class and to chapel, but also to sound a fire alarm. Fire was a constant threat in buildings made largely of wood with each room heated by a wood stove and lighted by kerosene lamps. Remarkably, none of them burned to the ground even though central heating was not introduced till 1907. But, whether legal or illegal, the sounding of the bell at night was sure to produce a good deal of frantic activity. More imaginative stunts included "borrowing" some faculty member's carriage, pulling it out into the country, and abandoning it; placing a wagon fully loaded with cordwood on the top of West College; and coaxing a cow up the stairways of East into the cupola on the roof, from which it could not be persuaded to descend of its own free will. These were Halloween stunts most likely to occur on that evening, but certainly ingenuity produced pranks on other nights as well.

Obviously, proctoring was a wearisome and arduous

task, and few instructors, male or female, could stand it for very long. This was true even of the superintendent of the Ladies Department, later known as the preceptress. The 19th-century equivalent of a dean of women, except that they lived in a dormitory, these ladies came and went with great regularity, often surviving for just one year. The record, 10 years, was held by the indomitable Mrs. Tracy.

It should come as no surprise that the women were more carefully "guarded" than the men as they were throughout the nation until well past the middle of the present century and for the same somewhat suspect reasons— women were assumed to be less able to take care of themselves, and parents had to be assured of the safety of their daughters on a coed campus. Like their 20th-century successors, the Ripon ladies resented what they felt to be discrimination, protested against it, and won an occasional victory. After a lengthy squabble in 1885, a rule requiring women, but not men, to be in bed by 10 p.m. was abolished. But the faculty balked when a group of ladies requested permission to join the lads at a roller-skating rink in downtown Ripon on Saturday afternoons: it was not thought proper for the fair sex to become involved in this "craze." To its credit, the *College Days* opposed the faculty's decision. But, actually, Ripon's parietal rules were not overly oppressive by Victorian standards, and the two sexes were more equally treated than one might have expected.

In one area, dormitory accommodations, women got much the better deal, especially after 1888, when Bartlett Cottage was built on land formerly used as a baseball diamond, a distinct defeat for masculinity. Lucy Bartlett of Oshkosh made the largest single gift ($6,000), asked that it be named after her recently deceased husband, and stipulated that it be called a cottage. A cottage it was not. Although the College went a bit overboard in announcing "that it will be unsurpassed in completeness of appointments and comfort by any similar building in the country," the *Ripon Commonwealth* for September 30, 1887, was correct in describing it as "more pretentious in appearance than any of the earlier buildings." It was also more comfortable and commodious, providing apartments for 44 women, with a separate study and bedroom for every two occupants, in this respect being far superior to any of Ripon's previous dormitories and most of its later ones. It quickly became the showpiece of the campus. It was the first building to have steam heat rather than woodstoves and, somewhat later, hardwood floors, electricity, and more or less modern plumbing. It even inspired a poem:

> Oh thou Bartlett! Noble Bartlett!
> Once again we sing of thee,
> Down the Ages may thou ever
> The Fair Queen of Ripon be.

The Bartlett women realized their good fortune and took pride in making an attractive residence, raising money for a piano and decorating their rooms with pictures, pennants, and pillows. It was a nice place to live and also to entertain in the comfortable parlors on the first floor, designed for both formal receptions and informal get-togethers. Bartlett soon replaced Middle College as the social center of the campus.

It is a little startling to learn that the Bartlett "yell" of the 1890s was "You just ask us; we'll say yes!" Perhaps opportunities to say "yes" were enhanced by the fire escape on the south side, which came to be called the "Romeo and Juliet balcony." But, except for Saturday night socials, men were allowed only one visit to Bartlett per week, the "squelch bell" sounded every evening but Saturday at 7:30 p.m. and Saturdays at 10; at both times "chasers" were summarily expelled by the proctors.[5]

The Commons in Middle College, managed by men students as helpers, provided board at nominal rates for preps, collegians, and faculty. Since the *College Days* never exploded into outrage, the food must have been at least adequate. In addition to the Commons, two co-ops or eating clubs served meals at even lower cost. The Economia Club for men, started in 1879, remained a fixture of the campus into the 20th century. Its success was due largely to the work of Mary Bessett, who served as its matron for more than 20 years, allowing the men to use her home on Congress Street (the present site of Merriman House) for their dining hall and club rooms. The members elected their own officers, who oversaw the operation, bought the food, and collected the assessments. Any money left over at the end of the school year was divided equally among the participants. For many years, the club was very popular; in 1887, for example, it had 45 members. In that year, a similar organization for women was established in Dawes Cottage, a small frame house just south of the present Memorial Gym, which was torn down in 1975. Smaller and more carefully supervised by the College than the Economia, it never enjoyed quite the same prominence, but nonetheless provided well-prepared meals for under $2 a week. So successful were these clubs that the College's own dining hall was reorganized on a cooperative basis in 1893. The fact that Mrs. Tracy had ceased to be matron by that time may have precipitated the change. Called the Cooperative Eating Club, it enrolled both students and faculty, elected its own officers (always students), and managed the facility with the help of a matron.

In the 19th century, the line between the curricular and the extracurricular was less clearly defined than it is today, especially in terms of faculty control. Since the College was a Christian family, what the students did outside class concerned the faculty as much as what they did in class and was considered just as integral a part of their liberal education.

Within the confines of the "college family," however, the students were allowed a certain amount of freedom as long as they used it responsibly, productively, and morally. They were given opportunities to develop organizational skills, assume leadership roles, and practice conventional social graces and were provided time for recreation. This freedom was real in the sense that almost all extracurricular activities were organized by student initiative with a minimum of faculty interference. If the students did not assume responsibility for them, they did not happen. Like their brothers and sisters elsewhere, Ripon students sponsored literary societies, a newspaper, oratorical contests, musical organizations, religious societies, and athletic programs; secret societies were, however, prohibited. Although it was hard for a school of Ripon's size to keep all this going at the same time, the students did so with reasonable success.

The college catalogs informed prospective students only that a wide range of extracurricular opportunities existed. Consequently, the best record of these activities was the student newspaper, *College Days*. Today, the *Days* claims to be Wisconsin's oldest college newspaper, and although it has not enjoyed uninterrupted publication since its founding in 1868, it is probably entitled to make this claim. From May, 1868, until March of 1874, it appeared under the name *College Days* as a monthly. For the next six years, it underwent a number of changes both in title and format, taking the name *Ripon College Quarterly* (1877-78), then *College News* (1879), and finally *Ripon College News Letter* (1879-81); but in January, 1882, it reappeared under the heading *College Days*. It has continued under that name as a monthly, a weekly, a biweekly, or a triweekly until the present day.

Originally, the *Days* was more journal than newspaper in the strict sense of the word, serving as a literary magazine, a humor magazine, an alumni newsletter, a campus newspaper, and finally, in the last issue of each school year, a yearbook. It also gave regular space to news from other colleges made possible by the exchange of publications. These publications were available to all students in one of the college reading rooms, but it is not likely that many of them received even a cursory reading. Clippings lifted from another school's paper made handy filler just as do *Intercol-*

legiate Press Bulletins today.

A typical issue of the *Days* in the 1880s (February, 1881), included an "Editorial" section with a number of short pieces on such things as the latest student craze at Madison (dressing like Oscar Wilde) and care of the Ripon campus when the ground was soft because of an early thaw. It carried longer, more serious efforts on "The Student's Responsibility to the World" and the "slanderous" comments in the town press concerning Ripon faculty and students. Then there was a poem by Miss Fanshaw, a junior prize oration by C. T. Kennan, and a synopsis of Professor Geery's lecture in the college chapel on Tennyson's "In Memoriam." And finally, there were two letters to the editor, one deploring rowdiness on other college campuses, the other urging attendance at an upcoming concert; four pages of "local" and "personal" news, most of it intended to be humorous; a page and a half of clippings from other college papers, and six pages of ads. Each issue contained 20 pages and sold for 15 cents a copy and $1 for the full year. A decade later, there would be more sports news and more news from and for alumni. Inevitably, the quality of the *Days* bore some relation to the size of the College Department. If one or two students were carrying most of the burden of publication, original composition was limited. Nevertheless, the paper was generally well edited and had an attractive format. Photographs did not appear as a regular feature until the late 1880s, when formal portraits and group pictures began to be inserted. These were most numerous in the "yearbook issue" published in June. Major changes in style and form did not occur until after 1910, when a much larger student body was able to undertake a more ambitious weekly paper, a separate literary magazine, and a separate yearbook.

Originally the *Days* was managed by the College Days Publication Association. During the years when it was published under other names, it was a private enterprise. From 1882 to 1905 it was managed by two of the campus literary societies, the Athenians (for college men) and the Ecolians (for college women); in 1905 it was taken over by the Oratorical Union. The literary societies were the primary force in the school's extracurricular program at least until the 1890s when athletic teams created a second outlet for student energy. Although their activities now appear to have been highly academic, they were conceived as a counterpoise to the regular educational program. In the first place, they were voluntary organizations run by the students with a social as well as an intellectual purpose. In the second place, their literary efforts, their debates, and their oratorical contests concerned topics more current and more worldly than those dealt with in class. Finally, the societies provided experience in composition, public speaking, and debate that augmented and applied the instruction received in rhetoricals. The professional careers anticipated by most college men and women in this period—law, the ministry, and teaching—called for special skills in these areas; hence, students wanted all the practice they could get. Although these activities involved significant efforts, the work was considered sufficiently different from that in regular courses to provide a healthy diversion.

At Ripon, literary societies had been formed by the pre-college students as early as the 1850s, with Booth War hero Hugh La Grange being one of the driving forces. When the College Division bloomed at the end of the Civil War, a number of new societies appeared almost immediately. The women were first to organize, establishing the Ecolian Society in 1864. Although membership required election, it was open to any woman registered in the College. The men followed with the Hermean Society and the Lincolnian Society two years later. In the beginning, both were open to preps and collegians, but in 1873 these groups were disbanded in favor of an Athenian Society for college men and a Philomatheon Society for male preps. The Ecolians, Athenians, and Philomatheons remained active throughout the century.

Once it was well established, each society was given a clubroom: the women in Middle College and later in

Bartlett; the men in West until 1883, when the Athenians moved into East. The rooms were used for meetings, social events, and libraries, which, small as they were, rivaled the College's collection at least until the 1880s. Their weekly meetings consisted primarily of organized debates on assigned topics as well as extemporaneous speaking and/or declamations. On occasion, however, there were parties and receptions, and, from time to time, the societies sponsored outside speakers for the school as a whole. The students requested joint meetings of Athenians and Ecolians; but, despite arguments that "nothing calls out the best and most active work of a literary society as do occasional visitors," the faculty said no. Following one such rejection, the *College Days* suggested that this stuffiness on the part of the faculty might explain why "so many Ripon students [were] found at Oberlin, Carleton, Madison, Beloit, and elsewhere."

The societies also sponsored all-campus oratorical and declamation contests, and eventually the Athenian Society joined the State Oratorical Association and participated in intercollegiate oratorical competition. Beloit College was the active promoter of this organization, which, at various times, included Lawrence and Milton. Beloit was usually the state champion; but Ripon's record was quite acceptable. A convincing win in 1890 was greeted with all the fervor of a present-day conference football championship. Actually, Ripon's participation was an on-again, off-again proposition during the 1880s when enrollments were unusually low, but in 1890 it rejoined the association and thereafter took part in interstate competition as well. These contests were always well attended, generating the kind of excitement that one would expect at an athletic event. The judges were drawn from all over the state and might include such well-known personalities as Governor (later Senator) Robert LaFollette, one of the great orators of his time. The *College Days* reported the contests with appropriate "color" commentary and generally included the texts of the winning orations. Since oratory was an art form that commanded universal respect, those who performed it well were the campus heroes of their time, especially since these events were Ripon's first venture into intercollegiate competition.

In popularity, the literary societies were rivaled only by the religious groups. Spontaneous religious revivals among college students had been fairly common before the Civil War, and Ripon had been the scene of at least one while it was only an academy. They were considerably less prevalent after the war, but regularly scheduled meetings, much like the earlier revivals, were frequent in the post-war years and often resulted in mass conversions. One such event was the Day of Prayer for Colleges, originated by Yale students in the 1830s and celebrated annually at many colleges, including Ripon; it was always scheduled well in advance for a particular day in late January or early February, with all classes canceled. The day's activities, planned by the student Christian Association, a voluntary organization of men and women who had actually been "called to Christ," included meditation and lengthy chapel services during which as many as 30 students might make public declarations of faith; for some, apparently, it was a major turning point in their lives. These events were always carefully reported in the student newspaper with vivid commentary on the extent and zeal of student commitment. Although there is some evidence that religious fervor was waning in the early 1880s, it revived again later in the decade when chapters of the YMCA and YWCA were organized.

These associations were part of an international movement founded in England in the 1840s. By the 1880s, they were well-established, well-organized, and well-financed on American college campuses, where they quickly took over most of the "Christian work," such as Bible study, prayer meetings (including the Day of Prayer), and the recruiting of missionaries for foreign service. The goal of the latter activity was nothing less than "the evangelization of the world in this generation."[6]

The Ripon College YMCA was formally organized in

1886; the YWCA, later that same year. The dedication of the men's meeting room, the first in the state set aside for that purpose, was a major event in the early history of the College with both the international secretary of the "Y" and the state secretary in attendance. The members of the Ripon YMCA threw themselves wholeheartedly into the activities of the state organization with its tried and true programs for Bible study, its workshops for campus leaders, its annual conventions, and its summer schools at Lake Geneva. But the Ripon women were not far behind. The first Wisconsin state convention of the YWCA was held on the Ripon campus with the national secretary of that organization on hand. The delegates came out four-square against dancing, card playing, and theater going. By the end of the century, the two religious associations were among the most vital student organizations on campus. If extracurricular piety at Ripon had lost some of its earlier spontaneity, it had certainly become much better organized.

In addition to the literary and religious societies, the College sponsored musical societies, always closely tied to the Music School, a separate division not yet integrated into the College. Singing groups and a college band were usually available for special events such as Commencement and might even undertake limited tours. Science clubs were organized on more than one occasion, and in 1886 a popular Biological Society was formed under the aegis of Professor Dwight Marsh "for the continuance of the study of Botany and Zoology" beyond the limit imposed by a one-year course.

The wave of the future was represented by the Athletic Association founded "for gentlemen" in 1877, primarily to organize track and field contests, and by separate clubs for baseball and "football" that came and went depending on student interest. The term "club sport," not then in use, would have been an accurate term since there were no coaches other than the team captains, no uniforms except as might be needed for physical protection, and no commonly accepted rules. Baseball was the first team sport to generate enthusiasm in the years immediately following the Civil War; as many as three student teams might be playing at the same time, occasionally in association with town players. Their schedule included high school and academy teams in the area as well as town clubs in nearby communities. Home games were played on the relatively level ground at the foot of the hill now occupied by Bartlett and Harwood Memorial Union. Apparently, Ripon was not able to field a team every year, but baseball was always a popular sport that was played pretty much as it is today.

This was not true of football. A game called football had existed for centuries, the object being to advance an inflated bladder toward an opponent's goal by kicking it; but after the Civil War, a unique American version of the game began to evolve by way of soccer and rugby, taking root on eastern college campuses in the late 1860s. Its rules were so various and so changeable that each game had to be preceded by negotiations concerning the shape of the ball, the number of players, and the rules of play. No record was kept of the regulations in the first reported contest at Ripon in 1881, an intramural game between members of the Economia Club and another organization known as the Spartans. Unfortunately, the game had to be called before the issue was decided because the ball burst. The next year, however, the College received a challenge from the men at Lawrence University, and what followed was the start of the oldest college football rivalry in the Middle West.

The Ripon squad, 11 starters and two substitutes, entrained for Appleton on Friday, November 17, 1882. Upon arrival, they were treated to a "social" and an oyster supper prepared by the young ladies of one of the Lawrence literary societies. The *Days* reported that it was "stacks of fun." Next morning at 10 a.m., the game began on a soggy field under threatening skies. To the dismay of the Ripon "eleven," the Lawrentians were using an oval ball in place of a round one, and they were playing on a field about a third the size of the one used for practice in Ripon. Nevertheless, the Ripon contingent pulled away to a 2-1 lead before the game was called on account of rain; they had been at it for an hour and a half. Apparently, they were playing a game more like rugby than modern American football. Still, everyone enjoyed it, and plans were made for a return match in Ripon the following year, a game that never took place. In fact, there were very few games for Ripon, even at the intramural level, until 1891 when more formal play was inaugurated under somewhat different rules.

Meanwhile, the major sports event of the year was the annual spring Field Day sponsored by the Athletic Association. At first, this was an intramural track meet made up of foot races, bicycle races, and a few field events such as the "running jump," "sledge throw," and "vaulting with pole." More frivolous events, including a sack race, a "Siamese Twin" race, and a 50-yard hop, added to the entertainment, and the afternoon was topped off by a tug-of-war. It was as much a social occasion as it was an athletic contest and brought the whole College as well as a good crowd of town people to the Ripon Fair Grounds, located just east of the current Ripon Foods plant. But in 1889, the Field Day acquired a more serious purpose when Lawrence University invited Ripon to participate in a joint meet that would include track and field events and a baseball game. When the Ripon men accepted the challenge, an annual event was inaugurated that took place either in Appleton or Ripon or possibly on neutral ground in Oshkosh. Relations between the student Athletic Associations of the two schools were formalized by an agreement signed in 1892. Some of the frivolous events were dropped from the games, but the social side of the meet was not neglected, as each school would extend its hospitality to any and all students who made the trip along with the contestants. Although women were not participating in the games, they were invited to go along for moral support and to cheer their men on to victory with carefully rehearsed "yells." Cheerleading costumes were undoubtedly different from today's, but some of the hoopla associated with later intercollegiate sports was beginning to find its way onto the playing fields of Wisconsin.

Ripon's athletic facilities in this era were scarcely worthy of the name. An open field at the base of the hill served for outdoor contests on campus until the construction of Bartlett Cottage in 1887. In that same year, however, John G. Ingalls, class of 1876, donated the land which became Ingalls Field. It was used for the first intercollegiate Field Day at Ripon in 1890 and has remained the site of all home track and football games to the present day. An adequate gymnasium for indoor sports, on the other hand, was harder to find. Kent Kennan had located an empty room in the basement of West that could be used by the men for a limited amount of physical training, and a room on the top floor of Middle was set aside for the women, but nothing even approaching a respectable gym floor was obtained until 1896, and this was still restricted within the remodeled confines of the West College basement. This proved to be more or less adequate for basketball as well as "light gymnastics" and was used by both men and women. Obviously, athletics in the modern sense had hardly arrived.

NOTES TO CHAPTER VI
NINETEENTH-CENTURY STUDENT LIFE

[1]"Reminiscences of K. K. Kennan," Archives.

[2]*1870-71 Catalogue*, 22.

[3]Clapp.

[4]*1876-77 Catalogue*, 28.

[5]Spencer.

[6]Hopkins, 29.

CHAPTER VII

TRANSITION
RUFUS C. FLAGG 1892-1901

*To the scientist, the universe presents
the aspect of one that has his eyes on
a mark and is stretching forward to a
goal. That goal includes not simply a
place of happiness for the saints, but
also the perfecting of the entire creation
of God, material and immaterial.*

Rufus Flagg

On February 16, 1892, the Board of Trustees elected
the Reverend Rufus Flagg third president of Ripon College. A
graduate of Middlebury College in his home state of Vermont
and of Andover Theological Seminary in Massachusetts, he
had received some of his preparation for the Congregational
ministry at the Chicago Theological Seminary, so he was not
a stranger to the Middle West. Flagg had returned to New
England to complete his training and then served a series of
three churches in Massachusetts and Vermont before coming to Ripon in his 46th year.[1] Trustee minutes say little
about his election, but there were two Middlebury graduates
on the board and the Selection Committee undoubtedly
utilized church contacts with the eastern educational establishment. He had had no previous academic employment,
but was well known as a biblical scholar. His inaugural
address reveals an awareness of educational trends, prefer-
ence for the small college over the university, and a commitment to Christian education, though he was more liberal
than his predecessor and undisturbed by the findings of
modern science and the new biblical scholarship.

The Ripon scene was no bed of roses. The College had just passed through troublesome times; a president had decided to resign after a protracted quarrel with some of his faculty, but had chosen to remain as a member of that faculty, teaching courses usually reserved for the president; and relations with the local church and with the community had been strained. Although some changes were called for, there was also need for tact and conciliation. This, Flagg seems to have provided, along with a necessary balance between innovation and stability. Alterations were made in the curriculum without serious controversy, and college enrollments improved modestly, topping 70 once again in 1896-97.

Flagg initiated the process of transforming a frontier missionary school into a modern provincial liberal arts college. In 1892 when Flagg assumed the presidency, Ripon College was made up of six divisions: the College with 39 students; the Preparatory School with 80; a "Select Course," best described as a junior college, with six; the English Academy, for students at the high school level not preparing for college, with 50; the School of Music with 63; and the School of Drawing and Printing with 13 for a total of 220 students (when allowance is made for double counting), fewer than 20 percent of whom were working toward a degree. Like many western institutions, Ripon was more academy than college. When Flagg left in 1901, the English Academy and the Select Course were gone; the College had an enrollment of 66; the Preparatory School, an equal number; the "Conservatory of Music," 40; and the School of Drawing and Printing, 33, for a total of 175 with approximately 40 percent working for their degrees. The overall decline in numbers was due primarily to the growth of public secondary schools; the increase in the number and proportion of college students was indicative of the direction the school had taken under Flagg's leadership. Although Ripon would continue to offer work in music and art, it was becoming more college than academy.

Reform of the rigid four-year curriculum had begun in the late years of Merrell's presidency. With a reduction in the number of required courses and the introduction of electives in each basic area of study (classical languages, mathematics, science, and philosophy), a student could take an elective course in most of his 12 terms and thus, if he wished, design a modest "major"; he could do this, for instance, by substituting elective math courses for no longer required philosophy courses. Certainly, with his approval and probably with his active encouragement, other changes occurred during Flagg's administration: a third college track leading to a bachelor of arts degree, more opportunities in the social sciences, a new course in biblical literature, and a faculty-directed program in "physical culture." A major expansion in the natural sciences was planned, but had to await the construction of a new science building.

The third track, known as the Literary Course, re- placed the so-called Select Course and substituted one year of French (Corneille, Molière, Racine) and one year of German (Goethe) for two years of Greek. No electives in either language were offered, but elective courses in English litera- ture were available. Introduced in 1883, the Literary Course became a popular alternative, attracting about a third of the college students by the end of the 1890s. The additions in social science resulted from Merrell's continuance on the faculty and the consequent necessity to find something for President Flagg to teach. The solution allowed Merrell to retain the capstone courses in psychology, ethics, and "Evi- dences" with the title professor of philosophy, while Flagg assumed Merrell's former classes in government and eco- nomics with the title professor of political and social science. Flagg also offered an elective in sociology and a new required course in New Testament History and Literature, a continu- ation of the preparatory-level courses in the Old Testament. Flagg's course descriptions for biblical studies claimed that "no sectarian or controversial use is made of the scriptures. They are studied simply as history and literature, and placed on precisely the same footing as other studies," a radical departure from previous practice.[2]

The required non-credit freshman and sophomore courses in physical education, evidence of both modernization and secularization, replaced the voluntary "gymnastics," which dated back to the 1870s. The "gym" was located in the bottom of West College, site of the old men's gym; the floor between the basement and sub-basement had been removed so that indoor games like basketball could now be played. The new facility had "baths" and dressing rooms for both men and women and was supervised by the director of gymnasium (the first director was also a professor of Greek) and a part-time instructor (woman) of physical culture; parents were assured that "due precaution is taken in the case of young women to prevent possible injury from overwork." The *Catalogue* stated that "an inexpensive gymnasium suit is required";[3] the only surviving pictures of the gym show a group of discreetly clad ladies indulging in calisthenics. Before long, women were playing their own version of basketball.

The reappearance of a "varsity" football team in 1891 was unrelated to the faculty's new interest in physical education, but the team's eventual adoption by the faculty was obviously part of this developing concern. Certainly, its return was related to the growing national passion for intercollegiate athletics and, particularly, football; even the smallest of colleges could not have escaped its influence for long. By 1890, the rules of football had been standardized so that everyone was using the same-shaped ball, the same-sized field, and the same system of scoring, and a recognizable game called American football was now being played on college and university campuses from coast to coast. The problem at Ripon was finding someone who knew the rules and who actually had played the game.

This problem was solved in the fall of 1891 when Le Roy Woodmansee enrolled in the School of Music. He was a transfer from Olivet College in Michigan, where he had played the game and, finding no team at Ripon, he proceeded to recruit one. As captain, coach, trainer, and fullback, he assembled a squad of 14 students and two alumni and taught them the game. He also convinced them that they needed uniforms, which they would have to supply at their own expense ($3.25 apiece), presumably the first uniforms worn by a Ripon team of any sort. They were made of white canvas and leather with a small red RC on the front of the jacket—no padding and no helmets, although the team picture suggests that they may have worn red stocking caps. Later teams had better equipment, but none had a better winning percentage: the 1891 "eleven" finished 3-0—against high-school opposition.

The early football teams did not have the whole-hearted support of the trustees, the faculty, or even the students at first, as indicated by small crowds at Ingalls Field. The game was so rough that it incurred the hostility of both the churches and the press, and there was serious doubt whether it should be allowed at all. But shortly the game caught on, and soon it was no longer a question of allowing it; it was a matter of taming it. For a few years, a "coach" who had played the game at Madison or Chicago was brought in just for the season, but in 1895 Frank Morton Erickson joined the faculty as professor of Greek and, because he had played at Chicago, he agreed to serve as football coach as well as director of the new gymnasium. This appears to have been the first clear instance of direct faculty supervision of an extracurricular activity at Ripon, another example of modernization.

But the best example of modernization during Flagg's presidency was the planning of a greatly expanded program in the natural sciences, perhaps the central development of the Flagg years. Very likely, the president was trying consciously to pattern Ripon after a contemporary New England college; and, although he found support from the faculty, notably Dwight Marsh, he had trouble, at first, with the Board of Trustees. Being Merrell's board, it was conservative to say the least, not apt to take great risks. If Flagg intended to make any major changes in the College, he would have to start with the trustees; and this he proceeded to do, quietly, but effectively. He was able to secure a number of appointments that really did change the temper of the board and, as a result, was able to get approval for a bold and ambitious move—the building of a hall of science.

The Board of Trustees was, and is, a self-perpetuating body with one-third of its 15 members, elected annually. Although they delegated power to the president, the faculty, and the students, the trustees retained final legal authority over the entire operation. At this time, the president of the board and of the College were the same; he was elected annually, thus serving at the pleasure of the trustees. Conversely, the board reflected the philosophy of the president; when they did not, they usually resigned. As is still true, a primary function of the board was fund raising. Although the president did most of the legwork, the trustees were expected to help and were chosen, at least partly, for their ability and willingness to do so. They tended to belong to the constituencies on which the College relied for support, either the church or the community. Perhaps, since the College was still receiving money from the Western College Society and the president made frequent fund-raising trips to the East Coast, the East was not represented on the board. Although the Western Society expected its colleges to raise half their funds locally, the largest single gifts, $10,000 and $20,000, came from Massachusetts as a result of Merrell's eastern trips. However, none of the presidents neglected Wisconsin in their search for men of means; two examples were Edward D. Holton of Milwaukee and Elisha D. Smith of Menasha. The former, a wealthy railroader and banker, a prominent abolitionist and Milwaukee Republican, and Merrell's staunchest supporter on the board, served as a trustee from 1864 until his death in 1892 and left the College a $25,000 piece of Milwaukee lakefront property.[4] Smith, owner of the largest and most successful "woodenware" company in the world, served from 1889 to 1899 and gave the College a substantial number of small gifts.[5] For many years, Middle College, now Middle Hall, bore his name; one of the Quads does so now.

Thereafter, the College began to rely more heavily on regional giving, particularly from the business community. As a New Englander, Flagg undoubtedly sensed the declining interest of eastern churches in western colleges. To counter this, he set about changing the composition of a board he considered too conservative in both theology and fund raising. One of his most happy choices was Orrin H. Ingram, a wealthy lumber baron from Eau Claire, who served on the board from 1892 until his death in 1918. He was recommended by Samuel Pedrick, a recent alumnus and a Ripon resident. While still an undergraduate, Pedrick had met Ingram at an oratorical contest between Ripon and Beloit during which Ingram had served as a judge and had, incidentally, expressed his admiration of President Merriman.[6] Ingram was to become the most generous contributor to the College in his time; his challenge grant of $15,000, successfully matched by an additional $25,000, made possible the construction of the new science building named in his honor.

Five years later, Albert G. Farr of Chicago joined the board, once again with an assist from Pedrick. Farr had married Alice Parkhurst of Ripon and spent many summers in Ripon with his wife's family; the Parkhurst home at the corner of Thorne and Ransom Streets was for years a sorority house. Pedrick knew the Parkhursts and, when questioned by Flagg on Farr's qualifications for board membership, gave Farr an enthusiastic recommendation. A partner in the Harris Trust and Savings Bank, Farr was a man of considerable stature in midwestern financial circles, something quite unusual for a Ripon board member. An advocate of bold planning for the future, he came to the board at a most opportune time. Like Ingram, he was to have his name placed on a science building; the Farr bequest of close to $1 million, received on the death of his daughter, Shirley, in 1956, was the largest single gift to the College up to that time.[7]

It was only a matter of time before Pedrick became a member of the board, apparently on Farr's recommendation. Although conservative politically, Farr agreed with Flagg that the board needed younger men with fresh ideas; Pedrick was 31 when he accepted election. His active association with the school had begun in 1886 when he entered the Preparatory Department. Before his graduation from the College five years later, he had served as an editor of the *College Days* for a year and as business manager and editor-in-chief for two years, participated in forensics, organized the first field day with Lawrence, and played center on Ripon's first "real" football team. Even during his three years at law school in Madison, he wrote the alumni section of the *Days*, successfully encouraging active alumni participation in the affairs of the College. At Pedrick's first meeting as a trustee, Farr engineered his election to the combined position of secretary and treasurer. In those days, the treasurer was, in effect, the business manager; the position required almost daily contact with the College. That he should be elected while just beginning his first term demonstrates the confidence he inspired in Flagg, Farr, and other trustees; he did not disappoint. Pedrick was a truly remarkable man. Although he never held elective office (he was a Democrat in a Republican town), he served on the school board, the library board, the hospital commission, and the Fond du Lac County Board, devoting his energies to turning Ripon into a modern city and strengthening the College at the same time. Not the least of his accomplishments was his monumental record of the city: his historical collections fill 87 scrapbooks and his genealogical records 41 looseleaf notebooks. All this on top of a private law practice.[8]

The crowning achievement of Flagg's administration was the construction of Ingram Hall. Beset on all sides with competition from the growing public school system, from the state normal schools, from colleges with both ethnic and sectarian constituencies, and from the undergraduate divisions of the expanding universities, it took real courage to construct a building of Ingram's size. It seemed to Flagg and the trustees that the best chance for growth and survival was to challenge the undergraduate college of the state university and to create a liberal arts college in the mold of the small New England colleges. To do this, it was necessary to offer a more modern curriculum, particularly in the sciences. Hence, in June of 1894, the trustees recommended the erection of a science building and directed the president to start looking for money. This was no easy task, since Flagg had just raised $50,000 to meet the conditions of the Holton legacy, and Ingram and five other trustees had contributed generously to this fund. But with the announcement in 1898 of Ingram's challenge grant of $15,000, roughly half the anticipated cost of construction, the planning process got under way and the trustees gave the final go-ahead in September of 1899. Of the additional $25,000 required by Ingram's challenge, $10,500 came in the form of major gifts of $500 or more; approximately $4,000 was raised in Ripon. In a reprise of the original staking out of East Hall, the trustees recessed their September, 1899, meeting and planted stakes outlining the foundation.   The building was completed and ready for partial occupancy in December, 1900, six years after the project was first considered. Located on ground now partly occupied by Todd Wehr Hall, it had 8,000 square feet of floor space, was constructed of red brick totally out of harmony with the other college buildings, and was not particularly well built—considerable remodeling had to be done before the building could be occupied. It took years for the College to grow into it, and it never fulfilled its original purpose of a complete science hall. In fact, it housed the library until 1931 and all of the academic departments except Art, Military Science, Music, and Physical Education until the construction of the Memorial Gymnasium in 1910 and the building boom of the 1960s and 1970s.

Flagg's dedicatory remarks, "Possible Spiritual Gains from the Advancement of Science," were, it turned out, his valedictory. He had submitted his resignation to the board in June, 1899, but a decision had been postponed until the dedication of Ingram Hall. Flagg had cited faculty discontent as his primary motivation, but he had not been popular in the community either. He may have been a bit of a snob, comparing both the College and the community unfavorably with those of New England. Perhaps he was a little too liberal, and Merrell's continued presence on the faculty must have made his position uncomfortable. Though not unappreciative of his achievements, some of the trustees, including the very influential Farr, thought it was time for a change. However, before taking final action, the trustees consulted the various constituencies of the College: the Reverend Robert T. Roberts, a trustee and graduate, mailed a questionnaire to the alumni; Farr did the same in the city. The respondents favored resignation; Farr had already concluded that the faculty were "practically a unit in favor of [a] speedy change in administration."[9] So, on December 19, 1900, the board formally accepted his resignation. Flagg went back east, where he served a number of churches, and in 1917 returned to Wisconsin as dean of religion at Northland College.

In addition to Ingram Hall, Flagg's achievements were not inconsiderable. While he may not have been personally popular, he had mended fences in both the church and the city. He had markedly strengthened the Board of Trustees, recruiting men of regional rather than merely local stature and shifting its composition, at least partially, from ministers to businessmen. He had succeeded in raising impressive sums of money. He had liberalized and modernized the curriculum and prepared the College for the 20th century. Ripon College was definitely in better shape than when he took office.

NOTES TO CHAPTER VII
RUFUS C. FLAGG 1892-1901

[1]"Rufus Cushman Flagg," *Pedrick Genealogies.*

[2]*1895-96 Catalogue.*

[3]*1886-87 Catalogue.*

[4]*Dictionary of Wisconsin Biography*, 175-76.

[5]"Elisha D. Smith," *Pedrick Genealogies.*

[6]"Orrin H. Ingram," *Pedrick Genealogies.*

[7]"Albert G. Farr," *Pedrick Genealogies.*

[8]"Samuel Pedrick," *Pedrick Genealogies.*

[9]*Ripon Historical Collections*, XXVIII, 304-11.

CHAPTER VIII

TRANSFORMATION
RICHARD C. HUGHES
1901-1909

*The large universities are overcrowded
and utterly unable to do for the undergraduate what the sturdy, well-
equipped and carefully managed small
college is doing with great success.*

Richard Hughes

Richard C. Hughes was the first Presbyterian (although Merriman had served a Presbyterian church in Green
Bay), the first westerner, and the first experienced college
administrator to be elected president of Ripon College. A
native of Ohio educated at the College of Wooster and at
Princeton and McCormick Theological Seminaries, he was an
ordained Presbyterian minister but had held only one pastorate in Iowa for four years before joining the faculty of Tabor
College in that state as professor of philosophy and psychology. In 1897, he became president of Tabor. His success in
that position led to his appointment at Ripon; perhaps the
trustees were deliberately looking for someone with administrative experience.[1]

Apparently Hughes' Presbyterian background raised
no eyebrows, since there was no public comment about it.
Although Congregationalists and Presbyterians had drifted
apart, still Brockway College had been adopted by both sects.
In 1903, President Hughes persuaded the Presbyterian Synod
to re-endorse Ripon College rather than establish its own
institution in northern Wisconsin, and for a time the College
was visited annually by committees representing both

churches. In fact, Hughes was more aggressively denominational than Flagg, but his motivation was practical rather
than sectarian: Ripon needed more students.

Shortly after Hughes' arrival, Ripon's religious ties
threatened to become an embarrassment. The Carnegie
Pension Fund was being established to underwrite retirement plans for colleges and universities, but "sectarian
schools" were not eligible. Both because two faculty members, ex-President Merrell and Professor Charles Chandler,
were ready to retire and because membership in the prestigious national program would enhance the College's reputation, Hughes was anxious to have Ripon accepted as a
charter member. Fortunately, he was able to persuade the
foundation that Ripon was nonsectarian.

This ability to have his cake and eat it too seems to
have been one of President Hughes' outstanding administrative talents. At the same time that he was emphasizing the
College's commitment to Christian education in its publicity
and encouraging the faculty to participate in community
church work, he continued Flagg's policy of loosening the
religious obligations of the students, for example, advising
but not requiring attendance at daily chapel. Thus, the
overall tone of his administration was less formal and less
severe than that of his predecessors.

The same "loosening" occurred in the curriculum
during Hughes' administration, continuing a trend initiated
by President Flagg. The number of required courses was
further reduced, the three-track option was replaced by a
system of distribution requirements and majors, the B.S.
degree was dropped, and a two-semester calendar was
adopted. By 1906, even the terminology had become modern. All graduation requirements were incorporated into
courses (there were no more rhetoricals); courses earned so
many "hours' credit" (one hour for each class meeting per
week except for laboratory sciences, which earned one credit
for every two hours in lab); 128 hours were needed for

graduation. A required core of courses for all students included eight hours of English composition; either 14 or 22 hours of foreign language depending on the amount of high-school credits (more than one language could be taken to fill this requirement, but no less than a full year of any one language was accepted); three hours of Bible; and four semesters of non-credit physical training. Also required were eight hours each in any three of the following: mathematics, a laboratory science (chemistry, biology, or physics), history, and philosophy. No later than the beginning of the junior year, each student was expected to choose a "major" consisting of 40 hours work in any one of seven "groups" and culminating in a senior thesis. The seven groups were classics, mathematics-physics, chemistry-biology, history-economics, philosophy, modern languages (foreign), and English-languages (English and foreign language combined). The faculty was not yet large enough to offer a major in all departments, but the group system was a workable compromise, one that still has merit today. In many cases, the groups were designed to prepare students for graduate work leading to a particular profession: mathematics-physics, pre-engineering; chemistry-biology, pre-medicine; history-economics, pre-law; classics, theological; and so on.

A student could meet all of the above requirements and still have either 31 or 39 hours of electives, depending on the number of high-school foreign language credits. The curriculum achieved this flexibility at the expense of Mental and Moral Philosophy. The number of requirements with a significant religious or ethical emphasis had been reduced to one—a three-hour course in the Bible taught primarily as literature; psychology had become an elective. In a sense, this was counterbalanced by an increase in the number of Bible-related courses and by the addition of two Congregational ministers to the faculty, but the new courses were all electives, and one of the ministers taught English literature. Meanwhile, all of the integrative courses of the senior year were gone; the great story no longer had a moral. The only common experience of the final year was the major thesis.

This radical overhauling of the curriculum seems to have been accomplished with a minimum of agonizing by the faculty. Most likely, the guiding hand of the new president was the dominant influence since the changes began immediately following his arrival; in addition, the pending retirement of ex-president Merrell undoubtedly helped. His departure in 1906, following several years of intermittent illness that kept him out of the classroom for extended periods, truly marked the end of an era. Merrell had been so important in the life of the College for so long that his presence inevitably impeded changes that ran counter to his own strongly held views. Although ties with the older philosophy of Christian education remained and a serious effort was made to sustain a Christian atmosphere throughout campus life, instruction was becoming increasingly secular.

Rapidly rising college-level enrollments—from 66 in 1901 to 209 in 1909—made possible a modernized curriculum. In turn, the new curriculum, together with modernization in other areas—physical plant, administrative structure, extracurricular activities, fund-raising, and student recruitment—helped increase enrollment. Hughes' previous experience as college teacher and administrator enabled him quickly to identify Ripon's needs and make changes to meet them. Despite his clerical and academic background, he got along well with the businessmen on the Board of Trustees, and together they altered the table of organization, such as it was. For a start, the president got a secretary. Perhaps this was due to the simple need for someone who knew how to use a typewriter, but the appointment was thought important enough to be listed in the *Catalogue*. A new system of accounting was introduced and placed in the hands of a professional bookkeeper. Similarly, academic record keeping was reorganized, and greater responsibility was given to the faculty secretary-registrar, Professor Chandler of the Mathematics Department. Dwight Marsh, Professor of Biology, became the first dean of the College, with the understanding that he was to be the chief administrative officer under the president. None of this was accomplished without friction, and the faculty occasionally complained that Hughes was too autocratic. Marsh and Chandler had some sort of squabble with the trustees, possibly over the use of Ingram Hall; the trustees declared their chairs vacant, i.e., they were fired, but the action was rescinded. Nonetheless, after Chandler retired and Marsh departed to the University of Chicago, the trustees changed the college by-laws to require "absolute loyalty" by the faculty to the trustees. Apparently, in these pre-academic-freedom days, the board expected the College to be run like a business and the professors to behave like employees.

The total effect of these administrative changes, together with a sharp reduction in Hughes' teaching load—he taught some psychology—was to enable the president to devote more time and energy to what we now call "development." There were no great windfalls for the endowment during Hughes' administration, but the continuing generosity of Ingram, Farr, and the Smith family, together with the final settlement of the Erwin Estate ($174,000 in all) and the long awaited sale of the Holton dock property in Milwaukee for $20,000, supplied funds needed for annual operations. Other gifts such as a Carnegie Endowment grant of $20,000 in 1905 (to be matched by another $20,000) were helpful in underwriting the College's expansion.

For the recruitment of students, Hughes implemented new tactics which had been previously recommended by President Flagg and by Professor Marsh serving as acting president after Flagg's resignation. In the past, Ripon had relied on the churches and on its own Preparatory Department as the source for college students. This strategy had merit as long as the Academy was one of the few places in northern and central Wisconsin offering college preparatory work. But, with the growth of public secondary schools and the resultant decline in the size of the Academy, the College was forced to seek elsewhere for students. It did so by what

Flagg and Marsh both called "advertising," in other words, visits by Ripon faculty to secondary schools and academies throughout the state during the spring term. Thus, the faculty became the College's first admissions counselors. These visits involved evaluation of the secondary school, talks with administrators and students, and possibly a public lecture. Depending on the outcome of the visit, the school might then be placed on an approved list, making its graduates automatically eligible for admission to Ripon.

As another means of advertising, members of the faculty also participated in the many lecture series often referred to at this time as the "Chautauqua Circuit." Professor Edward Clark of the Latin Department was the most popular speaker on the staff, making frequent appearances in Milwaukee and Chicago and, on occasion, in the East. The president, of course, was expected to do a great deal of speaking and/or preaching as a way of advertising the school and to be the College's best salesman. Hughes was an accomplished public speaker with an attractively relaxed style that contrasted sharply with the rhetorical style of the older preachers. On one occasion, he offered a series of six "Bible hour" talks for a Chautauqua meeting in Oshkosh. His first appearance attracted 36 rather hesitant listeners; his final talk drew 500. Hughes also did much more than his predecessors with promotional literature. The *Catalogue* was redesigned to serve as an admissions document; many more copies were printed and distributed each year to high schools and academies. Other special bulletins and brochures, designed for recruiting purposes, now became regular college publications. In all of them, the message was pretty much the same: small colleges had advantages over larger universities; Christian colleges provided better training for the whole person; and Ripon College had certain special advantages in location, curriculum, and tradition. It was all pretty low key, but perhaps more effective because of this.

Like other colleges in the state, Ripon had been losing

potential enrollees to the University of Wisconsin, now recognized as one of the finest institutions in the country. In solving this problem, the private colleges received unexpected help from the university's farsighted president, Charles Van Hise. Van Hise was more interested in expanding the graduate schools than the undergraduate college, and he actively sought alumni from Beloit, Lawrence, and Ripon, among others. Ripon had been sending many of its abler graduates to the University of Chicago; Van Hise believed that they ought to go to Madison. To this end, he established working relations with Ripon and other private Wisconsin colleges that could benefit all parties. The university made its list of accredited high schools available to the colleges, thereby establishing a common basis for the evaluation of secondary schools and encouraging common standards of admissions; also course credits for undergraduate work at Madison and at select private colleges became interchangeable. This working agreement meant that Ripon graduates had just as good a chance of admission to a Wisconsin graduate school as alumni of the university's College of Letters and Sciences.

Better advertising and better relations with Madison increased the scope of Ripon's drawing power. It remained very much a regional college with most students coming from Wisconsin, but it now drew from a wider area of the state. In the past most enrollees had come from within a 25 mile radius; in 1909, Hughes calculated the average distance to each student's home (except for foreign students) to be 68 miles.

Although growth solved many problems, it also created others, especially for an overworked and underpaid faculty now faced with larger classes along with the obligation to handle student discipline, supervise extracurricular activities, and help in the recruitment of students. Department chairmen were continually asking for additional staff and buttressing their requests with facts and figures supplied by national organizations and by comparisons with

other institutions. Not fully aware of or sympathetic to the
new academic professionalism, the trustees considered this
information irrelevant and added faculty reluctantly. Nor did
increased enrollment, as it often does, lead to higher pay.
Salaries for professors, the only rank above instructor,
increased only two percent during Hughes' tenure, ranging
from $1,100 to $1,500 in 1909. Nonetheless, faculty morale
seems to have risen, partly, at least, because of an improved
physical plant.

The interior of virtually every building on campus, including brand new Ingram Hall, which always seemed to
need repair, was renovated. Middle College, the main men's
dormitory, was renamed Smith Hall in honor of the generous
Smith family. A new dining facility, generally known as
"Alumni Commons," was located on the first floor of West
College, now more apt to be called West Hall; men occupied
the top floors, and the basement continued to serve unsatis-
factorily as a gym. The old Merriman home, today Hughes
House, was reacquired and remodeled as the president's
home. The little white schoolhouse, famed as the Birthplace
of the Republican Party, was saved from demolition and
relocated west of Bartlett; it served as the college museum
and housed the old "cabinet" until 1942 when it was moved
to a site near West Hall. It is now located on Blackburn Street
near the Republican House. A central heating plant for the
entire campus was constructed with funds donated by
lumber baron Sumner T. McNight. The campus was re-
landscaped, and the first cement sidewalks were installed;
the *Days* boasted that Ripon had the best college sidewalks
in the Midwest.

A new library and a genuine gymnasium remained
the most pressing needs. Hughes wanted to construct a joint
city-college library where Farr Hall now stands and believed
he could attract the interest of Andrew Carnegie, who was
building libraries all over the country. But the College and
various factions in the city could not agree on a site, and
rather than doom the entire project, Hughes dropped his

plan. However, he did help the city get funds from the Carnegie Foundation for a library building which now houses Pearl's House of Fashion on the corner of Watson and Seward Streets. As a stopgap measure, the combined collections of the College and the literary societies were moved into Ingram Hall, where they remained until the construction of Lane Library in 1930. Meanwhile, Hughes was having more luck with his plans for a new "Indoor Athletic Field" (the present Memorial Gymnasium). Although it was not constructed before he left in 1909, he had raised the necessary funds, mostly from alumni but also with substantial help from Farr.

Of all the early presidents, Hughes was the most ardent supporter of intercollegiate athletics, partly because he thought they attracted students. Although football was already being criticized for brutality and professionalism, Hughes believed that it could be made safe and clean through adequate supervision. Consequently, he played a leading role in forming the Wisconsin-Illinois Athletic Conference: Beloit, Carroll, Knox, Lake Forest, Lawrence, Marquette, Northwestern (Watertown, Wisconsin), and Ripon. In addition, he made certain that Ripon joined the National Intercollegiate Athletic Association (NCAA), formed in 1906. Playing by the new NCAA rules, Ripon won its first state football championship in the same year, with a record of 5-0-1.

Two years later, Ripon discovered to its horror, that the Lawrence football roster included an athlete who had played four years for "Pop" Warner's famous Carlisle Indians, starring the legendary Jim Thorpe; it was even rumored that the Lawrentian had played for pay. However, Lawrence claimed that Carlisle was only a prep school. Academically, this may have been true, but Carlisle played an intercollegiate schedule, which included Harvard and Yale, football powers in those days. When Lawrence refused to back down, a mass meeting of Ripon students and faculty voted to cancel the game despite the fact that the undefeated Crimson were favored to win. The Milwaukee press split on the issue, but the publicity probably did Ripon more good than harm.

In view of all that Hughes had done for Ripon College, his resignation in 1909 came with surprising suddenness and without adequate explanation. Just the year before, he had submitted a glowing report to the trustees: the college dormitories had been full to overflowing; Ingram Hall, for the first time, had been fully utilized; contacts with the public high schools in the state were now much improved; and relations with the state university had been stabilized. Hughes also announced that Ripon had been accepted as a charter member of the North Central Association of Colleges and Secondary Schools, not yet a full-fledged accrediting agency for colleges and universities but in the process of developing standards that would go into full effect for its members in 1912. Ripon could not have met these standards when Hughes took office in 1901; that it could do so in 1908 was perhaps his crowning achievement. But a whisper of scandal, apparently without foundation, involving the president and "some women employees in the office," threatened to cause the College some embarrassment. Pedrick's brief account of the affair insists that no immorality had been charged; the president was said to be guilty simply of "familiarity." Since there is nothing else to go on, we can only assume that the trustees knew more than we do or, more likely, that they were excessively sensitive to public gossip. In any event, Hughes offered his resignation and the board accepted it. The public explanation was that he had been offered a promising business opportunity in Madison. This may have been true, since for a short time he worked in a Madison insurance company. But he soon returned to the church, ending his active career as university secretary of the Presbyterian Church with supervision over the activities of his denomination.[2] That Hughes Walk, leading from Seward Street to Middle Hall, and Hughes House, headquarters of the Ripon College Society of Scholars, should bear his name seems little enough memorial to all he had done for Ripon College.

NOTES TO CHAPTER VIII
RICHARD C. HUGHES 1901-1909

[1]"Richard C. Hughes," *Pedrick Genealogies.*

[2]*Ibid.*

CHAPTER IX

GROWTH AND STABILITY
SILAS EVANS 1910-1917

The real college man stands for the
virile type of culture; for reality, sincer-
ity and genuineness. He knows what
he is in college for; is not ashamed to
support the things for which the Col-
lege stands in physical manhood, in-
tellectual power, wholesome friend-
ships and religious convictions. We
want a man who is healthy enough to
play and is also big enough to pray.

Silas Evans

In September, 1910, Silas Evans '98 became the fifth president of Ripon College. He served two terms (1910-17 and 1921-43), the hiatus being spent as president of Occidental College in Los Angeles. His second incumbency was the longest consecutive service in the College's history; furthermore, his policies and personality, even in his absence, dominated Ripon for nearly 35 years. Under his quiet leadership, the College grew from 267 students, 17 in the soon-to-be discontinued Academy and 84 in the Music School, to a consolidated college of 540. A campus of 10 buildings, not including barns and sheds, became one of 20 buildings; and an endowment of $200,000 increased to $600,000. Despite two world wars and the Great Depression, the Evans years were a period of amazing growth and stability; Ripon became a very successful provincial liberal arts college; even today it bears the imprint of his labors.

Born in Scranton, Pennsylvania, into a first and second generation immigrant family, he grew up in and around Cambria, about 25 miles southwest of Ripon, where his father was a minister in the Welsh Calvinistic Methodist Church. At the age of 15, he entered Ripon, spending three years in the Academy and four in the College. Although he worked part time "in harvest fields, as a janitor, and doing odd jobs around town," he was an honors student, with a flair for classical languages, and a natural campus leader.[1] He played four years of varsity football, either at halfback or end; took part in intercollegiate baseball and track; was active in debate, oratory, and the Christian Association; played in the college band and had a leading role in what may have been the first all-college play. Also, he served as president of the Athenian Society, vice president of the Athletic Association, captain of the football team, and sports editor of the *College Days*. Had anyone bothered to make such a choice among the 17 graduates in his class, he undoubtedly would have been elected "most likely to succeed." A number of trustees singled him out as a man to watch; he did not disappoint them.

Although his earliest ambition was to be a farmer, both his father and the Ripon faculty encouraged him to pursue a career either in the ministry or in education. He opted for a combination of the two. Upon graduation from Ripon, he entered Princeton University and, in 1901, emerged with both master of arts and bachelor of divinity degrees. Ordained as a Presbyterian minister, he accepted a position as professor of philosophy at Hastings College in Hastings, Nebraska, where he also served as assistant pastor of the Congregational Church. Two years later, he moved to Park College near Kansas City, Missouri, and in 1909 became professor of Greek and Hebrew in the University of Wisconsin Extension Service. One year afterwards, he took office at Ripon. He had not been the trustees' first choice; the Reverend David Beaton, a distinguished Congregational clergyman, turned them down because he had just accepted a call to the First Church in Janesville. The Search Committee then turned to Evans; no one ever regretted the choice.

When he assumed the presidency, Evans was barely 35, unusually young by the standards of the day though not uncharacteristic of later Ripon prexies. Actually, his youth may have helped in the first crisis he faced. After Hughes' resignation, there had been an interregnum during which Dean of the College Frank Erickson had run the school. In his attempts to modernize Ripon, Hughes had allowed the establishment of fraternities and granted students, in general, more freedom and self-government. In the absence of a president, a few students, all athletes and members of a Greek-letter group in Smith Hall, had pushed the new liberalization too far and got caught drinking in the dormitory. The faculty had dismissed five of them and disciplined the head of the house for failing to maintain proper order. When friends of the expelled students protested, in some cases rather vehemently, the state press exaggeratedly characterized their actions as an "insurrection"; with equal hyperbole, Evans called it a student rebellion. Anyhow, one of his first official acts was to "quell" the disturbance. He had always been a teetotaler and had served as president of the Prohibition Club in his junior year; quite naturally, he considered drinking on campus, in violation of college regulations and of Christian standards of conduct, a serious offense. Therefore, he upheld the expulsions, removed the house president from office, and required him to live off campus for the rest of the school year. Thus, Evans began his administration by getting tough, but did so in a way that, after the whole matter was talked out in chapel, won student support.

In graduate school, Evans had been impressed by Princeton President Woodrow Wilson's opposition to the university's elitish clubs as undemocratic. At Ripon, he came to a similar conclusion about fraternities and sororities and, no doubt strengthened in his resolve by the Smith Hall episode, decided they had no place on the campus. Consequently, they were banned. In making this move, he had the support of a majority of trustees and students, though not of

the alumni. The following year, a number of students who
were unhappy with the new regime, decided not to return,
but their loss was more than offset by successive larger
entering classes, attracted, it was believed, by the young
president's forthright stand.

For Evans, Ripon was still a Christian college, but its
Christianity was muscular in the style of British empire
builder Cecil Rhodes, founder of the Rhodes Scholarships, or
of Theodore Roosevelt, apostle of strenuous living. "The real
college man," Evans said, "stands for the virile type of
culture . . . physical manhood, intellectual power, wholesome friendships and religious convictions. . . . We want a
man who is healthy enough to play and is also big enough to
pray."[2] He desired a college dedicated to "democracy, scholarship, and Christian character . . . large enough to sustain all the varied activities of college community life and yet
small enough to tempt every latent capacity which the
student may have. . . ." At first, this meant 300 students;
later it meant 500. A strong believer in extracurricular
activities, he nevertheless feared overemphasis. "Extracurricular distractions loom too prominently in the modern
college." He wanted Ripon modern, but not too modern. He
also feared snobbery and extravagance, which he tended to
equate with fraternities and sororities. Like President Merriman, he intended to keep Ripon "near to the poor." "The
average boy or girl will always be welcome, if ambitious, hard
working, and purposeful." "We will cultivate the virtue of
economy. . . . Thrift is fundamental for moral character
and national prosperity." Ripon would be a college without
frills, as inexpensive as the state university. Nonetheless,
Ripon would "maintain stoutly a high standard of scholarship" and would "prepare students for the best professional
schools in the country."[3] In the achievement of these goals,
he was remarkably successful.

In part, his success was due to his keeping Ripon a
school primarily for rural central and northern Wisconsin, an
area he called "our legitimate territory." Reflecting his own

family heritage, he made a special effort to attract Welsh students, who tended to be concentrated in the region around Ripon, and even suggested always having a Welsh "representative" on the Board of Trustees. No one was ever denied admission because of race, color, or creed, but naturally the student body reflected the ethnic mix in "the College's territory." Judging from pictures in the *Crimson*, the first black student entered in 1911 (he stayed one year); the next black did not enroll until 1924 (he, too, stayed only one year); and there were very few Jewish students until after World War II. With regard to gender, Evans favored a ratio of two men for every woman, which probably reflected the available pool of prospective students anyway.   Consequently, Ripon came to be known as a men's college, a reputation that Evans was quite willing to live with.

Evans' skill as a public speaker became one of the College's greatest assets. He spent a great deal of time "placing the College before the state," believing this to be his "first duty." During the school year 1913-14, for example, he gave 70 speeches or sermons throughout Wisconsin (16 of them were commencement addresses at high schools). Soon, he was receiving many more invitations than he could possibly accept. During the summer, he was constantly in demand on the Chautauqua circuit and at Bible conferences throughout the entire country; he was invited back repeatedly to address church meetings in Illinois, Iowa, Michigan, Ohio, Missouri, Oregon, and California. On many occasions, his talks were broadcast on the local radio stations.

Evans the educator was never far removed from Evans the minister so that there was apt to be a moral or ethical point to all his talks. He was always ready to speak on current political and international affairs and had the knack of discussing controversial subjects without being himself controversial. Even his Wilsonian liberalism never seemed to offend his conservative Wisconsin audiences.

Public speaking engagements took Evans away from campus more often than he liked. He always taught courses in religion, but inevitably missed a good many classes, often relying on senior students to lead his required freshman recitation sections in Bible. The course required very little preparation on his part or on the part of the students. It was primarily an opportunity for freshmen and president to discuss contemporary moral questions relating to campus life, academic goals, and personal development, a kind of orientation course for college and for life. It continued his predecessors' courses in moral philosophy that used to come at the end of one's undergraduate career, but now, significantly, it was introduction rather than synthesis. Evans believed the course to be close to the heart of his responsibilities as president.

By the time Evans took office, accrediting agencies and educational foundations had begun to change the American college scene. At the end of the 19th century, this scene could only be described as chaotic. No one really knew what a college was, except that it fitted vaguely somewhere between a secondary school and a graduate school. Some academies were called colleges and some colleges were called universities. The time had come for some definitions and the imposition of some standards. These were first supplied by voluntary regional accrediting agencies, called "voluntary" because no institutions had to join them or accept their policies and recommendations, although almost all thought it advisable to do so. The first of these agencies was the New England Association; the second, founded in 1895, was the North Central Association, the largest of them all, extending from West Virginia to Oklahoma and including, of course, Wisconsin. Their original purpose had been to clarify relations between secondary schools and institutions of higher learning, especially regarding entrance requirements for the latter. They quickly became accrediting agencies. Standards for colleges, effective in 1912, were quite specific, much more so than they are today. All faculty should have a master's degree or its equivalent and should teach no more than 18 hours, with 15 recommended as the maximum. Every college should have at least eight liberal arts departments, with at least one full-time professor in each. It must have "a library and laboratory equipment sufficient to develop fully and illustrate each course announced"; "it must be able to prepare its graduates to enter graduate schools as candidates for advanced degrees." Maximum class size was set at 30. The physical plant should "insure hygienic conditions for both students and teachers." To be accepted for admission to an accredited college, a student had to present 14 "units" of acceptable work, distributed among English, foreign languages, history, mathematics, and science (none of the newfangled courses in the social studies were acceptable). To graduate, a student must have completed no fewer than 120 semester hours. Endowment should amount to $200,000, raised to $300,000 after World War I. The association even recommended "conservativism in granting honorary degrees."[4]

The new accrediting agencies received welcome support from private philanthropic foundations, two in particular. Between 1896 and 1919, the year of his death, Pittsburgh steel magnate Andrew Carnegie established no fewer than 22 charitable trusts, mostly concerned with higher education or international peace. One of these sprinkled the landscape with libraries. Another, the Carnegie Foundation for the Advancement of Teaching, established a pension fund for the under-appreciated and under-paid college teaching profession. Originally conceived as a free opportunity for qualified participants, it eventually evolved into the more practical insurance and annuity plan (TIAA-CREF) to which participating colleges, including Ripon, and individual faculty members made regular contributions. It had a tremendous impact on higher education because, in order to qualify, institutions had to meet certain criteria similar to and, in some instances, more stringent than those imposed by the accrediting agencies. For instance, while the regional associations recommended that 60 to 80 percent of the faculty members hold doctorates, Carnegie favored 100 percent. Actually, Carnegie did not enforce this figure rigidly, but his recommendation strengthened the growing emphasis on the Ph.D. as a prerequisite for college teaching. Furthermore, the Carnegie Foundation followed the policy of the accrediting agencies that member colleges should have an endowment of at least $200,000, later (in 1921) raising this figure to $500,000 when the regional associations were moving to $300,000.

Carnegie's chief rival in philanthropy for higher education was John D. Rockefeller, builder of Standard Oil, who established the General Education Board (GEB) in 1903. Rockefeller was richer, more sympathetic to denominational colleges, and less inclined to set minimum fiscal standards than Carnegie. Like Carnegie, he believed that most American colleges were undercapitalized and inefficiently managed; he also thought that helping colleges increase their endowments should be the main task of the GEB. By 1924, the board had given 291 colleges $60 million for their endowments with the customary provision that the recipients match these funds.

Ripon was fortunate in being placed on the charter rolls of both the North Central Association and the Carnegie Foundation; it also qualified for endowment grants from the General Education Board, though not without some difficulty. It had no trouble meeting academic standards for accreditation, but fiscal requirements did create some problems.

Like many college presidents before and after him, Evans believed that he had accepted his position with the clear understanding that he would devote virtually all his efforts to academic and promotional activities and then found that he was required to spend an inordinate amount of time raising money. "I only want to make it clear again," he told the trustees in 1913, "that I will be a college president . . . but I will not be a financial agent for any institution in the world."[5] Of course, he was wrong. By 1913, he was already involved in a capital campaign that may well have been the central achievement of his first term.

The heart of the College's financial difficulties was an inadequate endowment. In 1910, when Evans assumed the presidency, Ripon's endowment was just under $200,000. By the standards recently imposed by the Rockefeller and Carnegie Foundations and the North Central Association, this was not adequate for a first-rank liberal arts college. The College was relatively clear of debt because of the willingness of key board members to cover its annual losses and because of the generosity of these same trustees and a handful of friends when capital improvements became necessary. Even before Evans took command, the board, however, had decided on an endowment campaign of $350,000. Now it was up to Evans to push it through to a successful conclusion.

The goal was reached, although not without considerable clawing and scratching. Evans correctly judged that the foundations would have to provide the initial thrust for the campaign; so he did what he could to cultivate favor with the Carnegie Foundation and Rockefeller's GEB. Ripon had already received one gift from Carnegie and had qualified for his pension plan in 1906. The College had been able to use the influence of James A. Blanchard '71, justice of the New York Supreme Court and a personal friend of Carnegie. This connection was still available; thus, Evans found relatively easy access to the foundation. Rockefeller's board, on the other hand, was less accessible, and the first appeal for funds was unsuccessful. But persistence paid off, and a second application brought a modest grant of $50,000, which had to be matched by another $200,000.

The final report on the campaign gave the following breakdown:

General Education Board	$ 50,000
Carnegie Foundation	$ 35,000
Ingram Family	$ 50,000
Farr Family	$ 30,000
Other trustees and friends	$116,215
Alumni	$ 12,625

City of Ripon	$ 56,500
Victor Lawson	$ 10,000
Jones Estate	$ 5,100
Total	$365,440

Much of the match for the GEB grant, in other words, had come from the College's traditional sources: a few wealthy benefactors, including board members, and the City of Ripon.

However, successful completion of the campaign helped Evans reach a decision which had unfortunate consequences for the College. Suddenly, and completely to the surprise of the board, in May, 1917, he announced his acceptance of the presidency of Occidental College in Los Angeles. Ripon's trustees tried mightily to dissuade him, suggesting, correctly as it turned out, that he might not be happy among the reactionary sectarians of southern California and that Occidental's notoriously conservative board might not take kindly to his relatively liberal Protestantism. They even attempted to persuade Occidental to withdraw its offer. Despite impassioned pleas from faculty and friends and mass demonstrations by students and townspeople, Evans did not change his mind. He reminded everyone that he had announced his intention of staying only five years; he had actually stayed seven. He had brought the College successfully through what seemed to be a complete cycle. Ripon had been in financial difficulty when he arrived; it had been rescued from that difficulty. Student morale had been at a low ebb; it was now restored. Enrollment was up to capacity; the level of scholarship had improved; the faculty had been strengthened. Ahead lay more cycles of improvement but not new challenges. California, on the other hand, provided a "wider field" for him while he was still a young man. There is reason to believe that Evans may have been anticipating a future career in church administration at the national or even international level. At age 42, he was still young enough and ambitious enough to want something new.

NOTES TO CHAPTER IX
SILAS EVANS 1910-1917

[1]Thompson, "Silas Evans as a Student," *Alumnus*, June, 1943, 11-15.

[2]*College Days*, March 14 and 30, 1911; May 7, 14, and 21, 1913.

[3]*Ibid.*, Oct. 13, 1916, April 3, 1917, and Oct. 11, 1921; *Evans Papers*, Box #3, article by Evans for the *Milwaukee Journal* in 1924.

[4]Davis, 45-56, 61, 76-78.

[5]*Trustees' Minutes*, II, 478.

CHAPTER X

INTERREGNUM
HENRY C. CULBERTSON
1918-1920

Our dormitories should teach ideals of home in a wholesome and practical, but nevertheless cultural, way. The social life of the students should be governed not merely by rules but by the creation of a cultural atmosphere and a tactful training of these young men and women in ways which make cultured gentlemen and gentlewomen.

Henry Culbertson

Evans left Ripon in the summer of 1917; his successor, Henry C. Culbertson, did not arrive till October, 1918. During this interim, while the new president was engaged in war service, William Harley Barber, the Dean of the College, served as acting president. A native of Black Earth, Wisconsin, a small village near Madison, Barber attended the state university and, upon graduation, took a teaching job at Ripon High School. Although he liked the community of Ripon and the community was very enthusiastic about him, first as teacher and then as principal, his ambitions were not fulfilled by teaching at the secondary level. So, after four years, he left for a position as laboratory assistant at the Bureau of Standards in Washington, D. C. Then, two years later, in 1906, President Hughes called Barber back to Ripon, this time as professor of physics. He was to occupy this chair for the next 40 years, turning out a remarkable string of bright young physicists who went on to win national recognition in the service of government (mainly at the Bureau of Standards), industry, and education. He, in turn, was to gain national renown for his skill as a teacher.[1]

After returning to Ripon, Barber did enough post-graduate work at the University of Chicago to earn a master's degree, but he never got his doctorate, believing that a Ph.D. would not open up any greater opportunities than he already had. He enjoyed life at a small college in a small town, where he was able to participate actively in the management of both. He sat on the Ripon City Council, served as mayor of the city, and acted at one time or another as business manager, registrar, dean, and interim president of the College—always on top of a regular teaching load. Completely in tune with Evans' ideas of academic "efficiency," he worked with mar-ginal instructional equipment, most of the time as a one-man department, making certain that all his majors were thor-oughly grounded in the fundamentals of physical science, mathematics, and communication skills.

American entry into World War I in April of 1917 did not produce a wholesale rush to the colors by Ripon students. Some went; many others wanted to, but the War and Navy Departments deliberately discouraged any such drain on the nation's educational system. The British and French govern-ments had closed their universities, calling all their eligible men into military service. By 1917, this was thought to have been a mistake since both nations were losing an entire generation of their best minds. So, American college stu-dents were told to stay in school until summoned by the selective service system. On April 16, 1917, 10 days after the declaration of war, the Executive Committee of the board, with wholehearted faculty approval, voted to place the Col-lege on a "war footing." Military drill, required of all men and carrying some academic credit, began immediately without uniforms and with sticks in place of rifles; women learned how to roll bandages; and part of Ingalls Field (not including the football area) was set aside to grow potatoes for the Commons. Because of the government's interest in physical fitness, the trustees revoked an earlier wartime decision suspending athletics, though not in time for the 1917 football season. A number of war-related courses were added to the curriculum.

In the fall of 1918, the Student Army Training Corps (SATC) brought 200 soldiers to the College. Women students found themselves relocated completely off campus in the Hotel LeRoy (later the Davis Hotel), where all the ladies ate their meals, and in three of the four houses along the west side of Woodside Avenue: the president's home (now Hughes House), Scribner (later the dean's home at 416), and Harwood. The LeRoy, renamed the College Inn, was rather spartan, with inadequate heat and only one bathtub; nevertheless, the women chose to stay there rather than return to Bartlett when the SATC disbanded in December. Three months of use by the Army had turned "the cottage" into a shambles.

The presence of the SATC was short-lived because the war ended in November of 1918, but it was intense. Classrooms were filled with uniforms; bugles sounded throughout the day between first call at 6:30 a.m. and taps at 10 p.m.; men with real rifles drilled in the streets of Ripon and stood guard duty around the campus. Classes continued to function on a coeducational basis, but steps were taken to assure a decent separation of the sexes after hours. It was an exercise in patriotism with seriocomic overtones, but there was nothing lighthearted about its implementation.

The SATC led almost immediately to ROTC (Reserve Officers Training Corps), but, even more significantly, it sent to campuses thousands of enlisted men whom the Army thought qualified for college work but who would not otherwise have gone. They were discharged when the program ended, but both the government and the schools encouraged them to remain; many did so, using state bonuses for veterans (at least in Wisconsin) to pay for their new-found educational opportunities. As a result, the college population of the country increased dramatically. In 1920, it was half again as large as it had been in 1915, and this growth continued throughout the 1920s and 1930s. Like World War II, the Great War of 1917-18 was a major force in the democratization of American higher education.

The war brought other changes to Ripon College. For instance, the Army program was run on the quarter system, the intent being to have four full terms in each year. Ripon not only adopted the system during the war but chose to stay on it for the next 28 years. Moreover, the war had a lasting impact on the curriculum by encouraging a stronger emphasis on history and the social sciences. Courses dealing with national and international problems, introduced for the SATC as "war measures," tended to stay in the curriculum; approximately a third of the graduating class of 1925 majored in history or one of the social sciences.

During the war, 248 Ripon students and alumni served in the armed forces or the Red Cross, not including men enrolled in SATC. Nine lost their lives while in uniform, among them Latimer Johns of Randolph, Wisconsin, Ripon's first Rhodes Scholar. A graduate of the class of 1911, Johns was attending Oxford University when the war began. He immediately returned to the United States, enlisted in the regular Army field artillery and, after receiving his commission as a second lieutenant, saw extended action on the Western Front. He was killed on the last day of September in 1918 and, for conspicuous bravery under enemy fire, was awarded the Distinguished Service Cross. He was one of only two Ripon alumni killed in battle, the rest dying of accidents or illness. The Second World War was to take a much heavier toll.

Ripon's return to normalcy was complicated by the belated arrival of the new president. An Ohioan, Culbertson graduated from Cincinnati University, attended both Columbia Law School and the University of Chicago Divinity School, earned his B.D. in 1900, was ordained a Presbyterian minister, and in 1907 at the age of 33 (two years younger than Evans was when he became Ripon's president), was elected to the presidency of Emporia College in Kansas. His record there was so impressive that William Allen White, the famed newspaper editor and "Sage of Emporia," wrote, "If I were looking for a college president and could get Henry Coe Culbertson, I would look no further."[2] Although Barber told Evans that there was some difference of opinion about Culbertson among faculty and trustees, his election was unanimous. In fact, he had made a tremendous impression on both College and city in two visits to the campus. On the surface, there seemed to be no reason to expect problems. But Evans was a tough act to follow; comparison was perhaps inevitably unfavorable.

In many respects, the philosophies of the two men were similar. Both believed strongly in the small liberal arts college. Both emphasized "Christian character":

> We are exceptionally fortunate in having a faculty, all of whom are of the highest type of Christian character and I believe that faculty and students should be in the closest possible relationship of friendship and that every possible step should be taken to build up the Christian ideals of character and service in the minds of the student body.[3]

Both presidents were liberal in their religious views: "I do not believe in a narrow orthodoxy," the new president told the trustees, "but I do believe in the broad ennobling teaching of Jesus Christ as given in the Beatitudes and the Sermon on the Mount"; he also believed that the theory of evolution actually strengthened Christianity.[4]

Like Evans, Culbertson was immediately faced with a disciplinary problem, and he solved it in a way that would have pleased his predecessor. The SATC had just been installed, and Culbertson was appalled by the behavior of the troops just as Evans had been disturbed by the drinking in Smith Hall. Culbertson blamed the trouble on the unit commander.

[He] had none of the character or educational ideals
which would fit him for such an important position.
He had been a traveling man, and his moral ideals
were little short of a disaster to the institution. His influence and the influence of the young men of similar
type who came into the student body under the SATC
have produced a very serious problem indeed with
relation to upholding the ideals of character and
scholarship for which Ripon College stands.

Culbertson dealt with the problem, once the unit had been
disbanded, by simply expelling "a certain number of boys
who appeared to be a center of undesirable influences." Also,
Evans would also have taken heart from a report by the
preceptress (i.e., housemother) at the end of the critical year
1918-19. "It is very much to the credit of our young women
that none of them were carried away by the uniform, and that
they did not make the mistake made in so many colleges of
over-entertaining [a world-class euphemism] the young men
of the S.A.T.C. . . ."[5]
        But there were differences between the two men. Cul-
bertson wanted, partly for financial reasons, to strengthen
Ripon's religious connections and, for instance, sought endorsement by the Baptist Church of Wisconsin. While Evans
was a bit of a male chauvinist and put much emphasis on
"masculinity," Culbertson wanted more equal treatment of
men and women, believing that accreditation by the national
Association of Collegiate Alumnae would benefit the College.
Consequently, he recommended the addition of more women
to the Board of Trustees—there had never been more than
one or two—and succeeded in getting raises for some notoriously underpaid women faculty members. In addition, he
got separate dressing rooms for the ladies, which had been
incomprehensibly overlooked in the planning of the gymnasium. The eventual result was acceptance in the membership of the women's alumnae association.
        It is clear that Culbertson was less obsessed than

Evans with "economy," especially if it were achieved, at least partially, by inadequate faculty compensation. Pointing out that inflation had doubled the cost of living while salaries had risen by only a third, he strongly urged the board to close the gap. He also was less concerned with keeping the College "near to the poor." Although he believed in a "democratically inexpensive" Ripon, he wanted the College "to attract students, not because it is cheaper than the university, but because it offers distinctive educational advantages to rich and poor alike. There can be no democracy in a one class school. . . ."[6] In other words, the College should be made more attractive to the children of the well-to-do. One way to accomplish this goal was to improve Ripon's "cultural atmosphere," an aspect of college life which did not especially concern Evans and which had degenerated somewhat during SATC days. "Our dormitories," he told the trustees, "should teach ideals of home in a wholesome and practical, but nevertheless cultural way. The social life of the students should be governed not merely by rules but by the creation of a cultural atmosphere and a tactful training of these young men and women in ways which mark cultured gentlemen and gentlewomen."[7] With this aim in mind, he established a joint college-community fine arts series.

Whatever his strengths and weaknesses, Culbertson was unable to solve Ripon's severe financial problems aggravated by inflation during and after the war. In endowment and instructional equipment, the College was perilously close to the lower limit expected of an accredited school, and it had violated accepted practice by borrowing from endowment to purchase off-campus housing and cover annual deficits. According to the North Central Association, accreditation might have been lost except for wartime emergency. Thus, another capital campaign was absolutely necessary. Briefly, prospects looked good. The independent Christian colleges of Wisconsin (Beloit, Campion, Carroll, Lawrence, Marquette, Milwaukee Downer, Northfield, and Ripon) had formed a consortium, and Rockefeller's board had offered the member institutions challenge grants for endowment and operating expenses; Ripon would get $12,500 for expenses, including salary improvement, and $100,000 for endowment on a three-to-one matching basis. Although Culbertson devoted much time and energy to fund raising on behalf of the consortium, especially in the Chicago area, an effort which took him away from the campus when he might have profited from becoming more familiar with his new position and the people with whom he had to work, the campaign fell far short of the consortium's $5 million goal. Hoping to offset this shortfall through more efficient financial management, Culbertson endorsed a proposal by Trustee William R. Dawes to hire a consultant. An economist from the University of Chicago made a study and recommended that the College hire a professional business manager. In 1920, George R. Beach was appointed with a salary of $4,500. Although this was a sensible move, it did not have the enthusiastic approval of the board and was to have disastrous consequences for Culbertson.

Previously, the financial affairs of the College had been handled by the trustees through its officers and committees. Secretary of the board Sam Pedrick (a lawyer) was the closest thing to a business manager, but he relied heavily on Dean Barber (a physicist) and Herman Gatzke, Superintendent of Buildings and Grounds (a carpenter), in preparing and implementing the budget, and on Cashier Addie W. Horner (a housewife), for the collection and payment of bills. It may have been a management consultant's nightmare, but without doubt, it was extremely cost-efficient if only because it involved so little expense. The system of bookkeeping was actually a model of efficiency, thanks to Trustee Albert Farr; its only weakness was the College's inability to collect student fees on time. Relying on the argument that if it works, don't fix it, both Pedrick and Barber objected strenuously to Beach's appointment. To both of them, it was an unnecessary extravagance, the kind of thing that Evans would never have condoned. Pedrick resigned as secretary of the board,

though not from the board, and Barber asked for a renego-
tiation of his contract. He had been offered a position as
chairman of the Physics Department at Beloit with a much
higher salary. Ripon was paying him $2,800 a year and
providing him with a house thought to be worth another
$400; Beloit was offering him $3,600. Barber said he would
be willing to stay at a salary of $3,400, including the house,
if he could have a five-year contract as dean and chairman of
the Physics Department. In addition, he would have to have
assurance that the dean of the College would always serve as
acting president in the president's absence, that he would
have charge of all student-related financial affairs and all
expenditures for maintenance and operation of the college
plant, and that he would be directly responsible to the
president, not the business manager. It was a pretty bold
power play, yet it worked. He got everything he asked for
except the five-year contract (the board gave him two) and, in
the process, created an impossible situation for the new
business manager and further embarrassment for Culbertson.

It was clear by the fall of 1920 that Culbertson was in
serious trouble with important members of the board, especially the Executive Committee, consisting largely of local
trustees. They found him "difficult to work with," as did
Barber, and soon came to believe that Culbertson was on the
verge of a nervous collapse. He may have been. Pedrick
maintained that he was "under some mental stress that
interfered with his duties as president very seriously, although at times he would rise to the requirements of his
position and manifest remarkable capacity as an administrator and leader."[8] Exhausted by his war-time activities (he had
served with Herbert Hoover's Food Administration and spent
the summer of 1918 in Europe on a special assignment for
the YMCA), thrown into a difficult situation at the College,
faced with pressing financial problems, and constantly subject
to comparison with a popular former president, it was a
trying situation complicated by a crumbling marriage. The

hiring of a business manager was simply the last straw. According to Barber, the trustees asked Culbertson to resign toward the end of 1920, and he gladly complied. Under better circumstances, he might have been a successful president. Free of the trials of administration and an unhappy marriage—his wife divorced him shortly after his resignation—he returned to the ministry and, in Pedrick's words, "made an enviable record as a preacher and pastor."[9]

It is hard to believe that the Culbertson years seriously damaged the College. Although Dean Barber insisted that things were deteriorating to the point of crisis and that only Evans' return could save the College, Trustee John Wright told Evans that the College was actually in very good shape aside from the president's office. Wright's assessment would seem to be accurate, since 1919-20, Culbertson's only full year as president, was a banner year in almost every way. Returning veterans and remaining SATC students pushed enrollment up to a record 330 (it reached 370 the following year); new faculty were of unusually good quality; the football, basketball, and track teams won state championships; Ripon students captured the State Latin Cup for the third year in a row; and the Glee Club made its most ambitious tour culminating in a triumphal appearance at Orchestra Hall in Chicago. In addition, alumni from the Culbertson years were among the most loyal in the school's history.

In the meantime, Evans was experiencing problems at Occidental very similar to Culbertson's at Ripon. He had difficulties with key trustees, the religious "moss-backs" against whom he had been warned; unfortunately for him, they were wealthy moss-backs on whom Occidental relied for financial support. Predictably, they resisted his efforts to liberate both students and faculty from the dead hand of reactionary theology. Then, a crucial fund-raising campaign failed, as had Culbertson's. Evans felt compelled to offer his resignation. He later claimed to have the backing of four-fifths of the board as well as the enthusiastic support of students and faculty, so perhaps he hoped that his resignation would not be accepted. But it was, unanimously, in the summer of 1920. Since this happened several months before Culbertson's resignation in December, it may have sealed the latter's fate: the Ripon board may very well have got rid of Culbertson, hoping they could lure Evans back to Ripon. In fact, Ripon's Search Committee had contacted Evans before Culbertson had officially resigned.

In the fall of 1920, Evans took a temporary position as pastor of the First Presbyterian Church in San Diego. He had many options other than Ripon, some of them quite attractive. He was formally offered the presidency of two other small colleges, including Carroll in Waukesha, and was contacted by several other colleges and universities looking for presidents: Ohio State, Lafayette, Colorado College, and Lake Forest. He was also offered chairs in philosophy at Carleton, Lake Forest, and Reed and the possibility of a deanship in the proposed School of Religion at the University of Michigan. There were numerous vacancies in pulpits coast-to-coast. However, the most appealing were some openings in the national headquarters of the Presbyterian Church as well as the chance for the general secretaryship of the American Board of Foreign Missions. But, when this opportunity faded, the lure of Ripon proved irresistible, even though it might be considered a step backwards. "I had a sense of ownership in Ripon College," he wrote. In March of 1921, the Executive Committee offered him a contract with a salary of $6,000 plus moving expenses and accompanied it with a flood of letters and petitions from students, faculty, trustees, alumni, and townspeople. He replied by night letter (a form of telegram) to William Dawes, Chairman of the Search Committee: "Have burned all other bridges. I am accepting Ripon with hearty good will and enthusiastic purpose."[10]

Evans believed that his four years at Occidental had been a good learning experience, but he had no regrets about leaving. "California," he wrote to a friend in February of 1921, "has the religion of leisure, beset with isms, controlled in its religious thought too much by long-haired men and short-haired women."[11] He was back on campus in Ripon by May of 1921.

NOTES TO CHAPTER X
HENRY C. CULBERTSON 1918-1920

[1]"William Harley Barber," *Pedrick Genealogies*.

[2]"Henry Coe Culbertson," *Pedrick Genealogies*.

[3]*Ibid.*

[4]*Trustees' Minutes*, V, 695, 746.

[5]*Ibid.*, 692, 724, 730, 746, 750; *College Days*, May 7, 1918.

[6]*Trustees' Minutes*, V, 686, 696, 746, 750, 755.

[7]*Ibid.*, 695, 698, 728-29, 734, 745, 751.

[8]"Culbertson," *Pedrick Genealogies*.

[9]*Ibid.*

[10]*Evans Papers*, Box #1, "Return to Ripon," "Opportunities," "Personal: Occidental," and "Personal: On Return to Ripon."

[11]*Ibid.*, "Personal: On Return to Ripon" (letter to Fred Staff).

CHAPTER XI

A POOR MAN'S COLLEGE
SILAS EVANS 1921-1943

*You don't have much money up there,
but you have something better, and
that is the spirit of turning out excellent
men and women.*

Charles Slichter

This statement, made by the dean of Wisconsin's
Graduate School in the early 1920s,[1] aptly characterizes
Ripon throughout its history, but is particularly appropriate
for Silas Evans' second term. When Evans returned, the
College was broke, but it continued to produce able graduates. That it could do so was probably attributable to Evans'
reestablishing his earlier policy of "economy." Almost immediately, he informed the Board of Trustees that salary increases were out of the question and that administrative
costs must continue to be curbed. The latter statement was
at least obliquely aimed at newly appointed Business Manager George Beach, whose attempts at administrative reform
had thus far been blocked by Dean Barber and Secretary
Pedrick. If Beach hoped to win support from the returning
president, as he apparently did, his hopes were dashed when
Evans told the trustees that one person, Addie Horner, could
still run the business office by herself as she had done in the
past. Consequently, Beach, seeing the handwriting on the
wall, submitted his resignation, effective January 1, 1923.
The board accepted it as of November 1, 1922, continuing
his salary for the remainder of the calendar year, but
declining to pay his moving expenses to and from Ripon. This
thrifty attitude characterized Evans' entire second term, as it

had his first: faculty salaries remained scandalously low and the administration grew but slightly; in both respects, the College compared unfavorably with its competitors, but Evans' "efficiency" probably enabled Ripon to survive. When the Great Depression hit in 1929, the College became a model of economy for other institutions unaware that Ripon had always operated this way even in the Roaring Twenties.

The College was run by a skeletal staff of administrator-teachers: Dean Barber taught all physics courses with the help of student assistants; Dean of Women Gertrude Kingsland and Registrar Wilson Woodmansee had their teaching loads reduced from 15 to 12 hours in English composition and mathematics, respectively; Librarian Josephine Hargrave had a paid assistant but taught one course each term in library science. On the next level, Herman Gatzke handled maintenance with the help of students and the college horse, one person managed the Commons with the assistance of a cook and student help, another ran the heating plant, Miss Horner kept the books, and two stenographers acted as secretaries for the president and deans. Except for the housemothers in each of the women's dorms, some of whom had other teaching or administrative chores, that was it. The first significant addition to the staff was a field secretary, hired in the late 1920s to handle admissions, alumni affairs, publicity, including publication of the *Ripon Alumnus*, and miscellaneous other duties such as management of the Glee Club tours. In 1925, the total staff payroll aside from teaching salaries was under $20,000. Evans' salary that year was $6,000, considerably below that of his counterparts at Lawrence, Carroll, or Beloit.

But for all its efficiency and despite some help from Rockefeller's General Education Board and the joint Wisconsin college campaign, the College still operated with an annual deficit as high as $29,000 (the average was around $12,000) through the decade of the 1920s. The main problem was inadequate return from too small an endowment, which barely met the minimum required by the North

Central Association. The GEB was sympathetic and in fact offered a sum of $133,000 provided that Ripon could come up with an additional $266,000 and effect some reforms in its financial management. As previously mentioned, the College had borrowed from endowment to purchase off-campus housing and, since the buildings produced revenue in the form of student fees, they were carried on the books as endowment. The latter practice, in particular, violated guidelines established by the GEB as well as the Carnegie Foundation and North Central. Consequently, the Rockefeller Board demanded that Ripon stop listing dormitories as endowment and also free itself from debt. By giving generously of their own money and even borrowing funds on their own collateral, the trustees managed to balance the budget; they then turned to the more difficult problem of launching a $600,000 capital campaign, the most ambitious yet undertaken by Ripon. In 1923, the New York firm of Tamblyn and Brown was hired to manage the campaign, but this relationship did not work; the College dropped the New York agency, decreased the goal to $400,000, undertook the drive by itself, and raised the money by 1930.

In the meantime, however, the North Central Association had removed Ripon from its list of accredited institutions in 1927. While assuring the College that its academic standing was not in question, the association pointed out that Ripon's current enrollment of 400 required an endowment of $600,000. Once again, the trustees girded their loins and succeeded in raising the endowment to $602,862.62 (including pledges). Evans requested and received a re-examination by North Central; and, after a visit by President Seaton of Albion College, Ripon regained its accreditation. Despite receiving testimonials from the Universities of Michigan and Wisconsin, the episode was certainly a blow to college prestige and pride. However, both the problem and its successful solution had two beneficial effects: additional impetus to the capital campaign and awareness of the need for a stronger, broader economic base.

The College had become too dependent on the generosity of its trustees and the local community, now numbering 4,000 inhabitants. Sixty-five thousand dollars (16 percent) of the $400,000 was raised in the city during one rainy week of May, 1924. Throughout that week, a "clock" showing progress toward the $65,000 goal was mounted on the city building, and special issues of the *Ripon Daily Press* were published each day to stimulate local interest.[2] Of course, community support was a definite plus, but it also highlighted Ripon's continued provincialism. By 1930, seven of 25 trustees lived in the city, and two (Farr and Dawes) had strong local ties. Only four, including Farr and Dawes, lived outside the state; the other two were alumni. Board membership thus corresponded almost exactly to the College's "legitimate territory," but this territory was not prospering, largely because of the decline of the lumber industry, in which many of Ripon's wealthier board members earned their money. That other areas in Wisconsin were flourishing is indicated by the fact that, while Ripon was struggling to raise $400,000, Lawrence raised $3 million. For a short time, the College was free of debt, and the endowment inched toward $1 million, but the practice of borrowing from this fund to meet operating expenses and to finance new construction continued, with special permission from the GEB. Progress toward a stable financial base was painfully slow.

The generosity of the trustees was all the more remarkable since, although none seem to have been wiped out when the depression came in 1929, many had their fortunes drastically reduced. For the same reason, it became increasingly difficult to find a replacement whenever a resignation occurred. Nevertheless, Evans determined to enlarge the board in order to make the financial burden less onerous for individual members. With a legal charter limit of 30, the board had 27 trustees, including Evans. By making the president ex officio, the College could add four new people; three were added in 1936. In the next year, the College created a new position, chairman of the board, to be chosen from the 29 members. The first to hold the position was William R. Dawes, scion of a family notable in the country's annals since the Revolutionary War: William Dawes had helped Paul Revere on the famous ride; Rufus Dawes had served as an officer in the Iron Brigade, generally considered the outstanding brigade in the Union Army, and was one of the heroes of Gettysburg; and Charles G. Dawes became vice president of the United States 1925-29 under Calvin Coolidge. A native of Ripon and an 1884 alumnus, the second William Dawes was a successful, though not especially wealthy, Chicago investment banker. Serving on the board from 1907 to 1948, he was particularly successful at recruiting students and raising money in the Chicago area, a region that was becoming increasingly important to the College.[3]

After finance, the most serious problem Evans had to face early in his second term was the survival of ROTC. He had supported SATC at Occidental and believed that "if there is to be any form of national defense whatever, the R.O.T.C. is the most economical, scientific, idealistic and thorough form that a democracy can adopt. The R.O.T.C. is the safest and sanest."[4] According to Evans, the program attracted students. In addition, a civilian Army was less of a threat to individual liberty than a completely professional military, offering a "middle way" between "fanatical militarism" and "rabid pacifism." Furthermore, World War I had demonstrated that the military training required in all land-grant universities, including Wisconsin, was inadequate; well more than a year was needed to put in the field a poorly equipped and poorly trained Army. ROTC, it was hoped by Evans and others, would provide the great majority of officers for the previously established National Guard and the newly organized Army and Navy reserves, as well as supply a pool of inactive reserves for rapid mobilization in time of emergency. World War II proved these hopes to be sound.

Originally, the program at Ripon was purely voluntary. Students chosen for the advanced course were paid $108-$162 per year and received a uniform allowance of

$56.50. During the lean years of the depression, this pay and the uniform allowance, which provided an extra set of clothes, helped Ripon maintain its enrollment. To retain a unit, a college had to average an ROTC enrollment of 100, a considerable accomplishment for a coeducational institution with fewer than 400 students. But the requirement created no problems for Ripon. By 1927, 75 percent of the males were enrolled in the corps, with 50 percent of the upperclass men in the advanced course; in fact, the program could not accept all juniors who wished to continue their military training. So impressed were the trustees that, in 1927, they decided to make the first two years compulsory for all men unless excused by the faculty "for some important reason." According to the board, military training had developed "leadership, self-reliance, respect for authority, proper posture and carriage, and, above all, a sense of duty and obligation to his country."[5]

The State of Wisconsin has always taken pride in its military achievements: the Iron Brigade in the Civil War and the Red Arrow Division in World War I for instance. But Ripon was the only private college in the state to apply for a unit. So there was something in the background of Riponites to account for ROTC's popularity: perhaps men from rural and small-town areas were not in the least embarrassed to wear their uniforms. Even the ladies were supportive; each company of the battalion had a "sponsor" chosen from the more popular women on the campus; on ceremonial occasions they, too, were entitled to wear uniforms.[6] An early 1920s *Crimson* unabashedly referred to Ripon as the "West Point of the Middlewest."[7] Not only was the program popular, it was also highly successful, in fact remarkably so. The unit repeatedly won top honors in the annual government inspection, earning distinguished ratings in 1929-30, 1930-31, 1934-35, and 1938-39, and usually fielded one of the best rifle teams in the Sixth Corps Area, which, of course, included several much larger land-grant universities. The 1922-23 squad set a world record for indoor shooting with

Army equipment; the women also organized a crack team. In 1939, four of six Sixth Corps ROTC graduates receiving regular Army commissions, a mark of real distinction, were from Ripon. Seven Ripon alumni have become generals: James Banville '23, Advisor to Chiang Kai-Shek, Chief of the Personnel Division, and Secretary of the Reserve Officers Association; Harley Jones '26; Ralph Olson '26, Adjutant General of the State of Wisconsin; William Blakefield '39; James Hall '41; Gerald Bethke '57; and Rudolph Ostovich '63.[8]

Yet, occasionally ROTC was threatened. In the early 1920s, a cutback in defense spending jeopardized the program, but Evans saved it by pointing out to the Army the Ripon unit's rapid growth and remarkable success. Then in the 1930s, pacificism reared its head. At a meeting at Lake Geneva in October, 1934, the Wisconsin Congregational Conference adopted a resolution obviously aimed at Ripon:

We reaffirm our conviction that compulsory military training in high schools, colleges, and universities serves no true educational purpose, tends to distort fundamental values, is inconsistent with the best American traditions and with Christian ideals, and is out of harmony with the purposes of a Christian college.

A handful of alumni criticized the program, one of them objecting because it "teaches young men not to be critical." And, when the Days complained that the administration was pressuring the paper to refrain from criticizing ROTC, the national press accused the College of censorship, a claim Evans vehemently denied. The president also received hate mail, including one letter that called him "a war-monger of the worst type because you profess to be a Christian"; the College was pilloried in one newspaper for using "Girl Bait," in other words, female sponsors, to lure males into ROTC.[9]

Evans replied that the program was not "militarism" but merely part of national defense and vastly superior to a professional army. "It is not armies that create war," he insisted, "it is wars that create armies." In any event, ROTC weathered the storm. And a decade later, when other colleges were clamoring to get on the ROTC bandwagon, Evans remarked that "we have some of the wicked sense of vindication and poetic justice."[10]

The depression affected Ripon less severely than it did most institutions because it had a reputation for being a "poor man's college," hence affordable. In 1923, students paid $50 per quarter for tuition and fees as well as $20 for room rent; meals at the Commons cost $5 per week. By 1930, the comparable figures were $60, $28, and $5.50; by 1940, $78, $35, and $5—not much higher than the charges at the University of Wisconsin. For a time, Ripon, Lawrence, and Carroll had a gentleman's agreement to keep their student expenses comparable, but this seems to have lapsed in the 1930s, giving Ripon a comparative cost advantage. Scholarship money was minimal, but the trustees in 1933 provided $3,250 for $50 grants to "needy and worthy students" and a year later offered full tuition to high schoolers ranked in the top five percent of their class. Furthermore, government assistance, often thought to be a phenomenon of the 1960s and 1970s, was available. In 1933, the state established a loan fund, from which in the first year alone 73 Ripon students borrowed amounts ranging from $60 to $150. These loans carried no interest as long as the student remained in school, but were expected to be repaid at five percent interest within two years after graduation. Federal aid began in the same year under the Emergency Relief Act, through which Ripon received $450 per month to be applied to the tuition of 30 students who performed a variety of campus jobs, mostly with the maintenance staff. Two years later, the program was taken over by the New Deal's National Youth Administration, which paid an average of $15 per month for work grants; 20 percent of the students benefitted from this program in 1936-37, presumably a typical year. Director of Athletics Carl Doehling, with the title assistant to the president, administered the program with no extra pay and at first without released time. Also, downtown jobs in hotels, restaurants, and stores were fairly plentiful.

Another factor enabling Ripon to sustain enrollment was beefed-up promotion and publicity. With his heavy schedule of Sunday sermons, service club talks, and secondary school commencement addresses, President Evans continued to be Ripon's best advertiser. To increase the College's visibility and bring prospective students to the campus, Ripon sponsored high-school basketball tournaments and track meets, hosted speech contests under the auspices of the locally headquartered National Forensic League, and in 1940 persuaded the American Legion to locate Boys State on the campus every summer, a practice which still continues. In the 1930s, a "Friendship Weekend" brought high-schoolers to Ripon in May for banquets, dances, and "tin can derbies," an event somewhat similar to an antique car rally. The various forensic teams and musical organizations spread the name Ripon throughout the state and northern Illinois. All these activities were coordinated by a field secretary, later called a student secretary; an alumni secretary was later added. This position reflected the fact that Ripon's most successful recruiters were its alumni. In poll after poll asking students why they chose Ripon, the greatest number mentioned some kind of contact with graduates of the College.

Curricular innovation was not a characteristic of the Evans years. Graduation requirements remained stable: English composition, Bible, two years of foreign language, exposure to three of four areas (later changed to four of five with the expansion of the social sciences)—history, literature, mathematics, science—and a major with one or more cognate minors. Between 1925 and 1929, the College tried unsuccessfully to increase income through a summer school. More significant were the 1936 introduction of a three-two cooperative program in engineering with the Massachusetts Institute of Technology and a final decision on the role of music in the curriculum. Music had always been part of the offer of the College, but until 1909 it had been taught only at the academy level. The musicians received only certificates or diplomas, but through their musical organizations and public concerts they added significantly to the cultural life of both the College and community. Then in 1909, President Hughes hired Elizabeth Battle Bintliff as director of the School of Music in the hope that it might develop into a full-fledged conservatory. In keeping with Hughes' decision to drop the Preparatory Division, the school would offer only college courses and its graduates would receive a Bachelor of Music degree. "Battle" Bintliff had received her training at the Oberlin Conservatory of Music; had established studios in Janesville, St. Paul, and Milwaukee; and had served as head of the Olivet College Conservatory in Michigan for 16 years before coming to Ripon. She labored mightily and with some success for 19 years, but never developed a first-rate conservatory. In her 1925 report to the trustees shortly before her resignation, she remarked that her school had become little more than a department of the College. In 1926, the College dropped the music degree, and Bintliff's successor, Harold Chamberlain, another Oberlin graduate, seemed content with a music major leading to a B.A. Since the number of musicians declined precipitously during the depression, this was probably a sensible solution. However, music continued to flourish extracurricularly.

Barber's fame as a teacher of physics led to Ripon's being asked to join 19 of the country's most distinguished small liberal arts colleges in a cooperative program with M.I.T. Under this arrangement, a Ripon student could attend Ripon for three years and M.I.T. for two years, receiving degrees from both institutions. All parties benefitted. M.I.T. gained large numbers of outstanding liberally educated upperclass students at virtually no recruitment cost and at a time when engineering schools were beginning to recognize the values of the liberal arts but were ill-equipped to provide them. Association with the most prestigious engineering school in the country attracted large numbers of students to Ripon. If they could not handle the rigorous required freshman courses in science and mathematics, many of them stayed anyhow and majored in other subjects. If they went on to M.I.T., they shortened their course of study by a year and received two degrees instead of one. Even after subtracting the few students who skipped their senior year at Ripon, the net gain in numbers for the College was significant. Ripon's three-two students did very well, having no difficulty competing with students from the other colleges. Their success led to the development of other combined programs, such as one with the Medill School of Journalism at Northwestern University. During the Evans years, the College placed considerable emphasis in both its publicity and its curriculum on pre-professional training, not only in engineering and journalism but in such fields as agriculture, "Christian Service," commerce, law, library science, medicine, nursing, and teaching. The results were not entirely satisfactory, since the curriculum became cluttered with courses like Agricultural Economy, College Journalism, Elementary Law (taught by Sam Pedrick), and Mechanical Drawing, which earned transfer credits to professional schools.

A high proportion of Ripon faculty had attended small liberal arts colleges like Ripon and had then done graduate work at the leading universities in the country, such as Wisconsin, Chicago, and Columbia. Although only three of 33 had earned doctorates in 1922, the ratio had increased by 1943 to 11 of 37, even including physical education, music, and military science where the Ph.D. was not expected. About a third were women, but only two of them (Elizabeth Bintliff and Grace Goodrich) held senior appointments (professor or associate professor) during the 1920s and the number had dropped to one (Constance Raymaker, economics) by the end of Evans' administration. By this time, possession of a Ph.D. had become nearly prerequisite for promotion, and women were still the victims of discrimination in graduate schools. Actually, Ripon may very well have employed more women teachers than most other coeducational colleges.

In Grace Goodrich, the College had one of its very best teachers. She was a 1906 alumna, had done post-graduate work in classics at the University of Wisconsin, receiving her doctorate in 1913 after additional work at the American School of Classical Study in Rome (1909-10) and Bryn Mawr College (1911-12). Accepting an appointment at Ripon in 1913, she remained at the College for 26 years, teaching Latin, Greek, and archaeology. In 1933, she became dean of women—announcement of her appointment was greeted by cheers in the College Chapel—and continued teaching and deaning until her unexpected death in 1939. "She had that rare quality," wrote one of her students, "of making each of us feel singled out for special interest." She loved to hold her classes out of doors and to treat the entire class to "Ripon College Specials" at Reichmuth's, an ice cream parlor on Watson Street. Evans called her the "most beautiful spirit to grace the halls of Ripon College." By the sheer force of her personality, she made the classics live, providing the kind of instruction that justifies the survival of the small liberal arts college.[11]

Somewhat surprisingly, the depression did not appreciably affect the faculty's standard of living. For one thing, the teachers absorbed increasing enrollments by accepting a heavier teaching load, so that the student-faculty ratio became 15-1, occasionally higher. In 1932, as the depression hit bottom, the entire college staff was asked to take a 10 percent pay cut, not high by national standards. The faculty agreed, but asked that it be considered an annual "donation" to the College rather than a permanent reduction. The trustees accepted this euphemism, promised to restore the cut as soon as possible, and actually did so in 1936 and 1937. The non-teaching staff was given a comparable cut without any promise of restitution, but it too had its pay restored by 1937. Before the cuts, a full professor at Ripon was making between $2,600 and $3,200; the corresponding rank at Beloit was getting $3,200-$5,000; at Lawrence, $3,000-$4,000. Maintenance workers at Ripon earned about $1,000. But the cost of living was falling much faster than salaries; even with the 10 percent cut in pay, Ripon's staff were actually getting raises in terms of real income. In this respect, they were better off than their successors in the 1950s when many worked at Green Giant and other local industries in the summer in order to make ends meet.

Perhaps this is one reason why the following faculty stayed so long at Ripon: Edwin Webster (history), 41 years; Barber (physics, dean, registrar, acting president), 40 years; Leone Oyster (chemistry), 39 years; Doehling (physical education, assistant to the president), 37 years; Augustus Barker (chemistry), 36 years; Clifford Moore (history), 36 years; Phillips Boody (English), 31 years; Josephine Hargrave (librarian), 31 years; Clark Graham (English, education, dean), 29 years; Harold Chamberlain (music), 29 years; Harris Barbour (philosophy), 28 years; James Groves (biology), 27 years; Goodrich (classics, dean of women), 26 years; George Dudycha (psychology), 25 years; John "Daddy" Becker (Spanish), 24 years; Wilson Woodmansee (mathematics, registrar), 23 years. These figures do not include campus fixtures who taught only part time or not at all, such as Bruno Jacob (speech, National Forensic League), Esther Barber and Elizabeth Chamberlain (music), Sergeant Arthur Peters (24 years with the ROTC), Horner (cashier for 23 years), and Herman Gatzke (superintendent of buildings and grounds for 40 years). Such longevity may not have been unique among small colleges in the early 20th century, but it helps to explain the consistency of Ripon's offerings as does the fact that many of the junior faculty on short-term appointments were Ripon graduates. The curriculum changed about as fast as the staff.

Thus, the hallmark of the Evans years was stability.

However, stability has its negative as well as its positive side. So does a reputation for being a poor man's college: such an image may be very appealing to the son of rural parents during depression years, but much less so to the daughter of sophisticated parents in the Milwaukee and Chicago suburbs as the country moved from depression to prosperity. While the years rolled by, it became increasingly apparent that the College needed some new buildings: a gymnasium large enough to accommodate both men and women as well as both varsity athletics and intramurals, an attractive social center, an enlarged dining hall, a home for the fine arts, more on-campus dormitories, an adequate library, improved science facilities, space for administrative offices, and even faculty housing. All of these needs were not fulfilled till the 1970s, but a start was made late in Evans' second term. First came Lane Library, built in 1930 with funds from Rollin B. Lane, a former student who had left before graduating to study law in the East. After he received his law degree, Lane returned to Ripon as a young attorney, then moved to Milwaukee and finally California, where he amassed a fortune in banking and real estate in booming Hollywood. Costing $100,000 and providing shelves for 100,000 titles, the library was built near the site of the old Athenian Hall, which was moved to Ingalls Field to serve, until very recently, as a dressing room for football and track. Thirty thousand books were moved by the ROTC cadets in one day in 1931. Both West and Ingram Halls were remodeled, with classrooms and faculty offices occupying the refurbished first two floors of Ingram and military science taking over a newly remodeled basement in West.

But on January 7, 1931, nine days before the move to Lane Library, a disaster struck the campus and complicated further plans to improve campus housing. Shortly after noon, when most of the students were at lunch, a fire erupted and completely gutted Smith Hall. The fire alarm was activated, but the driver of the city's pumper suffered a fatal heart attack, the engine wound up in a ditch, and the fire department was 45 minutes late. In the meantime, students tossed their belongings out the window and did what they could with fire extinguishers. But flames quickly engulfed the whole structure, the roof collapsed, and the interior was a total loss, though the outer walls remained intact. Luckily, the fireman was the only casualty. For the rest of the school year, Smith men found temporary quarters in other dormitories and nearby private homes. The gutted interior was rebuilt as it had previously existed, so that the job was almost finished when a large crowd gathered at Commencement in June, 1931, for the dedication of Lane Library.

The physical plant, however, was by no means Ripon's only problem; the College was ill-equipped on all fronts to meet the needs and tastes of vastly increasing numbers of high-school graduates seeking admission to colleges and universities. To attract its share of these students, Ripon needed not only an expanded physical plant, but also a larger administrative staff, especially admissions counselors. To handle what was hoped to be an increased enrollment, the College had to hire more teachers and, in order to lure them to the campus, pay them higher salaries and give them lighter teaching loads. As the nation began to recover from the depression, inflation destroyed the faculty's previously favorable financial position. Salaries became so low as to make it difficult even to subscribe to professional journals. There was no sabbatical leave program, no fund to subsidize travel to professional meetings, and no time to do research on campus. The College was falling behind the times, and its poor man's image was becoming somewhat of an albatross.

All this was recognized by Evans' dean, Clark Graham, a graduate of Grinnell with a master's from Columbia and a doctorate from Wisconsin. He had joined the faculty in 1916 as a kind of "utility humanist" in composition, creative writing, journalism, drama, forensics, and education before becoming professor of English and eventually in 1925, dean of the College. He shared Evans' views on the value of extracurricular activities and the virtues of the small private

college: "We are striving," he said, "to be a college with a
personal touch, with the idea of identifying ourselves in a
friendly way with the students' needs and capacities—intellectual, physical, and moral."[12] More strongly than Evans, he
believed in the pure liberal arts as opposed to pre-professional training and in a curriculum more attractive to women,
as well as equal opportunity for them in athletics, drama, and
forensics. He was more in tune with the time and thought
that Ripon's provincial image was causing the College to be
"outdistanced by more progressive schools. . . . We do not
possess in our physical plant a type of 'front' which charac-
teristically appeals to the richer students."[13] These views he
summarized in a lengthy 1936 report to the trustees. Many
of them he was successful in implementing, for instance,
relaxing the "Madison connection" and eliminating pre-
professional courses designed for transfer credit to the
graduate schools there. Others were not achieved for decades and during the terms of later presidents. In selling one
of his strongest convictions, interdepartmental courses, he
was no more successful than his successors in the dean's
office. If Evans was unhappy with Graham's report to the
board, he never said so, seeming to realize that Ripon must
change. Despite their obvious differences of opinion, they
worked well together, and together they shaped the College
of the 1920s and 1930s.

In their attempt to give Ripon "more that air and appearance of success" through an extensive building program,
Evans and Graham found an able and enthusiastic supporter in Shirley Farr, now serving as vice president of the
Board of Trustees.[14] Like her father, she wanted the College
to grow in size and stature and was ready to use her
substantial inherited wealth to serve this purpose. After
matriculating at the University of Chicago, she did some
graduate work and briefly taught history at both Chicago and
Ripon. Poor eyesight forced abandonment of her teaching
career, but she served on the editorial staff of the *American
Historical Review* and was a prominent member of the

American Association of University Women. Since she recognized the urgent need for long-range planning, she was probably instrumental in hiring Thomas Tallmadge, a well-known Chicago architect, to plot the physical expansion of the campus. The Tallmadge Plan, enthusiastically endorsed by the board in 1938, envisioned men's housing in the Tri-Dorms and two adjacent buildings, women's housing in Bartlett and two other adjacent buildings, a new dining hall south of the gym on the corner of Seward and Elm, a northward annex to the gym for women's athletics, a new classroom building on the present site of Farr Hall, a new heating plant to the rear of the gym, and an outdoor theatre behind Middle Hall. It was an impressive plan, proposing a uniform style of architecture, lacking only a student union (unless space could be made in the dining hall) and, obviously, making no use of what is now known as the Lower Campus. But like most master plans, it lasted only till a new president developed his own scheme. Furthermore, Tri-Dorms was the only structure designed by Tallmadge and located where he thought it should be (he died in 1940). Nonetheless, the plan laid out clearly what Ripon had to do in the way of physical expansion.

After reviewing the Tallmadge Plan, the board authorized construction of Tri-Dorms and the heating plant. The latter was largely subsidized by Miss Farr; the former by a series of major gifts: one from Clarence Shaler, a retired industrialist and sculptor ("Young Abe Lincoln" between Todd Wehr and Farr Halls as well as "Genesis" at the top of the hill between West and Middle Halls are his creations), another from J. W. Wright of Ripon, a long-time trustee, and a third from the Evans family. The two wings were named after Shaler and Wright; the center, after President Evans. A grand game of musical chairs followed: three fraternities, previously occupying Duffie, Sanford, and Woodside moved into the Tri-Dorms; the sorority located in Bartlett was shifted to a renovated Duffie, freeing Bartlett for freshman and independent women. Meanwhile, the brothers in Merriman, fearing competition from their rivals in the brand new Tri-Dorms, built a home of their own under a complicated arrangement whereby construction costs, ownership, and responsibility for maintenance were shared with the College. New Merriman replaced Sanford House; Old Merriman became Bartlett Annex as overflow quarters for freshman women.   Ingalls Field was sold to the city under a very favorable arrangement: the College had priority for football games and track meets. All this occurred in 1939-40; in the following year, the locker rooms at the south end of the gym received a second floor to "provide equal facilities for women."

Still a year later, Evans proposed, and the board accepted, plans for a combined social center and dining hall, as well as rooms for meetings and recreation; a grill; a book store; and offices for student publications, the admissions staff, and the members of the Physical Education Department. World War II delayed construction, but the building was ready for partial occupancy in 1942 and full occupancy in 1944. The structure, which cost $150,000, was named the Frank J. Harwood Memorial Union in honor of a trustee who had died in 1940. The international situation put further construction on hold for a decade.

Evans began thinking of retirement in the late 1930s, but felt he should not leave in the midst of campus expansion. When he became 65 in 1941, he made his first formal offer to step down. However, the Union was still under construction and, for many reasons, the trustees weren't ready to face the prospect of finding a successor to a man who had run the school for so long, had made it what it had become, and *was in fact Ripon College*. Consequently, they asked him to remain on a year-to-year basis, set July 1, 1943, as the official resignation date, but gave him the right to leave earlier if he wished. He chose to stay till the terminal date. Locally, there were appropriate ceremonies, and congratulatory messages poured in from all over the country. But wartime constrictions, particularly on travel, prevented students, alumni, friends, and fellow educators from making full acknowledgement of his achievements.   Yet in their hearts and minds, all Riponites knew what he had meant to them and their college.   He had presided for 29 years, far longer than any of his predecessors or successors, and he had left his stamp on the institution as no one else ever had or probably ever would.

NOTES TO CHAPTER XI
SILAS EVANS 1921-1943

[1]Undated *Ripon College Bulletin* (circa 1922), 9.

[2]See the *Ripon Daily Press* for the week of May 6, 1924, bound with the *College Days.*

[3]"Hector Dawes," *Pedrick Genealogies.*

[4]Article from the *Wisconsin Reservist*, July, 1927, in *Evans Papers*, Box #3, "Personal: ROTC."

[5]*Trustees' Minutes*, V, 290; VI, 41-42, 55-56.

[6]See pictures in the *Crimson* 1922, 109 and 1924, 139.

[7]*Crimson*, 1922, 108.

[8]See *College Days*, Sept. 22, 1959, for a history of military training at Ripon.

[9]"Personal: ROTC," *Evans Papers*, Box #3; *Alumnus*, Jan., 1934, 6-7; June, 1934, 13.

[10]Letter to Rev. Leonard Parr, "Personal Papers, 1935-42," *Evans Papers*, Box #1; *Alumnus*, March, 1934, 4-5, 8, and June, 1934, 13.

[11]"Wickliffe Goodrich," *Pedrick Genealogies.*

[12]"James Clark Graham," *Pedrick Genealogies; Trustees' Minutes*, VI, 77 and 340ff.

[13]*Alumnus*, Oct., 1935, 2-12; March, 1936, 12.

[14]"Albert G. Farr," *Pedrick Genealogies.*

CHAPTER XII

AN INTIMATE COLLEGE
STUDENT LIFE UNDER EVANS

*The most priceless gifts of Ripon, that
small, private, liberal arts college where
I spent the four most stimulating years
of my life, were the personal nature of
the educational process, the warmth of
relationships between student and
student, the rapport between student
and faculty.*[1]

So wrote Pearl Pierce Dopp '25, recipient of Ripon's
Distinguished Alumni Citation in 1975 and the Ripon College
Medal of Merit in 1989.

There had always been extracurricular activities,
both authorized and unauthorized, at Ripon, but they had
been somewhat restricted by the size of the College, Victorian
prudery, and the religious atmosphere. With the less severe
attitudes of Hughes and Evans, the growth of the student
body, and the example of other institutions, particularly the
state universities, "outside" activities increased exponen-
tially during the 20th century without any apparent relaxation of academic standards. The various Christian organizations survived into the 20th century, but their main function
under Evans was to perform services similar to those now assigned to the Orientation Committee; they also published the
first *Student Handbook*. Monthly vespers at the Congregational Church continued, featuring outside speakers, usually ministers, though they did not inevitably choose religious topics, but the Day of Prayer for Colleges ceased to be
a major break in campus routine. The literary societies gave
way to fraternities and sororities; publications and forensics,
previously independent, came under the control of a board of

Brockway College, founded in 1851.

Ripon College in the 1880s.

1: Reverend William E. Merriman, first president of Ripon College (1863-76);
2: Reverend Edward H. Merrell, second president (1876-91);
3: Reverend Rufus C. Flagg, third president (1892-1901);
4: Reverend Richard C. Hughes, fourth president (1901-09);
5: Reverend Henry C. Culbertson, sixth president (1917-21).

David P. Mapes, founder
of Brockway College.

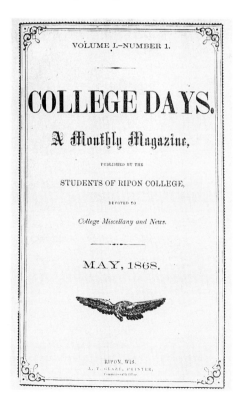

Students of the 1950s salute a Brockway banner
of the 1850s.

Alvan Bovay, first secretary of
the Board of Trustees.

Cover of the first issue of *College
Days*.

The Economia Club, 1887.

Clarissa Tucker Tracy,
"Mother of Ripon
College."

Bartlett Cottage, built in 1888.

Ripon's first football team, 1891.

Women's gym class in basement of West College.

O.H. Ingram, Trustee
(1892-1918).

Biology lab in Ingram Hall in the early 1900s.

Ingram Hall, built in 1900, razed in 1969.

Field Day: Ripon versus Lawrence in the 1890s.

Greek tragedy, early 1900s.

Albert G. Farr, Trustee
(1897-1913).

H. Phillips Boody,
member of the faculty
(1915-46).

Reverend Silas Evans, fifth president (1910-17,
1921-43).

J. Clark Graham,
member of the faculty
(1916-45).

William Harley Barber,
member of the faculty
(1906-46).

Grace Goodrich,
member of the faculty
(1913-39).

Men's Glee Club leaving Ripon on tour in 1926.

Smith Hall fire, 1931.

Student high jinks in the 1930s.

Shirley Farr, Trustee (1914-55).

Women's gym class in the 1920s.

Spencer Tracy receiving
an honorary degree in
1940.

Eastern Debate Team, 1922. (Bumby, Tracy,
MacDougall)

Pi Kappa Delta, honorary forensics fraternity founded in 1921.

Don "Red" Martin
and Carl Doehling,
members of the
faculty (1930-40
and 1924-61).

"Siberia": post-World War II housing for men.

The 10 "most beautiful women at Ripon College," selected by Spencer
Tracy in 1935.

Ver Adest, 1948.

Homecoming parade in 1947.

Miss Wisconsin, 1957:
Lynn Holden, Class of
1958.

Freshman women "button" for sophomore
"hellers" in the 1950s.

Installation of Phi Beta Kappa, 1952.

Grand March: Junior Prom, 1947.

"Winter Wonderland": the campus in the 1940s.

"Present Arms": the ROTC in Memorial Gym, 1950.

Al Jarreau, Class of 1962.

Frances Lee McCain, Class of 1966 (far right), and cast of "The Rape of the Belt," in 1962.

Harrison Ford, Class of 1964 (far left), and cast of "Three Penny Opera" in 1963.

Basketball action in Memorial Gym, 1967.

Freshman Pajama Parade: Homecoming, 1962.

"David vs. Goliath": from November 8, 1963 *College Days.*

College Bowl Team, 1963.

"Flower Power": Ingram Hall in the process of demolition, 1967.

Red Barn Theater fire, 1964.

Cheerleaders celebrate a Ripon touchdown in 1967.

Gail Dobish, Class of 1976.

Rugby action in the 1980s.

Hitting the line in the 1970s.

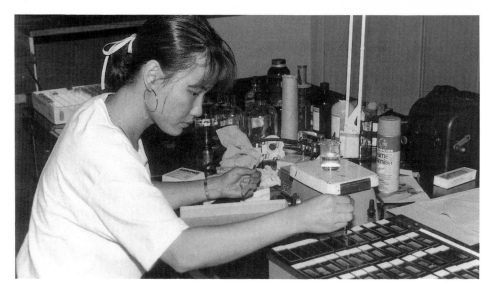

Biology lab in the 1980s.

1: Samuel N. Pickard, Trustee (1931-73); 2: Clark G. Kuebler, seventh president (1943-55); 3: Frederick O. Pinkham, eighth president (1955-66); 4: Bernard S. Adams, ninth president (1966-85); 5: William R. Stott, Jr., 10th president (1985-).

Dormitory living in the 1980s.

Chemistry lab in the 1980s.

Aerial view of the campus in the 1980s.

faculty, students, and trustees. The undergraduates seemed to welcome the change because, with coaches and faculty advisers, the forensic and athletic teams achieved remarkable success competing against much larger schools. Together with touring musical organizations as well as an occasional play, they earned fame and publicity in the Milwaukee and Chicago press. Furthermore, the calendar became increasingly crowded with proms, balls, and less formal parties.

Nothing epitomized the new era more clearly than the emergence of fraternities and sororities, though at a later date than in many sister Christian colleges in the Midwest and even within the state (Beloit, for instance). The first mention of a Greek letter club appeared in the *College Days* of 1895, though secret societies may have existed earlier. In that year, a group called Sigma Pi Phi was organized for some unexplained purpose and proceeded to elect officers, among them Silas Evans, so it must have been a respectable organization; it lasted only a couple years. In 1904, seven women moved into Lyle, the first of the off-campus houses acquired by the College to accommodate growing enrollment. This solution to the problem of overcrowded dormitories obviously gave impetus to the fraternity-sorority movement. Under the sponsorship of Mrs. Hughes, these young ladies formed Alpha Gamma Theta, the first officially approved Greek-letter society. About the same time, eight men sought permission to organize a fraternity. It took them two years (during which time they were meeting sub rosa in a room above a Watson Street grocery store) since they were asking for more than the Lyle girls did: secrecy (expressly forbidden by college policy) plus the right to own their own house and serve meals there. But after getting a faculty adviser, Professor Oliver Marston of the History Department, they were formally recognized as Alpha Omega Alpha. Next came two more sororities, Kappa Phi in 1907 and Delta Pi Sigma in 1909, which were given meeting rooms in Bartlett by Dean of Women Mary Harwood. Since she thought day students and independents should have equal opportunity, in 1910 she gave them a lounge in Ingram.

But there was still only one fraternity, and when the year's rushing results were announced, male resentment brought a sudden, if temporary, end to further expansion. Twenty-four men in Smith Hall had petitioned to form a second group and won faculty approval, subject to ratification by the trustees. Both faculty and trustees had always been sharply divided on the subject, the two sides using the same arguments still in force today: responsibility and self-government versus elitism and incompatibility with the ideals of the College. Dean of the College Frank Erickson, accepting the latter arguments and believing that a student union would better accommodate the students' obvious social needs, urged the board not only to reject the Smith petition but to abolish the whole Greek-letter system. The situation was complicated by the drinking problem in men's dorms, particularly Smith, mentioned in the chapter on Evans' first term. Harley Barber, Chairman of the Committee on Housing, favored simply requiring the offenders to live off campus; Erickson thought this solution would increase the consumption of alcohol. For once, Barber lost an argument. The board concluded that fraternities served no "purpose other than affording an opportunity for club life," cost more money than they were worth, diverted time and interest from the students' "legitimate college work . . . with no corresponding compensation," and, consequently, that fraternities should "be dissolved as quickly as possible." Of course, this ruling caused the demise of sororities also. But the end result was the immediate reemergence of the Greeks as clubs with non-offending names. The trustees retaliated by banning the clubs in 1912 and five years later became more explicit: off-campus rooming houses were prohibited from serving meals (with a few exceptions), using Greek letters, taking men from dormitories, pledging members, and wearing club pins. "It must never be forgotten that neither wealth nor social position, but ability and character are the standards by which our students are judged," the board said.[2]

Once again, however, the students outfoxed their elders: their houses were fraternities and sororities in every respect except the privilege of choosing their own members. By 1924, even the president capitulated. He told the trustees that Greek-letter groups existed in every house and dormitory and he saw no way to abolish them; both human nature and college housing arrangements led to their formation. Since, fortunately, the locals as yet had none of "the objectionable features of the National and recognized Fraternities," such as rushing, pledging, and initiating, he was willing to throw in the towel to prevent "something of a revolution."[3]

So once again, Ripon became a Greek-letter campus, with eight fraternities and five sororities (listed in note four), most of which existed as locals for 30 years under rules established by interfraternity and intersorority councils. Nonetheless, the question of nationalization arose almost immediately when the Bartlett women in 1925, were invited to join Theta Upsilon. Somewhat surprisingly, considering Evans' views on nationals, the trustees, with the president's concurrence, proposed a two-year trial. Although Dean of Women Gertrude Kingsland supported the sorority system, believing that it brought "a more attractive class of young women to Ripon" and improved "the moral tone of the campus" by removing "the deception of sub rosa organizations," she reported after the two-year trial that "the majority of the girls prefer the democracy of many local sororities to a campus divided between local and national groups." Evans, of course, supported this view and in 1927 recommended that the trustees return to a system of locals only; they accepted his recommendation, giving little heed to the fact that many nationwide organizations were seeking chapters at Ripon. So the Bartlett women were forced to reorganize as a local under a new name, Kappa Sigma Chi.[5]

The College experimented briefly with allowing the fraternities, but not the sororities, to own or lease their own houses. Evans believed that such an arrangement would encourage pride and responsibility as well as add some money to the endowment through the payment of sale or rent money. But only Tracy and Merriman Houses signed leases, and the whole idea soon collapsed, probably because of the depression.

In addition to owning the houses, Ripon exercised greater control over fraternities and sororities than most other colleges. The modern system of rushing and pledging did not exist. Since there were no freshman dorms, new students, except for a few who had previous contacts and made their own choices, were distributed more or less arbitrarily among the various houses and usually became members of their assigned fraternity or sorority. Thus, virtually the entire student body, including "townies" so inclined, lived in Greek-letter units. There seemed to be little or no discrimination based on race, religion, wealth, or social background, a tradition that survived the shift to nationals in the 1950s and 1960s, much to the consternation of the parent headquarters.

Another source of control was the Commons, where all students ate their meals, despite protests from the ladies that the menu appeared to be designed for truck drivers and a request from Dean Kingsland that her girls should have a separate dining hall. Of course, as is still true, the various groups tended to congregate in certain sections of the Commons and interhouse rivalries were keen, but the system worked pretty well till the student body outgrew the Commons and some fraternities were given permission to run their own eating facilities.

As was mentioned in the chapter on 19th century student life, the earliest forms of student government were organized around "classes," that is, freshman, sophomore, and so forth. But, as living groups began to flourish, they became the organizing principle. In the fall of 1920, the Men's Student Council, with all houses and the YMCA represented, was formed; its main function was to channel student complaints to the faculty. Shortly thereafter, the ladies followed suit with the Women's Self Government Association (WSGA); it differed from the Men's Council in being more broadly based—all women were members—and in exercising certain judiciary powers, i.e., enforcing the policies of the dean of women. With the legalization of the Greeks in 1924, the men's organization was replaced by an Interfraternity Council. An Intersorority Council soon followed, but it was not a substitute for the still semi-judicial WSGA. All three bodies, though justified as developing responsibility, were not so much "self-governments" as instruments of control for the faculty and deans. In other words, students were encouraged to enforce rules, but had little say in making them.

Perhaps because they were fenced in by more rules than the men, the women were more inclined to question certain policies. They did not take kindly to having freshmen assigned to their houses, preferring to choose their own sisters after inspecting the whole crop of newcomers. But, in turn, this system of rushing and pledging created a need for even more regulations in order to ensure fair and equal opportunity. In 1932, the Intersorority Council, with the encouragement of the dean of women, forbade the presence of honorary members (usually faculty wives), alumnae, and men (presumably handsome campus heroes) at rushing parties. These parties, limited to one per house, could not be held in the homes of local members and could cost no more than $15 apiece. Paradoxically, the dorms accommodated the ladies' rushing and pledging system while, at the same time, giving the dean of women more control.

The practice of "hazing," not unique to this country, was both an extension of the older interclass rivalry and an integral part of the initiation ceremonies of fraternities and sororities. The "green" freshmen were subjected to ingenious kinds of physical and psychological indignities, all intended to test their mettle, instill discipline and respect for their elders, introduce them to Ripon's traditions, and enable sophomores to reproduce the tortures inflicted on them by students who were now juniors. All newcomers had to wear green "beanies" and to "button" all upperclassmen, that is to salute them by touching their beanie buttons. Freshman women had to tie their hair in green bows and adorn their evening gowns with green ribbons. Their male classmates were required to wear green ties and were allowed to smoke only corncob pipes and nowhere but in their rooms. Any breach of the rules was subject to discipline by the sophomore class. Naturally, the punishments sometimes got out of hand, so that 1917 saw the first attempt to control hazing. Though the rules remained, enforcement was shifted from the sophomore class to the presidents of the houses, who, it was hoped, would put on the brakes. This shift caused the editor of the *College Days* to wax indignant. Hazing at Ripon was mild, he thought, compared to that in other colleges, and he was probably right. Furthermore, he considered the practice "constructive," spurring the frosh to "nobler things. We must return to some form of hazing, or the College will deteriorate."[6] He need not have worried: there was no way hazing could be abolished.

Another tradition was the "secret" freshman party, customarily held during the first week of school, which the sophomores were expected to find and crash. On one such occasion in October, 1917, the frosh arose at 1:30 a.m., gathered at Ingalls Field, and rode in haywagons to Rosendale, where a dance hall had been rented. Although some sophomores were decoyed to Fairwater, most of them arrived in Rosendale shortly after the freshmen. Following a brief, harmless scuffle, the elders were allowed to join the youngsters' party. Presumably, they all returned in time for breakfast. The use of wagons placed a limit on distance, but the advent of the horseless carriage introduced all kinds of new and dangerous possibilities so that the faculty, in 1927, outlawed the parties and imposed a total ban on automobiles.

By then, the houses had taken over freshman hazing via the rituals of pledging and initiating: the use of the paddle, the performance of "pledge duties," and the long midnight walks in the country. These more or less private practices were augmented by public displays such as the autumn Saturday morning downtown parade of freshman men in outlandish costumes, usually in drag, for which a committee of seniors awarded prizes to the "cleverest and funniest acts." A sizeable crowd of both college and town folk always lined the parade route much to the delight of the press and the embarrassment of the administration. This relatively harmless event, as well as other forms of public hazing, were finally outlawed by the Interfraternity Council.

The faculty was disturbed by any form of hazing; so was Dean Clark Graham. But his attempts at further reform were no more successful than previous ones. In 1936, he reported that on the whole, the sophomore mind has dominated, and we have suffered "periodically from eruptions of hazing which at best have been silly, and at worst have been dangerous, and which have on occasion alienated families and even whole towns from Ripon College."[7] But the eruptions, both interclass and fraternal, continued well into the 1950s and 1960s, with time out during World War II, when they were deemed inappropriate.

However, the "social calendar," prepared by a committee of one member from each house, caused little consternation among faculty and administrators. A typical example, 1926-27, listed 56 events, most of them dances, all chaperoned, all "dry," and all rather decorous. They came in all sizes: large—the Junior Prom and the Military Ball—, medium—the Homecoming Dance, the Waiters' Ball, and the Eastern Star Formal—, and small—requiring only a Victrola and scheduled after basketball games, Wednesday supper, and so forth. Those were "big band" days, playing "swing," "sweet," "hot," or "Latin," although the tango, considered by the dean of women to be dangerously excitable, was briefly banned; the waltzes and fox trots, of course, permitted some polite intimacy.

The Prom and the Mil Ball were highly formal:

tuxedoes or "tails," evening gowns and corsages, lavishly decorated settings (usually in the gym or the armory downtown), a name band, and a grand march led by the king and his queen. Each couple had small, neatly printed "programs," listing each dance and with a space provided for writing in the respective partners: a full program would prove to the male that his date was not a "wall flower."

The only concern of Evans and his faculty was whether the spring house parties became too exclusive, too expensive, or too distant, thus requiring overnight privileges. Ultimately, house parties were banned and attempts made to encourage all-college social events, such as the annual spring picnic at Silver Lake, an all-day outing, which required a special train and a 35 mile ride to Wautoma. Nonetheless, fraternities and sororities remained central to Ripon's social life and still do.

Relationships between students and faculty were frequent and friendly, but strictly conventional. The teachers were expected to do a lot of entertaining, both formal (Sunday dinners and afternoon teas) and informal (listening to records and radio, with students taking turns on the earphones), and chaperoning parties large and small, near and far. In these activities, the Evanses contributed more than their share. Students had social obligations, too; senior women, for instance, were expected to make the rounds of all faculty homes before graduation and could pop in on faculty wives in the afternoons. All this is what made Ripon special and still does today, though under greatly changed conditions.

On relationships between the sexes, evidence is harder to come by. When Jessie Fox Taintor, a graduate of 1873 and an English professor from 1905 to 1921, returned for his 50th reunion, he remarked that boys were still boys and girls were still girls, they were still traipsing off into the woods, they were still seeking dark corners, and they were still making love to each other, more openly but "just as effectively" as they had always done.[8] But, "effective" lovemaking must have been much more difficult to arrange than in later years. Although the religious atmosphere was on the wane, Ripon was still a "Christian" college, women were locked into their dormitories by 10 p.m. on week nights and 11 p.m. on weekends, housemothers were omnipresent, *in loco parentis* was in full flower, there was great concern for womanly virtue, and, if roller skating was no longer considered "over-exciting," movies definitely were. But love has always laughed at locksmiths, and there was always the great outdoors.

"Christian character" was very important to President Evans, so much so that the College kept a "character record" on all students, evaluating them for "good habits, loyalty, industry, honesty, initiative, good manners, respect for law and property values, forensic, musical, athletic, social, and varied other activities," including church attendance for those who chose to attend. A student failing to establish a satisfactory record could be considered "unfit for Ripon College."[9] Such evaluations were not really new, but the relentless, systematic gathering and recording of information as well as the explicit threat of expulsion were. Some students considered the system militaristic—it was, in fact, partly developed by Captain George T. Rice of the ROTC; today it might be considered Orwellian. But Evans managed to quiet student fears—after all, it was for their own good, and apparently, no student was drummed out of school because of it.

The campus was still somewhat puritanical and provincial. Faculty could smoke on campus only in their offices; men students in their rooms, but not on the campus, the athletic fields, or the city streets. Female liberation appeared only in hairdos and dress styles. Gambling and drinking were definitely taboo. These were, of course, the days of prohibition (1919-33), but Wisconsin never took kindly to temperance movements and the downtown taverns provided near beer legally and regular beer illegally with only occasional interference from federal marshals; venturesome males could also visit the "speakeasies" in Fond du Lac and

Oshkosh. With the end of prohibition, alcohol naturally became easier to obtain, and beer appeared in the fraternities and at many house parties. Yet, drinking was seemingly not excessive, partly because of bans on automobiles but mostly because of Ripon's clientele. Despite Dean Graham's hopes for a more sophisticated, more affluent, and less regional student body, Ripon remained largely a rural and provincial college, though less so than previously. In 1940, 329 of 430 students came from Wisconsin, with 79 from Illinois. Although more men and women were coming from Milwaukee and Chicago, neither city sent as many as the City of Ripon; somewhat surprisingly, a higher percentage of Milwaukee-Chicago students required financial aid than students from other areas. Similarly, although the number of Roman Catholics increased, the students remained predominantly Protestant; seldom was there a Black or Jewish student. Likewise, the career goals of the alumni do not suggest upper middle class origins: in some years, 75 percent of the graduates sought public school teaching jobs.

Early in the 1930s, Ripon had a chance to purchase, for the proverbial "song," the huge Victor Lawson estate, present home of the Green Lake Conference Center, owned by the American Baptist Assembly. Lawsonia would have provided a spectacular location for a new campus on the lakeshore, but Evans feared it would change the character of the College.

Having himself been "a big man on campus," President Evans believed in and enthusiastically supported athletics and extracurricular activities, and he had reason to be proud of Ripon's remarkable record in forensics. In February of 1922, the Eastern Debating Team left the Midwest for an extended tour of the Atlantic Coast states. After a warm-up against Illinois Wesleyan, they headed for Maine to challenge Colby and Bowdoin, which happened to be debate coach Phillips Boody's alma mater. The Bowdoin contest ended in a split decision against Ripon, but the dissenting judge, a Harvard professor, was so convinced the Wisconsin team had won that he lodged a formal protest. After defeating Colby, the Riponites returned home via Boston, New York, and Washington. They were an especially talented group, consisting of Curtis MacDougall, who became dean of the Medill School of Journalism, Harold Bumby, who became a successful Milwaukee industrialist, and Spencer Tracy, who became the greatest film actor of his time. And for Tracy, the trip was the turning point of his life. After a short hitch in the Navy during World War I, he finished high school at Northwestern Military and Naval Academy in Lake Geneva and entered Ripon for the winter term of 1920-21, intending to become a doctor. But he was not much of a science student and directed his energies largely towards forensics and acting. Since he was the most argumentative student on campus, Boody recruited him for debating; and, since he was more mature looking than his classmates and had a phenomenal memory for lines, Clark Graham recruited him for the stage. In fact, Graham was so impressed that he suggested an acting career and wrote a letter on Tracy's behalf to the American Academy of Dramatic Arts in New York. So, when the debate team arrived in New York, Tracy presented himself at the academy, read some lines from a one-act play in which he had appeared at Ripon, and was immediately accepted for admission. According to an article he wrote for *The Forensic of Pi Kappa Delta*, after his return to Wisconsin with the debate team he talked things over with his family as well as Professor Boody and left for New York. He returned to Ripon 18 years later as the College's most famous alumnus and received an honorary Doctorate of Fine Arts in June, 1940; his wife, Louise, also received an honorary degree in 1976 for her work in schools for the deaf—their son was a victim of the handicap.

Tracy's stay at Ripon was happy and productive in areas other than academics. During his sophomore year, he was voted "the cleverest man on campus," served as president of his fraternity in West Hall, founded a group called the Campus Players, and was admitted to Pi Kappa Delta, the national honor society in speech. During his years of success, he always gave credit to the College, especially to Boody and Graham, for giving his life direction. He once wrote, "I owe whatever success I had to the start I got at Ripon College, to Professors Boody and Graham. I shall always be grateful."[10]

The so-called Eastern Team were not the only outstanding debaters trained by Boody. Two others were Allan Michie '36, journalist, author of a dozen books, and Radio Free Europe broadcaster, and especially Bruno Jacob '22. These two, together with MacDougall, were elected Alumni Phi Beta Kappas. Boody, after graduating from Bowdoin and earning a master's degree at Columbia, joined the Ripon faculty to teach English literature, dramaturgy, and speech for 31 years. His success was such that he attracted to the College the best high-school debaters in the state and shared with Harley Barber, Tracy, and later Jacob the distinction of spreading the name of Ripon throughout the Midwest and beyond. Eventually, he shifted his interest to the stage and founded the Mask and Whig Club, which produced more than 100 plays by the time of his retirement in 1946. He published college texts in all three of his fields of expertise: two in speech and one each in English composition and acting.[11]

Boody had been preceded as debate coach by Professor Oliver Marston of the History Department in 1910, when Ripon's debaters complained that other colleges enjoyed a competitive advantage by having faculty coaches. Then in 1911, Dean Erickson created a new position and appointed E. R. Nichols Professor of English Composition and Public Speaking. Nichols stayed long enough to help his students establish the first chapter of Pi Kappa Delta in 1913, modeled on the Kansas State Prohibition Oratorical Association, of which he had been a member. Grace Goodrich, Professor of Classics, suggested the society's motto, PEITHO KAE DIKAIA, meaning "the arts of persuasion, beautiful and true." Among the nearly 400 chapters of the society, Ripon has always played a leadership role and, in 1919, published a high school manual, *Suggestions for the Debater*, which eventually sold 35,000 copies at 25 cents apiece.

One of the stars attracted to Ripon by Boody was Bruno Jacob of Valders, Wisconsin. He was the student manager on some of Boody's most successful teams and the author of *Suggestions for the Debater* while still in college. After graduation, he became assistant coach and manager of debate trips, but achieved his greatest fame as founder of the National Forensic League. This came about when a teacher who had been using Jacob's book wrote to ask whether high-school students could join Pi Kappa Delta and, if not, was there an organization they could join? Since the answer was "No," Jacob went to work, discovered through correspondence with debate coaches that there was strong interest in a society for secondary-school forensics, and in 1925 chartered the NFL. Beginning with 20 schools in 13 states, it grew to its present size of 1,689 chapters and 606 affiliates in all 50 states and the Territory of Guam. For many years, its headquarters were on the campus. Until his retirement in 1969, Jacob served as NFL's national secretary; Ripon Alumni Secretary Reinhold Gehner '30 called the society "the greatest advertising medium Ripon College has."[12]

Although they never achieved as much national recognition or covered so many miles as the debate teams (one group logged 4,000 miles in 1926), Ripon's musical organizations gave more concerts and to larger audiences. Between March 8 and April 24, 1922, the Men's Glee Club gave 27 concerts in 23 cities; the women's group performed 11 times outside Ripon. Logistics became so complicated that the College hired a part-time manager. In this position, Sam Pickard began his long and fruitful association with the College. He had grown up in the house now occupied by the Ripon Historical Society and might have attended the College had he not accepted a position with the First National Bank instead. About the same time, President Culbertson established the College's first fine arts series, which included the

Minneapolis Symphony. But Pickard saw that town-gown cooperation could lead to a much more ambitious program and created a joint venture called the Famous Artists Course with himself as manager. With an annual fee of only $5 for students and $10 for adults, Pickard was able to schedule such headliners as opera singers Ernestine Schumann-Heink and Amelita Galli-Curci, dancers Isadora Duncan and Anna Pavlova, Sousa's Band, and a number of major symphony orchestras.[13]   After he left Ripon in 1932 for the National Manufacturers Bank in Neenah, the program continued somewhat sporadically and prospers today under the sole sponsorship of the College. During the Culbertson-Evans presidencies, there was a lot of good music on the campus in addition to the Glee Clubs and the Artists Course: dance bands, a town-gown symphony orchestra, a choral union, and a versatile organization which served as a pep band at athletic events, a marching band for ROTC, and a touring "show band." Under the leadership of Arch MacGowan in the 1920s and 1930s, it advertised itself, perhaps justifiably, as "the best college band in the state."

Because of the small size of the school, the *College Days* for years had served as newspaper, literary journal, humor magazine, alumni newsletter, and yearbook all rolled into one. As the College grew in the 20th century, the *Days*, amoeba-like, began to split into separate parts. First, in 1907 came the *Crimson*, the yearbook. In 1942, it received an All-American rating from the National Scholastic Press Association. Next to appear, in 1920, was a literary magazine the *Scribbler*, under the direction of Professor Boody. About the same time, an issue of the *Bulletin* featured alumni news. This, in turn, gave way after 1927 to the *Ripon Alumnus*, first a bimonthly newsletter, then a quarterly magazine published by the Alumni Association. As it gradually yielded these functions, the *Days* became a weekly paper covering campus news in an eight-page format, with occasional special issues put out by one of the classes or by the women or featuring a big event such as Homecoming. Like the *Crimson*, the *Days* earned an All-American rating (in 1939). A board of students and faculty, with occasional advice from the administration, appointed the editors, established general policy, and occasionally exercised the right of censorship. But, since wide off-campus distribution made the *Days* a kind of mirror for the College, all parties were inclined to cooperate. Only compulsory ROTC caused much of a rumpus.

Both the newspaper and the yearbook covered athletics extensively; so did local and "big city" papers, unlike today when it is sometimes difficult even to find scores in the *Milwaukee Journal*. Until after World War II, Ripon's was essentially a masculine three-sports program: football, basketball, and (not very successfully) track, with occasional forays into baseball. For these, the facilities—Ingalls Field and the Indoor Athletic Field (Memorial Gym)—were adequate. Briefly, the latter had a dirt track around the perimeter with a basketball court in the middle and balcony seats on two sides. Plans called for expansion of the gym, but except for an addition to the front, which provided office space for the P.E. staff, they never came to fruition. As it did in forensics, the appointment of professional coaches established a winning tradition. The first of the professionals was Frederick Luehring, who became director of athletics in 1906 and, though trained in physical education, also was a professor of sociology. He won three small-college state championships in football and two in basketball before moving to a distinguished career as director of athletics at Minnesota. He was succeeded, in 1917, by Harold Olsen. Like many Ripon coaches, he had been a star athlete at Wisconsin and came to Ripon immediately after graduation. In four years, (his tenure was interrupted by service in the Army Air Corps) his teams captured seven championships in football, basketball, and track, a three-sport record that has never been surpassed. He left Ripon in 1922 to become basketball coach at Ohio State.

Two years later, Carl Doehling arrived. Nowadays, it is too easy to forget all that Doehling did for Ripon College. It was he who established its modern programs both in health and physical education and in intercollegiate and intramural athletics. A graduate of Colorado A. and M. with a degree in civil engineering, he had been a successful high school coach in Minneapolis. During his tenure of 37 years, he introduced an academic major in physical education, established the college infirmary, served as assistant to the president in the administration of student aid, taught an occasional section of English composition, and handled a major share of the coaching duties, particularly in football and track.   He expanded the varsity program to include tennis, golf, wrestling, cross country, and baseball. In his own eyes, however, his most important achievement was the building of a program in intramurals, something that had never been completely lacking at the College but previously had no effective organization. His motto was, "A man for every sport and a sport for every man," and he succeeded in making it pretty much of a reality. Using the fraternity system as the basis of scheduling and his physical education students as officials, he initiated competition in 12 different sports. Although most of his efforts were directed toward athletics for men, he ultimately established programs for women, including them in the academic major, intramurals, and intercollegiate schedules. He won 15 conference championships, and he was certainly one of the major figures during Evans' second term. Subsequently, he was elected to both the Wisconsin Football Hall of Fame and the Ripon College Athletic Hall of Fame. At his funeral in 1985, retired Chaplain Jerry Thompson noted that Doehling had worked his way through college playing the violin and, after his retirement, composed lyrics and melodies for the mandolin; he was, said Thompson, "the model of the Renaissance gentleman—the combination scholar, athlete, and musician."[14]

For the most part, intercollegiate competition was restricted to two conferences: a group of small Wisconsin colleges known as the Big Four or the Big Five (Ripon,

Lawrence, Beloit, Carroll, and sometimes Northwestern of Watertown) and the Midwest Collegiate Athletic Conference, which Ripon joined in 1922. At that time, the member colleges were Ripon, Lawrence, and Beloit in Wisconsin; Carleton and Hamline in Minnesota; Coe and Cornell in Iowa; and Knox and Milliken in Illinois. Unlike his predecessor, Doehling was willing to play an occasional game of football not only with state schools like Oshkosh but with major athletic powers of the Western Conference (Big Ten). The rationale behind contests with the Big Ten was almost entirely financial. A guaranteed gate for a game in one of their big stadiums was too tempting when money was so difficult to raise by more conventional means. During the late 1920s, Ripon played Wisconsin, Iowa, Minnesota, and Chicago one or more times, usually losing rather badly but sometimes surprising their much bigger foes. Between the two world wars, the Big Ten often scheduled "a practice game" or two, usually the first of the season and always at home. Occasionally, they would play double-headers against two smaller foes, dividing their squads into halves of more or less equal ability. On one such occasion in September, 1928, the Redmen stunned a Chicago split team 12-0; in those days the Maroon, coached by the legendary Amos Alonzo Stagg, was still a football power. It was one of the great upsets in Ripon athletic history, perhaps equaled only by the Redmen's shellacking the Wisconsin Jayvees in the late 1970s. The nickname Redmen first appeared in the 1920s. Its origin is obscure, but one theory is that it was due to "Red" Martin, one of Ripon's football immortals; in other words, the "Crimson" players were Red's men.[15] Actually, however, the name outdated Martin's arrival on the campus. Anyhow, Doehling liked the name, and it stuck.

Despite his enthusiastic support, President Evans kept athletics in perspective. Under both NCAA and conference rules, freshmen were not eligible, and at Ripon a player could be dropped from a team for sub-standard academic performance at any time during the season. Of course, remuneration was strictly forbidden; so was gambling. Evans threw two players off the basketball squad in 1922 when he learned they had played for pay before entering college. After he noticed betting in the stands at a 1917 basketball game against Carleton, he threatened to cancel the rest of the season should further gambling occur.

No account of student life under Evans would be complete without mention of college pranks: Evans' students were inveterate and imaginative pranksters. In its winter issue of 1982, the *Ripon College Magazine* printed a picture of an automobile occupied by three young ladies and standing on the porch of the Congregational Church; the editor asked if anyone could identify the photograph. In a subsequent issue, Carl Griffin '35 wrote: "Of course—I recognize the picture. It is of 'Caroline.' No, that is not the name of any of the girls," but of the car, a Model-T Ford "roadster" with one seat and an open space for a trunk, owned by a succession of presidents of Duffie.[15]

In the same issue that Caroline's picture appeared, that prolific author Anonymous listed other undated pranks:

Malted milk balls placed in the hubcaps of a car on a 90-degree day. . . . A for sale sign placed in front of Middle Hall. . . . A snake strategically placed on a towel rack in a dorm room. . . . A snowman built with loving care in someone's dorm room. . . . Peanut butter on the stair rails in the Commons. . . .[16]

Probably no one came to Ripon during the Evans years just to play jokes. But many certainly enrolled because of its reputation in forensics, music, publications, athletics, and ROTC.

NOTES TO CHAPTER XII
STUDENT LIFE UNDER EVANS

[1]Pearl Dopp, *From the Top of the Tree*, 56-57. See also her letters in the Ripon College Archives.

[2]*Trustees' Minutes*, III, 326-37, 331, 351-52, 364-66, 374; *College Days*, May 20, 1910, March 14 and May 30, 1911.

[3]*Trustees' Minutes*, V, 945; *College Days*, Oct. 7, 1924, and June 15, 1925.

[4]The original six fraternities—Alpha Omega Alpha (Woodside), Theta Sigma Tau (The Elms, later Sanford), Delta Sigma Psi (Smith), Omega Sigma Chi (Hilltop, later Duffie), Phi Kappa Pi (Merriman), and Alpha Phi Omega (West)—were joined by Lambda Delta Alpha (Tracy) and Alpha Phi Kappa (Men's League). The sororities were Delta Delta Beta (Bartlett), Delta Phi Sigma (Harwood), Alpha Gamma Theta (Lyle), Pi Delta Omega (Parkhurst), and Kappa Sigma Chi (Women's League).

[5]*Trustees' Minutes*, V, 956-58, VI, 11, 45, and 57; *Alumnus*, #3 (1927), 13; *College Days*, June 15, 1925, and Oct. 4, 1927.

[6]*College Days*, Feb. 6 and Oct. 16, 1917.

[7]*Ibid.*, Oct. 18, 1932.

[8]*Ibid.*, June 11, 1923.

[9]*Ibid.*, Jan. 16, 1923; *Ripon College Bulletin*, Jan., 1923.

[10]*College Days*, Nov. 10, 1972, 7. See also Tracy's article "Professor Boody Pointed My Nose Toward the Stage" and Boody's "Spencer Tracy at Ripon" in *The Forensic of Pi Kappa*

Delta in the Ripon College Archives. The standard biography is Larry Swindell, *Spencer Tracy. A Biography*; somewhat more "muckraking" is Bill Davidson, *Spencer Tracy: Tragic Idol.*

[11]See "Henry Phillips Boody" in the *Pedrick Genealogies* and scrapbooks donated to the Ripon College Archives by Elizabeth Boody Blodgett. '39

[12]*Alumnus*, Oct., 1933, 4 and 11.

[13]See "Mrs. H. W. Pickard," *Pedrick Genealogies* and Dorothea Wilgus Pickard, *Call Me Sam.*

[14]*Ripon College Magazine*, Nov., 1985, 7.

[15]*Ibid.*, Winter, 1982, 12.

[16]*Ibid.*

CHAPTER XIII

TURBULENT DECADE CLARK G. KUEBLER 1943-1954

The best bulwark of defense for the free enterprise system is free and independent institutions of higher learning.

Clark Kuebler

To replace Silas Evans, the Board of Trustees' Search Committee sought "a young man in vigorous health, with a high scholastic standing, successful administrative experience . . . who was also a thorough Christian gentleman."[1] The committee found such a man in Clark G. Kuebler, a 35-year-old professor of classics at Northwestern University, a student personnel officer, and a prominent Episcopalian layman. He had graduated from Northwestern summa cum laude, studied at Princeton and in Munich before receiving his doctorate from Chicago in 1940, and, after teaching part time at his alma mater, had received a full-time appointment as a professor of classics with some administrative responsibilities.[2] When he assumed office on July 1, 1943, three things were abundantly clear: 1) he was a bird of a different feather from any of his predecessors; 2) he intended to change Ripon College radically; and 3) in attempting to do so, he faced some daunting obstacles.

To take each of these in turn, he was the first bachelor, the first layman, and the first non-Congregationalist-Presbyterian to preside over the College. More specifically, he was about as different from Evans as anyone could be. Evans' background and experience were rural and provincial; Kuebler's, urban and cosmopolitan; Evans was low key and "well-rounded"; Kuebler, brilliant, dynamic, intellectual. Although both were effective speakers, they appealed to different audiences: Evans was most at home addressing a small church congregation, a high-school commencement, or a rural Rotary Club; Kuebler, a national symposium of church leaders, a college commencement, or 2,000 sailors at the Great Lakes Naval Training Center. Evans was folksy and human; Kuebler could be spellbinding, witty, profound, as the occasion demanded. They were alike only in their devotion to religion, but here again, as will appear, there were differences.

The new president was determined to transform Ripon from a somewhat old-fashioned, respected, regional college into a modern, prestigious, national institution. He wanted to upgrade the faculty, raise the percentage of Ph.D.'s, and extend the recruiting area beyond the Midwest; expand enrollment, especially by attracting more female students; decrease attrition; broaden and enrich the curriculum, particularly in those areas which would appeal to women; assemble a larger and more professional administrative staff; stabilize the College's finances, especially by increasing the endowment; improve the cultural atmosphere; give the faculty more say in the running of the institution; upgrade student housing; nationalize fraternities; and secure a chapter of Phi Beta Kappa, perhaps his most single-minded obsession. These interconnected goals were ambitious, to say the least, and accomplishing them would be difficult. In addition, they would make many older faculty, alumni, and townspeople uncomfortable, since Ripon would no longer be the institution they had known and loved. But transformation was absolutely necessary if the College were to achieve a front-rank status in a changing world.

World War II, much longer and more devastating in its consequences, had caused disruptions far beyond those of World War I. Nine alumni had been killed or died in service during the earlier war, only two of them in battle; 57 suffered the same fate in the second war, a majority killed in combat. The ROTC program was largely responsible for the high casualties since the infantry training offered at Ripon funneled most of its cadets into high-risk assignments, whether they had received their commissions or not. Actually, the highest casualties were in the Class of 1946, mere freshmen when they were called into service. It was their misfortune to be in college as part of the "Enlisted Reserve Corps" in 1943, when the Army began gearing up for the great offensives of the following year. In the spring, Ripon (along with many of its sister colleges) was emptied of all its available men to fill the needed combat divisions. Juniors in the advanced ROTC program were allowed to stay in school and complete their training, but the rest were ordered to duty as enlisted men. Ripon as a civilian school almost disappeared. The following fall, it reopened with 177 students: 31 men and 146 women.

Before the spring of 1943, the war had changed the College very little. Enrollment during the first year of the war (1941-42) had reached an all-time high of 503. The next year, it dropped to 466 largely because of the draft, but the College had enrolled one of its biggest freshman classes, consisting largely of men attracted by an ROTC program that promised draft deferment and a commission upon graduation. As a result, student life was able to continue pretty much as usual. Some of the more frivolous activities associated with fraternity and sorority life, notably hazing, were suspended for the duration; the Student Council was renamed the War Council; an experimental women's military course was introduced; students were encouraged to participate in various drives to sell war bonds and stamps and to collect strategic materials such as tinfoil for war industries; but, for the most part, academic and extracurricular activities remained unchanged. And the same was true of the lives of the faculty and administrators. Only a few of them were called into military or other government service, and the rationing of food and gasoline affected their standard of living very little.

In the summer of 1943, however, all this changed. As

in the First World War, the government had decided to use college and university campuses for Army and Navy training programs; and Ripon, because of its distinguished ROTC, had been chosen as one of five colleges in the Sixth Service Command to have an Army Specialized Training Program (ASTP). It took two years to get the program organized, but once it was ready, all Army inductees were screened following their basic training, and some of those considered qualified for college work were assigned to one of the units for intensive instruction in mathematics, physics, chemistry, English, history, geography, mechanical drawing, and physical education. They were taught by the existing college faculties, but were given standardized tests, prepared and graded by the Army. They lived in college housing, but under Army discipline, rising at 6:30 a.m. and retiring at 10:30 p.m., after a full day of classes and required study hours. Upon completion or termination of the course, they were either sent to an officers' candidate school, assigned to positions as technical non-commissioned officers, or returned to the ranks. The programs were initiated, interrupted, and cancelled at the convenience of the service, but, despite their uncertainty, they enabled a number of schools, including Ripon, to stay open with their faculties more or less intact during the last two years of the war.

Ripon received its first contingent of just more than 400 soldiers in June of 1943. Tri-Dorms, Smith (Middle), West, Parkhurst, and Tracy Halls were given to the Army; Harwood was reserved for the handful of civilian men expected in the fall; Bartlett, Duffie, Lyle, and new Merriman were kept open for women. Sororities were permitted to retain their identities even when forced out of their own houses, but fraternities were disbanded. The new Union dining hall became the Army mess; the old Alumni Commons in West Hall was reopened for civilians. Although efforts were made to make the ASTP men feel a part of the College, even to indoctrinate them with some of the school's traditions, they were never truly integrated either academically or socially. Their classes were separate, and they lived by Army rather than college rules. Moreover, there were unforeseen problems. For many of the men, Ripon was a first introduction to small-town America—they had been exiled to the sticks. Others had started college somewhere else and felt that Ripon did not measure up to their former alma maters. The women seemed cold or snooty, despite the existence of a date bureau in Bartlett, and there was nothing to do. Unlike the Navy, the Army did not allow its trainees to participate in intercollegiate athletics, so the entire varsity sports program had to be cancelled. Anyhow, the concentrated schedule of classes and study hours permitted very little social life. Still, most of the complaints were just part of normal Army griping, and the men freely admitted that they would rather be in Ripon than in North Africa or New Guinea. From the standpoint of the faculty, the program worked very well, indeed. Army personnel who could not or would not do the required work were immediately transferred; those who remained were exceptionally good students.

Unfortunately, ASTP was abruptly cancelled in March of 1944, its men reassigned in time for the summer offensives. They were not considered Ripon alumni, so any casualties they may have suffered were not counted as part of Ripon's total. Their places were taken by a smaller contingent of 250 17-and-18-year-olds waiting to be drafted but organized into an Army Specialized Training Reserve (ASTR). Their academic program was like that of ASTP and continued through the end of 1944, when they too were reassigned. During the last quarter of that school year, Ripon had only 183 students; Lawrence had 400 and Carleton 600. This disparity was almost entirely the College's own fault. For reasons of economy, patriotism, and ingrained masculine bias, Evans had, in effect, surrendered the institution to the Army, made little effort to enroll civilians of either sex, fashioned both the curriculum and the extracurriculum to suit male needs and desires, and reduced the admissions staff while Ripon's competitors were expanding theirs, especially to attract women.

Kuebler moved immediately to solve these problems. To recruit students of both sexes, he hired more admissions counselors; to lure women, he began to improve and expand housing, course offerings, and activities. Faculty recruitment for 1944-45 included an artist-in-residence, who also taught art courses (Lester Schwartz), an addition to the Music Department (William Peterman), and an instructor in women's physical education (Marjory Lyons). Naturally, it took a while for these moves to pay off. But, fortunately, the sudden end of the war during the summer of 1945 caused a quantum leap in enrollment; former students returned and even larger numbers entered Ripon for the first time, both groups taking advantage of the landmark federal legislation popularly known as the G.I. Bill, which practically guaranteed all veterans a full education, paying for tuition, fees, room, board, and books. Enrollment jumped from 183 in 1944-45 to 452 in the spring of 1946 to 689 in the fall of 1948, the maximum size of the College up to that time. Veterans alone could have filled Ripon to capacity; but, since most of them were men, sole reliance on this source would have accentuated the sexual imbalance; in fact, the male-female ratio rose from two to one to three to one and remained so for several years. Also, a golden opportunity to raise academic standards would have been lost. To prevent both happening, the College adopted a kind of double standard for admission. Returning Ripon veterans were automatically readmitted, but all others were required to meet certain criteria: class rank in the upper 40 percent for men and 25 percent for women. Even then, certain exceptions were made since the trustees did not want a student body composed largely of egg heads. Consequently, despite some discomfort on the part of the president, the Admissions Committee was allowed to admit "well-rounded" young people, especially male athletes, who did not meet the new standards.

Housing the increased enrollment created severe problems, complicated by the preponderance of veterans and the understandable desire of the Greeks to reclaim their former homes, which had been appropriated by the Army. What seemed simple enough to students was actually a complex problem of logistics, i.e., finding space to fit the sizes of the various groups and, at the same time, making efficient use of all available room. To accommodate the overflow, the College first purchased a number of houses near the campus, some for students, some for faculty, and then shuttled people in and out. Inevitably, this involved expensive remodeling of the houses as it became necessary to accommodate first faculty, then women, then men; but the situation was gradually improved by the construction of new buildings: first the temporary "barracks" for veterans, then the "faculty apartments," which were also intended to accommodate married students, a new phenomenon for Ripon College.

Ill-suited to Wisconsin winters, the barracks were pre-fabricated huts 100 feet x 20 feet provided by the government as emergency, low-cost housing for veterans. After two years, rental fees went to the College. Early in 1946, a group of five were built behind Smith (Middle) Hall; a few months later, three more appeared in "Siberia," the area now occupied by Kemper Hall and the adjacent parking lot. Though the vets were crowded three or four into rooms designed for two, they reacted with remarkably good humor. As soon as possible, the barracks were abandoned and eventually dismantled in the 1950s. On the other hand, the faculty apartments, built on the corner of Lincoln and Oak Streets, proved somewhat more durable. Composed of 16 units, they were constructed by a private company of college trustees and managed by the First National Bank until they were eventually purchased by the College. To this day, they provide low-cost housing for faculty, staff, married students, and even occasionally townspeople.

When the dust finally settled, four sororities and three fraternities had reacquired their old homes in Duffie, Harwood, Lyle, Parkhurst, Merriman, Smith (Middle), and West; but a new sorority (Pi Tau Pi) had no real home of its own. Among the displaced fraternities, Alpha Omega Alpha was in Bartlett, Omega Sigma Chi and Delta Sigma Psi in Smith, Theta Sigma Tau in Hall House on Woodside, Lambda Delta Alpha in the Pedrick House at 523 Watson and, later, in the Barker House (originally President Merrell's home) on the present site of the Pickard Commons. Tri-Dorms now housed freshman women, Old Merriman metamorphosed into the infirmary, and Tracy became a multi-purpose building: a home and a studio for the artist-in-residence as well as headquarters for the Speech Department and the National Forensic League. Disgruntled groups deprived of their former accommodations were assured of space in a contemplated new quadrangle, but this was a long time in coming.

Returning veterans comprised nearly half of the student body (306 of 644 in 1946-47, 289 of 677 in 1947-48), and they were different from previous generations of students: older, more experienced in the ways of the world, and, generally, more serious about academics. Many were first-generation collegians determined to make the most of an opportunity they had never expected to enjoy. Some had difficulty in adjusting and dropped out, but most stayed and became a dominant force in campus life. Returning Riponites had revived former traditions: freshman hazing, beanies, buttoning, hell week; the Junior Prom and the Mil Ball, to which were added such new events as Sadie Hawkins Day and a Beaux Arts Ball. Naturally, they were aided in both these revivals and innovations by the conventional younger students. ROTC flourished once again, with special provision made for former enlisted men who wanted to earn commissions. After a two-year lapse, Doehling's varsity teams regained their pre-war lustre, with the return of former stars like Teddy Scalissi and the arrival of new talent like "Doc" Weiske. A football championship in 1948, Doehling's 25th year, pleased everybody.

But large numbers of war vets disdained college hoopla, which they considered trivial and juvenile. They were not easily hazed and not necessarily eager to join fraternities.

Especially, those living in barracks preferred to form their own clubs and created a new minority of "independents." Many came from cities both within and outside Wisconsin rather than the rural areas which had previously supplied Ripon with most of its students. And their life styles were different, particularly in drinking and dating.

Since Kuebler believed "provincialism" to be a major obstacle to improving Ripon, this change in Ripon's constituency was very much to his liking, and he resolved to accentuate it. The newly expanded admissions staff recruited not only in Wisconsin and northern Illinois, but also in Minnesota, Michigan, Indiana, and downstate Illinois, concentrating heavily, for reasons of efficiency (greater yield per visit), on city schools. The expansion and improvement of the state colleges was hurting Ripon in the rural areas anyway. To attract and retain more sophisticated city students, Kuebler tried to improve the cultural atmosphere of the campus, and in one area, music, he had marked success. The recently appointed William Peterman, who also became dean of men, invigorated the musical program, built a touring choir of 80 voices, and produced the famed annual variety show called *Ver Adest* (*Spring Is Here*), patterned after the WAA-MU musical at Northwestern, Peterman's alma mater. Written and produced by students, such a project was an ambitious undertaking even for a university like Northwestern with graduate schools in music and speech, but Peterman made a go of it at Ripon. Getting it ready took nearly a year and involved a large proportion of the student body in writing, set designing, performing, and promoting. In 1946 and 1947, the shows were staged in the Municipal Auditorium on the present site of the Savings and Loan Association, but beginning in 1948 the College had its own theatre, a surplus Army movie house reassembled north and west of the Tri-Dorms. Although some faculty complained that the whole College had to shut down while Peterman put on his review, it was the big event of the year for the entire college community and the town; and for those who participated, playing to packed houses four times annually to audiences from a wide area of the state, it was the highlight of their college career. Peterman produced seven shows between 1946 and 1952, took time off to work on his doctorate at Northwestern, returned for one more production in 1954, and then left to become musical director at New Trier High School in Winnetka, Illinois. *Ver Adest* did not survive his departure, but it had probably run its course anyhow. Certainly, it had added vitality and excitement to a campus struggling to find itself in the midst of postwar readjustments.

Even before assuming office, Kuebler knew that Ripon's administrative staff needed a major overhaul. Almost immediately, he asked Harry Wells and James Brooks, the two top men in Northwestern's business office, to study the college's bookkeeping, to suggest improvements, and to find a replacement for Jasper Pickett, who had just retired as business manager. They did all three: William Ellis, former business manager at Alma College in Michigan, succeeded Pickett and structured an up-to-date system of budgeting and accounting; Brooks was elected to the Board of Trustees.

Kuebler believed that the attrition rate could be reduced by expanded student services and professional counseling. Consequently, a dean of men was hired and a bureau of testing and career planning was organized by James Dudycha, Professor of Psychology, and James Andrews, newly appointed professor of education. When Barber retired both as teacher and part-time registrar in 1945, Elva Boettcher became full-time registrar. Lucille Hawkinson, a professional dietitian, took over the food service; and Kuebler acquired an executive secretary in Harry Cody, Jr. '33 to direct fund-raising and long-term planning. These appointments, together with the expansion of the Admissions Office, doubled the size of the administration, although it remained smaller than that of Ripon's closest rivals. Despite this fact, the board, accustomed to Evans' leaner, less expensive staffing, accepted the additions reluctantly.

It was not only the administration that needed upgrading; the faculty needed it also. According to Kuebler, only the physical sciences were strong; the social sciences were "spotty," the humanities "weak," and the fine arts "inadequate." In-breeding and provincialism were the main culprits: too many faculty were Ripon alumni and too many had done their graduate work at Wisconsin and other midwestern universities. Too few held doctorates, had been elected to Phi Beta Kappa, attended professional meetings, or accomplished productive scholarship. Too many taught in more than one department. The new president attacked these deficiencies and achieved considerable success. He did his own recruiting with scarcely any consultation with the academic departments. Although he did not ignore such prestigious midwestern graduate schools as Chicago, Northwestern, and Michigan, his main target was the Ivy League: Columbia, Cornell, Harvard, Princeton, and Yale. Given Ripon's low salaries, he had to concentrate on hiring instructors and assistant professors, who either already had their doctorates or were very close to them. Turnover was high because of supply and demand and the Ripon pay scale. Nonetheless, the new faculty roster was impressive.

Curricular reform, including higher admission standards and strictly enforced graduation requirements, was high on Kuebler's agenda as they had been on Dean Graham's under Evans. In the past, almost any student who had graduated from an accredited high school with a certain number of credits was assured of admission. If an applicant's ability to handle college courses was doubtful, he was admitted on probation; in fact, many such students could not do the work and left, either voluntarily or involuntarily, thus compounding the problem of attrition. Consequently, Ripon began to pay more attention to class rank and "test scores," as the eastern schools had been doing for nearly a quarter-century.

At the same time, the College adopted a new set of graduation requirements, effective with the class entering in 1946. Henceforth, students would have to demonstrate competence in English, foreign language, and mathematics, through either testing or course work. Those deemed deficient in composition or mathematics had to take non-credit courses in those subjects; those who had received entrance credits in a foreign language had to elect the second-year course or enroll in the first-year course without credit. Graduation requirements included a year of composition, a year of English or classical literature, a year of American or Modern European history, a year of laboratory science, two years of physical education, two years of military science for men, and a semester of hygiene for women; with some exceptions, all these requirements had to be met by the end of the sophomore year. To graduate, a student had to pass 124 semester hours, achieve a C average, and complete a major of at least 24 credits. When these requirements were put into effect, the College returned to a semester calendar with a five-and-a-half-day week.

In attempting, simultaneously, to raise both admissions and academic standards, Ripon faced a dilemma because enrollment, temporarily swollen by the influx of veterans, had declined from 675 in 1948 to 593 in 1950-51 to 482 in 1953-54. The College had not yet been able to overcome the handicaps cited earlier: an admissions staff still too small and inexperienced, an inadequate student aid budget, substandard housing (especially for upperclass women), and a male-oriented curriculum. Despite the previously mentioned faculty appointments in art, music, and women's physical education, the male-female ratio had become three to one. A rich, well-endowed institution could surmount these obstacles. But Ripon's endowment in 1950 was around $1 million, if one included off-campus houses and the Union. When inflation was factored in, endowment was being seriously eroded.

Of course, tuition and fees could be raised, and they were. Between 1946 and 1954, tuition rose from $300 to $474, board from $216 to $435, and room from $120 to about $230, depending on the accommodations. But these increases tended to compound the problem by driving students into the cheaper state institutions. The obvious solution was a capital campaign to fatten endowment. This solution was tried but, as will be seen later, with disappointing results, largely because much of the money raised was pledged to the construction of new buildings like Marshall Scott Hall. And, as usually happens, the capital campaign tended to hamper annual fund-raising for operating expenses. Unfortunately, Ripon did not have a rich constituency. The alumni, many of them school teachers, ministers, and missionaries, were too few, too poor, and too badly organized to be of much help.

In the meantime, the faculty, especially the bright young Turks recruited by Kuebler, were becoming restive and by Ripon standards somewhat militant. The salary scale, already low by national standards, did not keep pace with inflation; the top salary was only $3,600; the sole fringe benefit was the Teachers Insurance and Annuity pension plan, to which both the faculty and the College contributed. Even relatively senior faculty had to work in the local canneries in the summer, to move into smaller homes, and even to give up their automobiles. Twice, the faculty requested a small cost-of-living bonus. In 1947, the request was granted, but in 1948 the trustees stated that all future raises would be based on merit alone.

At this point, the local chapter of the American Association of University Professors (AAUP) kicked up its heels. The chapter had existed for some time but largely as a kind of benign professional discussion group. Now, it was taking on the character of a grievance committee and as such enrolled almost the entire faculty. In 1950, it asked the administration for a copy of the salary scale but was rebuffed by the trustees. Thereupon, the members of AAUP voluntarily, but anonymously, reported their salary and rank and published their own scale. Especially since the report revealed some embarrassing inequities, the trustees were not pleased.

However, at Kuebler's urging, the board did agree to

adopt a written tenure policy. Tenure is an academic state of grace all but guaranteeing permanent employment to a teacher after a certain length of service to the profession. Once granted, it could not be withdrawn arbitrarily because the department chair or the dean did not like a particular person or, more significantly, because the trustees did not like a faculty member's religious or political views. Its primary purpose was not so much to guarantee a job but to protect academic freedom, in other words, the right of a teacher to investigate and present his or her convictions. This right had existed at Ripon since the turn of the century, but a policy had never been committed to paper or formally endorsed by the board. Since tenure policies recommended by national AAUP were in effect in most of the better schools, including those in the Midwest Conference, Kuebler considered the adoption of a similar policy another step toward aligning Ripon with the best institutions in the country. So, he persuaded the trustees to adopt a statement of tenure and academic freedom very similar to that recommended by national AAUP, but without any reference to that organization. Kuebler had the good sense to realize that certain rights claimed by AAUP, specifically the right to investigate any alleged violation at a particular college and to blacklist that college if it refused to correct any violation proved to exist, would be anathema to the trustees. The policy, adopted in writing by the trustees, secured tenure for an assistant professor after seven years, an associate professor after four years, and a full professor after three years and stipulated that a tenured teacher could not be dismissed except for "moral or social conduct unbecoming to a member of a college faculty; failure to cooperate with others in carrying out established college policies; permanent loss or serious impairment of physical or mental capacities; the discontinuance of offerings in the academic or professional field of the faculty member; financial exigency of the College which is demonstrably *bona fide*." Furthermore, any decision to dismiss a tenured faculty member could be made only by "a board composed of the president, the dean of the College, a faculty committee and a committee of the Board of Trustees"; faculty members had the right to appear before this board "in any cases where the facts were in dispute." All this was quite in accord with AAUP recommendations and is still in effect today. But the final section of the board's policy stated:

> Nothing in this agreement shall be construed to affect the right of the Board of Trustees and the Administration to raise or lower the faculty scale. . . . This policy may be amended by the Board of Trustees at any time.[3]

In the view of some Ripon faculty, these concluding statements vitiated the whole agreement.

These were not happy times for the country or the College; after all it was the era of the cold war and, at least temporarily, of rampant McCarthyism. Like most boards throughout the U. S., Ripon's was solidly conservative and Republican, composed almost entirely of businessmen and corporation lawyers. To them, academic life in general and particularly faculty, who spent 15 hours a week in the classroom, had three vacations during the school year, and took the whole summer off, were somewhat of an arcane mystery. Many trustees probably felt like the apocryphal farmer, who asked a college professor how much time he devoted to teaching classes. When told 15 hours, the farmer remarked, "Well that's a long day but then the work ain't heavy." Furthermore, Ripon's board was uneasy about the bright, young, articulate easterners Kuebler was hiring. If not actually communists, they might be "fellow travelers" or "parlor pinks," sympathizers with the New Deal and the Fair Deal, which threatened free enterprise. It hadn't been like this in the good old days when they could sit back, let Evans run the College, bask in the glory of their position on the board, and give generously whenever Ripon needed a little money to balance the budget. Now they confronted a growing deficit, a declining enrollment, an obstreperous faculty, and an ambitious president who wanted to remake the College, spend lots of money, and probably had little business sense. So the trustees began to play a more active role in the running of the College. The key groups were the Executive and Budget Committees, which often met together, sometimes as frequently as once a month. Of necessity, this joint committee consisted of local trustees: businessmen from Neenah, Fond du Lac, and Oshkosh, and occasionally as many as three Ripon bankers.

Kuebler was caught squarely in the middle. Politically, he was quite conservative as well as a staunch believer in capitalism. "The best bulwark of defense for the free enterprise system . . . is free and independent institutions of higher learning; they stand or fall together," he said. When a conservative Republican Educational Foundation was established in Ripon and located in the Republican House, Kuebler was elected to its board. But he felt he had the right to appoint teachers on the basis of academic merit regardless of their political views and to defend them after their appointment. Some trustees wanted to discourage faculty "from taking an active part in politics"; another stated that the board must "be able to assure potential donors that the philosophy of Ripon College was of a kind which would encourage the growth and teaching of the free enterprise system." Yet the president realized that Ripon could never be recognized nationally as a first-rate institution unless it supported academic freedom.[4]

With enrollment declining rapidly, the trustees were inclined to relax admissions standards or at least allow the director of admissions to admit some borderline applicants without the approval of a faculty committee. They were also inclined to blame the high attrition rate (60 percent in 1953) on poor teaching rather than poor students. Consequently, the Executive Committee recommended that teachers giving a high proportion of low grades be dismissed. Fortunately,

Kuebler took no action, exercising a kind of pocket veto.

In these troubled times, Ripon was fortunate to have Sam Pickard, President of the National Manufacturers' Bank in Neenah, as Chairman of the Board of Trustees. Elected to the board in 1931, he had become its chairman in 1950. Politically, he was a conservative Republican, but he was a reasonable and enlightened man. If Ripon's football team was of greater immediate concern to him than the History Department, he was genuinely interested in private higher education and gave generously of his time and money to make it work at Ripon. He had been instrumental in the hiring of Kuebler, as he was also in the choice of both Kuebler's successors, and he wanted the new president to succeed. Although he was anxious to have Ripon turn out well-rounded, patriotic young men and women, he knew it was the faculty's responsibility to control the academic program.

The problems facing Kuebler and Pickard, particularly, and Ripon College, generally, were aggravated by the personality of a new dean. Clark Graham had resigned in 1945 to accept the presidency of Yankton College in South Dakota and was replaced by Edward A. Tenney, Professor of English at Cornell University, who had a bachelor's degree from Oberlin and a doctorate from Cornell. He had been both gassed and wounded as a marine in World War I and had taught English at West Point during World War II. He had published extensively on English prose style and had written biographies of Andrew Dickson White, first president of Cornell, and of Thomas Lodge, Elizabethan poet, playwright, and novelist.[5] Known to his friends as "Red," he had many of the characteristics of people with red hair. A rigid disciplinarian and a believer in high academic standards, a selective admissions policy, and strict enforcement of academic honesty, he could react violently and articulately whenever his authority or his values were challenged. In a contest between quality and expediency, he came down hard for the former. Here, he had the uncompromising support of the faculty and, for a time at least, of the president. He felt strongly that the trustees were wrong in lowering standards to maintain enrollment and that they should make up their minds whether Ripon was to be a liberal arts college of Phi Beta Kappa standing or "a community college with community standards." The root of Ripon's problems lay in the board's reluctance to give the faculty full control of academic affairs, in the lack of communication and understanding between teachers and trustees, and in the latter's tendency to view faculty-board relationships as an employer-employee conflict rather than "a partnership of equal sharing in a great responsibility." In hopes of improving the situation, he advocated faculty representation on the board or at least election of two liberal educators from outside the College. But the board thought that Tenney was the problem. With too rigid enforcement of the new graduation requirements and of policies prohibiting plagiarism—he had annoyed the trustees with a too-candid report on the prevalence of cheating—he was driving students away, thus exacerbating the attrition rate. And, in giving Ripon a reputation for toughness and refusing to countenance even minor exceptions to admissions requirements, he was discouraging potential applicants. In the fall of 1951, Tenney had been granted a year's leave of absence to study at Yale under a Ford Fellowship. The board took advantage of this opportunity and dispatched Kuebler to New Haven with an ultimatum: Tenney could either return to Ripon as a professor of English with a reduced salary or take an additional year's terminal leave at his old salary; the president apparently offered no objection. Although both Tenney and his wife had enjoyed living in Ripon, he chose the second alternative. Not, however, before issuing an angry document entitled "Ripon's Administrative Problems and Its Relation to Our Present Discontents," in which he blasted the trustees and also accused the president of "double dealing," i.e., saying one thing to the faculty and something quite different to the board.[6] Tenney subsequently accepted a position at Indiana

State in Terra Haute. The whole affair was very embarrassing to Kuebler. It damaged his credibility and widened the
break between faculty and trustees. Ironically, he seemed to
have come down on the side of financial exigency and lower
academic standards just as he was realizing his primary
academic goal—winning a chapter of Phi Beta Kappa—and
just as the pool of available high school graduates and the
number of applicants were on the rise.

Very early in his presidency, Kuebler began looking
forward to celebrating Ripon's Centennial in 1951 with
appropriate pomp and circumstance. He enjoyed pomp and
appreciated circumstance. He hoped that a major capital
campaign preceding the celebration would enable the College
to enter its second century with new buildings and an
increased endowment. During the centennial year, a series
of events would highlight Ripon's achievements, its role in
contemporary society, and its promise for the future. Installation of a Phi Beta Kappa chapter would be the crowning
event. It was a well-conceived agenda that both succeeded
and failed, and in its triumphs and disappointments revealed
much about the College's leadership.

Kuebler first went to work celebrating Ripon's heritage, particularly its ties with Ripon, England, an important
educational center in the seventh and eighth centuries; in
fact, many historians viewed St. Wilfrid of Ripon's Monas-
tery as one of the fountains of western higher learning.
Kuebler especially wanted a visible symbol of Ripon's relationship with that ancient tradition. Episcopal Bishop
William T. Manning of New York suggested a copy of the
Ripon Cathedral mace and actually interceded with the
cathedral and the British government to have the copy made.
The mace was then designed and fabricated by Edward West,
Canon Sacrist of the Cathedral of St. John the Divine in New
York. To provide a physical link between the two Ripons, a
piece of stone cut from the crypt of St. Wilfrid's Church, now
buried beneath the present cathedral, was encased in the
ornamental silver emblem atop the staff. On November 19,

1946, West presented the mace to the College; Sir Francis Evans, British Consul General of New York, gave the address; and both men received honorary degrees.[7] Today, the mace is still being carried by the faculty marshal in formal academic processions.

However, many alumni saw the event as another example of the new president's disdain for Ripon's past, particularly the historical ties between the College and the Congregational Church. One disgruntled Congregationalist commented somewhat acidly:

> Ripon College was founded by a rugged group of individualists whose religious heritage was rebellion against all that Ripon Cathedral signifies, so this cherished hunk of rock at the end of a stick has little symbolism for college or community. A chip off good old Plymouth Rock at the end of a sliver from the Mayflower would be more appropriate. . . .[8]

Kuebler assured everyone that he was not denying the Wisconsin Congregational connection. He had, indeed, invited Superintendent Theodore Faville to give the opening invocation and prayer at the convocation, but the Episcopal Bishop of Fond du Lac gave the closing prayers and benediction; and to add to the confusion, it all took place in the Scott Street Lutheran Church. Kuebler probably used this particular building because it accommodated a larger audience than the Congregational Church; it was used by his successors for baccalaureate services at commencement until this event was cancelled altogether. But Kuebler continued to emphasize the British connection and opened college convocations by taking the mace from the faculty marshal, placing it on a rack beneath the podium, and bowing in approved high-church style. All this evoked memories of old rivalries between Congregationalists and Episcopalians dating way back to the days of the Brockways. Present-day use of the mace is much less ceremonial and lacks the high-church flavor.

In other respects, however, Kuebler's Anglican ties were clearly beneficial, most notably in attracting a number of outstanding students, some preparing for the priesthood, others merely coming from Episcopalian families. Two of the former group became bishops: Richard Kraft '58 in South Africa and Antonio Ramos '59 in Costa Rica. Even after Kuebler resigned, church leaders continued to send postulants to Ripon.

In the meantime, the Second Century Campaign got off to a good start with a four-day academic conference at the 1947 homecoming weekend. The roster of speakers was impressive: historian Paul Buck, later to become dean of Harvard College; Edward Teller, often called the father of the hydrogen bomb; and Oscar Rennebohm, Governor of Wisconsin. But after receiving pledges of $400,000 (a third from the City of Ripon) out of a projected $5 million, the campaign ran out of steam. It was Kuebler's intent to activate the old Tallmadge Plan: completion of the gym with a swimming pool and improved facilities for women, a new classroom building on the present site of Farr Hall, and a freshman women's dorm with a dining hall. To these already ambitious plans, Kuebler added a chapel and two fraternity-sorority quadrangles. If these dreams came to fruition, Ripon could accommodate 750 students. But these goals proved to be well beyond the College's means. Only Scott Hall and a renovated gym were completed; the former housed men, not women, and had no dining room; the latter contained no swimming pool and not much for the women. Even these modest achievements were difficult to accomplish, and the trustees even considered applying for a federal loan. But enough money was scraped together so that the two buildings, though still unfinished, were dedicated at the 1951 Commencement, with the physical education building renamed Memorial Gymnasium in honor of Ripon's war dead.

No money was raised for endowment.

Even though it was extended to 15 years, the Second Century Campaign was never completed. The New York firm that had advised the College recommended no further fund drives until the alumni became better organized and more corporate support could be identified. The best way to achieve the second objective, the trustees decided, was to publicize Ripon's dedication to free enterprise and to build the 1951 centennial year around this theme. The celebration would begin with a birthday party for faculty, students, and townspeople on January 29, the date of the College's first charter. In May, there would be a Centennial Convocation featuring nationally known scholars who would discuss some major academic issue and receive honorary degrees. The annual commencement exercises would recognize distinguished Ripon alumni. Finally, in September, leaders in business, industry, and government would gather to examine the ongoing struggle between "free enterprise and statism." This event would serve as a springboard for a renewed fund drive to raise $600,000 to $1 million, half for the fraternity quadrangle and half for endowment.

Almost nothing went exactly as planned. Bad weather forced cancellation of the birthday party, and the Centennial Convocation had to be revamped and rescheduled for the fall. But commencement weekend, incorporating some of the events originally planned for the free enterprise symposium, was a huge success. Its emphasis was twofold: 1) recognition of distinguished alumni and 2) Ripon's commitment to free enterprise. Harriet Davies '01, a missionary to India; James Dunlap '10, Professor of Classics at the University of Michigan; Arthur G. Hayden '01, a civil engineer; William F. Meggers '10, of the National Bureau of Standards; and Carl P. Russell '15, a naturalist in the National Park Service, received honorary degrees; 19 other alumni were awarded citations. The Reverend Walter Courtenay of Nashville delivered a baccalaureate sermon which was a classic statement of cold-war conservatism. Senator Robert Taft of Ohio, generally considered to be Mr. Conservative Republican, gave the commencement address, attracting 2,100 people, the largest crowd since 1940 when Spencer Tracy was honored.

In place of the cancelled Centennial Convocation, Ripon played host to the popular radio program "Town Meeting of the Air." Carried by 267 stations of ABC on November 6, 1951, it featured Norman Cousins, editor of the *Saturday Review of Literature*, Harvard historian Crane Brinton, Yale philosopher Theodore Greene, and General Leslie Groves, head of the Manhattan Project, which developed the atomic bomb. It was presented "live" before a packed house in the newly refurbished Memorial Gym and, of course, gave the College welcome national exposure.

Kuebler's chief disappointment was failure to install a chapter of Phi Beta Kappa during the centennial year. It was his "first and greatest ambition . . . and the most significant single goal in Ripon's history," the one national academic and institutional accreditation the College lacked, the most prestigious honor a liberal arts school could receive, and the best possible way to begin the second century. An initial application late in Evans' second term had failed. Most of Kuebler's reforms had been directed toward insuring success in a second attempt. One necessity was the hiring of faculty who had been elected at other institutions. By 1949, this goal had been achieved, Ripon's PBK teachers had formed a preliminary organization, and a second application was made. Although an inspection team worried about the size of both the endowment and the library, they recommended approval. Their recommendation was accepted at the next national convention, and the Ripon chapter was installed on December 12, 1952. There was one unforeseen repercussion. Some members of Phi Alpha, the local scholastic honorary founded by Dean Graham in 1938, assumed and possibly had been led to believe that they would automatically receive PBK keys. Unfortunately, this was an entirely erroneous assumption. According to the Ripon chapter's charter, undergraduates could qualify only by fulfilling certain very specific requirements. As for alumni, Ripon could elect three every three years, and the chief criterion was distinguished achievement after graduation, not grades earned in college.

About a year after the installation of Phi Beta Kappa, Kuebler informed the trustees that he was considering an offer from another institution. On August 4, 1954, he announced his decision to resign, effective at the end of the calendar year. The new position was that of provost at the University of California-Santa Barbara; provost was the top job at each branch in the state system. Kuebler may have aspired eventually to assume the system's presidency. If so, it was not to be, since he abruptly left Santa Barbara not long after taking office. He subsequently became president of the Campanhia Nacional di Cimento Portland in Brazil.

Clark Kuebler was the most controversial president in Ripon's history. He had ardent admirers, many of them fellow Episcopalians, and equally fervent critics; not many Riponites took a middle position. Almost everyone agreed that Ripon had to make changes if it wanted to move out of the backwater into the mainstream and compete with the better liberal arts colleges of the Middle West. Possibly, only a president as dynamic and aggressive as Kuebler could have gotten the job done; he did get it done, partially. But in so doing, he alienated many senior faculty, alumni, and Congregationalists, thus compounding the problems of admissions and fund-raising. Furthermore, his reach exceeded his grasp: he never found the financial resources to accomplish all that he wished. Thus, he left behind a double legacy: on the one hand, a necessary job partially done and, on the other, an institution riven with low morale, instability, and uncertainty. He had certainly steered the College in the right direction; he left to his successors the task of healing wounds, while at the same time restoring and maintaining momentum.

NOTES TO CHAPTER XIII
CLARK G. KUEBLER 1943-1954

[1]*Trustees' Minutes*, VI, 396.

[2]"Clark G. Kuebler," *Pedrick Genealogies*.

[3]*Trustees' Minutes*, "President's Report," Nov. 17, 1949; Feb. 9, 1950.

[4]*Trustees' Minutes*, "President's Reports," June 15, 1945, and Jan. 29, 1951; "Board Minutes," Jan. 22, 1953.

[5]"Edward A. Tenney," *Pedrick Genealogies*.

[6]*Trustees' Minutes*, May 22, 1952.

[7]"Memorabilia Personalia—The Mace," *Kuebler Papers*.

[8]*Wisconsin Congregational Church Life*, Jan., 1947, 41; *College Days*, Oct. 28, 1952.

CHAPTER XIV

PROGRESS AND PROSPERITY FRED O. PINKHAM 1955-1965

*The shouts and the cheers have stilled
now and the campus is going about its
normal business. To a casual observer
things seem just about the same now
as they did before that first afternoon
of November 3. But such an observer
would be wrong. During five, hectic,
thrilling weeks, Ripon looked into its
heart and liked what it saw. And the
College would never be the same again.*

Report from Ripon College

On August 16, 1954, the Executive Committee of the Board of Trustees authorized Chairman Sam Pickard to appoint a Presidential Search Committee consisting of five trustees (including Pickard), two faculty members, and two alumni. The full board on March 5, 1955, accepted the committee's recommendation that Dr. Fred O. Pinkham become Ripon's eighth president (counting Evans' two terms as one) to take office on April 1. A graduate of Kalamazoo College and Stanford University, Pinkham had served as assistant to the president of George Washington University and as executive secretary and co-founder of the National Commission on Accrediting. At 34, he was one of the youngest college presidents in the country. He brought with him an attractive family of five, and everyone was happy to see children in the president's home once more. Shortly after assuming office, he appointed Robert P. Ashley as Dean of the College, Professor of English, and Coach of Tennis. Ashley held a bachelor's degree from Bowdoin and an M.A.

and Ph.D. from Harvard; he had taught at Harvard, Washington and Jefferson, and the United States Military Academy; had served as assistant dean and tennis coach at Washington and Jefferson and also had coached tennis at Harvard. In addition, he had published two historical novels for teenagers as well as a biography of English novelist Wilkie Collins and co-edited an anthology of Elizabethan fiction. The division of responsibilities between the two administrators was simple, logical, and clear-cut: the dean was responsible for the faculty, the curriculum, student life, athletics, and admissions; the president, for everything else. Both men were products of and true believers in the small liberal arts college.

In an informal report to the trustees on May 12, President Pinkham listed the critical problems facing the College: inadequate faculty salaries, low student morale, deplorable upperclass housing, high attrition, poor student grades, and lack of agreement among faculty on the nature of the College. Pinkham later added to his list the need for long-range planning and a new science building, stating that "Ripon is in serious danger of losing its outstanding record in science education. . . . We have lost several excellent prospective students who decided, after visiting our laboratories, to attend better- equipped institutions."[1]

Before these problems could be addressed, however, the new administration became entangled in a controversial proposal for the establishment of a School of Conservative Thought on the Ripon campus. It was proposed that the school publish a periodical entitled *The Conservative Review*, as well as books and pamphlets, conduct summer seminars, develop a research library, and, overall, establish "an intellectual center for developing and promulgating conservative ideas" so that "researchers and scholars from all over the world can look to Ripon as the world center for the study of conservatism." According to Pinkham, such a project would prevent one party (the Democratic Party, although it was not mentioned by name) from dominating "the national scene for a long time" and both parties from ceasing "to differ significantly on basic issues."[2] Although the school would function largely in the summer, would use funds outside the college budget, and would be in "no way directly connected with the faculty, student body, curriculum, or other phases of the undergraduate programs," the proposal immediately attracted violent opposition. It was savaged by the Wisconsin press. The *Madison Capital Times* intemperately labeled the proposal "another example of how big business in the country is moving to take over educational institutions" and with equal hyperbole noted that "Ripon has long been known as an institution controlled by and dedicated to the aims of big business interests who support it with contributions."[3]

This was too much even for one of the most liberal faculty members, Paul Aldus, Chairman of the English Department. In a letter to the editor of the *Days*, Aldus denied that "there is no freeplay of ideas here, and that the faculty are either hand-picked or circumscribed in their proper duties and responsibilities." He went on to say, "This is my eighth year here. At no time. . . has there been the slightest suggestion of interference on the part of the administration or the trustees with the faculty in the classroom."[4] Nonetheless, the faculty had predictably voiced its disapproval, by a vote of 31 to 10, on the grounds that a conservative institute would "compromise the character of the College," be harmful to both its academic reputation and its public relations, and "tend to produce a monolithic faculty."[5] The student newspaper followed suit with some eloquence:

How can one doubt that under the proposed relationship Ripon would cease to be a healthy college? Or that many of the best professors would feel morally obligated to leave the campus? Nor can students afford to forget . . . that the degree of Ripon College would be seriously cheapened. . . . The finest traditions of 100 years are imperiled. Let us not stand idly by.[6]

In the same issue, the *Days* reported that 351 students, about 70 percent of the total enrollment, had signed a petition opposing the institute. Realizing that he had a tiger by the tail, President Pinkham told an all-college convocation that opposition to the proposal has caused "me to wonder if it is now a good idea. . . . I do not think it is going to be continued over the disapproval of the faculty and the student body."[7] Pickard later announced that the trustees would not impose any plan on the students and faculty members.

The Conservative Institute having gone down the memory hole, the administration was free to address the problems cited by the president. Actually, some progress had already been made, particularly in the areas of low grades and student attrition. At the trustees' meeting of October 18, 1956, Pinkham reported a "consistent pattern of improvement in the academic life at Ripon": the number of failing grades had steadily declined and 40 more students had returned for the fall term than in the previous year. This improvement was due, he said, to "counselling by the deans, earlier closing hours for freshmen, more selective admissions, and smaller class sizes."[8]

Throughout the 20th century, Ripon's educational philosophy has remained remarkably consistent. Although the faculty flirted with such mild experimentation as pass-fail and satisfactory-unsatisfactory options, they never succumbed to the no-grades mania or the no-requirements craze. Instead, they adhered consistently to some variation of the distribution system so that, when other institutions abandoned freewheeling and returned to structured curricula, they returned to a position which Ripon had never left. The posture of the faculty was simple and logical: by age, training, and experience, they knew better than students what was good for them. This is not to say that the curriculum never changed. It did. But whatever changes were made, although often significant, were relatively minor and always within a conventional framework. In the summer of 1958, the dean and three faculty members attended a curriculum conference sponsored by the Danforth Foundation at The Colorado College in Colorado Springs. These four formed the core of a steering committee, which after several months of deliberation recommended changes in the graduation requirements, adopted by the faculty on April 1, 1959. To the already existing required courses in English (12 hours), foreign language (14 hours), Modern European History (six hours), laboratory science (eight hours), military science (four hours), and physical education (four hours), the faculty added six-to-eight more hours of science (not necessarily requiring a laboratory), six hours of philosophy, six hours of fine arts, and six hours of social science. With pardonable hyperbole, Pinkham stated, "This is the biggest thing that has happened to Ripon in 15 years."[9]

In the summer of 1962, the dean and another faculty trio attended an additional Danforth conference in Colorado Springs. This second quartet recommended a significant addition to the orientation program for incoming students. In an attempt to introduce an academic component, all new students were sent a copy of William Golding's novel *Lord of the Flies*. After their arrival on campus, they were divided into small groups to discuss the novel with faculty volunteers. Subsequent years featured such works as Jonathan Swift's *Gulliver's Travels*, George Orwell's *1984*, Aldous Huxley's *Brave New World*, Robert Heilbroner's *The Future as History*, and Lionel Trilling's *The Liberal Imagination*.

Occasionally, Ripon could be innovative. Beginning in 1960, the College began building its Commencements around a theme and granting honorary degrees to dignitaries distinguished in areas suggested by the themes. For instance, the 1961 Civil War Commencement featured historians Bruce Catton, who gave the commencement address, and Clifford Dowdy; MacKinlay Kantor, author of the novels *And Long Remember* and *Andersonville*; and Raymond Massey, star of the Robert Sherwood play *Abe Lincoln in Illinois*. Notable honoraries in other fields included psychologist B. F. Skinner; economist Paul Samuelson; actor Frederic

March; conductor Arthur Fiedler; novelist John Updike; Helen Merrell (granddaughter of President Merrell) and Robert Staughton Lynd, authors of *Middletown*; stage director Tyrone Guthrie; James Webb, head of the National Aeronautics and Space Administration; Donald Hornig, Special Assistant to President Johnson for Science and Technology; and Warren E. Burger, soon to become Chief Justice of the U. S. Supreme Court. Excerpts from Burger's 1967 commencement address, published in *U.S. News and World Report*, are said to have caught President Nixon's attention and to have partly caused Burger's appointment as chief justice.

With foundation support, Ripon initiated, in 1962, a unique Guest Professor Program, under which eminent people actually appeared in classrooms rather than merely give a convocation address and lend their presence for a day or two as usually happens. The program brought to the campus historian Samuel Eliot Morison, political scientist and statesman George Kennan, poet-critics John Ciardi and Mark Van Doren, visionary architect Buckminster Fuller, and others.

Ripon was one of the first colleges in the country to abandon the traditional first-semester calendar beginning in mid-or-late September and ending in mid-or-late January. Originally designed to accommodate a rural economy, it increasingly made little sense, giving the students and faculty no break until late November, providing a day or a weekend at Thanksgiving, recessing again over Christmas, holding a couple weeks of classes in January, scheduling final exams in mid-month, then sending the students home again till the second semester began in February. The brainchild of Professors Erwin Breithaupt and Thomas Jones of the Art and German Departments, the new 1965-66 calendar brought the students to the campus in late August, gave them a week off halfway through the term, and allowed them to complete first-semester classes and finals before Christmas, thus eliminating the worst features of the old schedule: the uninterrupted first two months and the frequently chopped up second two.

The late 1950s and the decade of the 1960s were years of unprecedented prosperity and growth on all fronts, made possible, for the most part, by rising enrollments (from 554 to 931 during the Pinkham administration). Most significant, perhaps, was a quantum leap in average faculty salaries from $4,429 to $11,009, resulting in a huge boost to faculty morale. Similar increases in enrollment and faculty salaries were, of course, occurring throughout the country.

New majors were introduced in art, chemistry-biology, combined foreign languages, Latin American studies, Russian, and speech. One-man departments like art, political science, and psychology were expanded, and certification in elementary education became available. One result of these curricular improvements was a shift in the ratio of men to women students from three-one to three-two. Ripon's reputation in economics and the physical sciences and the distinguished record of its participants in the three-two program with M.I.T. had attracted a largely male constituency, but the increased offerings in art, education, foreign language, and psychology and the later addition of anthropology and sociology made the curriculum more attractive to women.

Russian had entered the curriculum through a highly concentrated one-semester course offered by Henry Smith of the German Department in 1957. Then in 1958, Waclaw Jedrzejewicz joined the faculty as visiting professor of slavic studies under the Whitney Foundation program for emeritus faculty; he had just retired as chairman of the Russian Department at Wellesley. Dr. "J" remained at Ripon for five years, offering year-long courses in Russian language, Russian literature in translation, and Russian-Central European history. Probably the most distinguished faculty member in Ripon's history and certainly one of the few with international stature, he had been Poland's first glider pilot and had served as ambassador to Japan and minister of education for pre-World War II Poland. At the 1990 Awards Day, represented by his son Thomas, he received an honorary doctorate in absentia.

A number of interdepartmental courses—Art and Religion, Art and Psychology, Great Works of Eastern Literature, Great Works of Western Literature—were introduced. One of the most innovative and imaginative of these, a 10-hour course in Concepts and Methods of Science, was organized by Dino Zei of the Physics Department to enable non-science majors to meet the science requirement without taking departmental courses designed for majors. Unfortunately, the course was never wholeheartedly supported by the faculty and was unfairly criticized by the students as too difficult: statistics proved it to be no more demanding than beginning courses in other disciplines. It was eventually replaced by topical courses given by the individual science departments for non-majors.

Perhaps the most significant academic event during the Pinkham administration was the formation in 1958-59 of the Associated Colleges of the Midwest, consisting of the 10 colleges in the Midwest Collegiate Athletic Conference: Beloit, Carleton, Coe, Grinnell, Knox, Lawrence, Monmouth, Ripon, and St. Olaf; Colorado, Lake Forest, and Macalester subsequently joined the consortium. Its main, though not sole, purpose was and still is to enable the member colleges to sponsor off-campus programs which they could not afford singly, thus providing uncalculable enrichment for both students and faculty. The Associated Colleges, sometimes alone and sometimes in collaboration with the Great Lakes Colleges Association, established overseas centers in London, Florence, Hong Kong, India, Japan, Russia, Costa Rica, and Yugoslavia; in this country, ACM students can study the humanities at the Newberry Library in Chicago, urban studies and urban education (also in Chicago), and science at Oak Ridge (replacing the Argonne National Laboratory near Chicago) or the Wilderness Field Station in northern Minnesota (summers only). In addition, the College itself operates exchange programs with Bonn University in Germany and with the College of Ripon and York St. John in England; students can also hone their language skills in Paris, Madrid, and Toledo in programs jointly operated by Ripon College with Academic Year Abroad of New York or the University of Minnesota and can study politics, foreign policy, and criminal justice in Washington, D.C.

What might be called the "nationalization" of Ripon continued apace during the Pinkham years as the College became an increasingly national rather than merely regional institution. In the 1960s, Illinois began contributing slightly more students than Wisconsin and larger numbers began enrolling from other states, particularly from the East Coast with Massachusetts leading the way; enrollment divided roughly into thirds: one-third each from Illinois, Wisconsin, and everywhere else. This phenomenon resulted not only from more extensive recruiting by the admissions staff, but also from nationwide publicity. Representing Wisconsin in the Miss America Contest of 1956, Lynn Holden '58 won the talent contest and was named "Miss Music America" after a performance on the piano. Lynn proved she had brains as well as beauty and musical talent by earning election to Phi Beta Kappa. A year later, Natalie Lueck '59 followed in Lynn's footsteps as Miss Wisconsin in the Miss Universe Contest. Welcome academic recognition resulted from an article in the *American Journal of Physics*, which pointed out that Ripon produced more eminent physicists per 100 graduates than any other college in the country as measured by the number of entries in *American Men of Science*. This distinguished record was due to the teaching skill of Harley Barber, longtime professor of physics; the College made him an honorary doctor of science at the 1958 Commencement.

But nothing could match the publicity received during the most exciting weeks in college history when Ripon participated in the televised General Electric College Bowl, a kind of Information Please program featuring four-man college teams. During the 1962-63 academic year, Ripon received an invitation to participate; Robert Hannaford of the

Philosophy Department was appointed coach; extensive tryouts, in which 100 students participated, were held; and a team consisting of Sandra Miller '65, Stephen Peters '65, Robert Schneider '64, and David Stankow '65 was selected. The team made its debut on November 3, 1963, with a thrilling comeback win over Brooklyn Polytechnic Institute. This was followed by equally exciting victories in successive weeks over Texas A&M (7,000 students), Wooster College, and Georgia Tech. A fifth contest, against the University of Massachusetts, was cancelled because of the assassination of President Kennedy. After a week's hiatus, Ripon lost its chance for the maximum allowable five victories by losing to Bowdoin College, despite having beaten the Maine school in rehearsal; the strength of the Bowdoin team was indicated by its retiring undefeated after five wins. It is almost impossible now to sense the excitement and pride generated during these five weeks as the entire college community spent an hour on Sunday afternoons glued to the television set and watched the little college in Wisconsin defeat four institutions, three of them several times its size. Very fittingly, the *College Days* front-paged a David and Goliath cartoon showing two small scholarly-looking Riponites confronting a huge cowboy and an equally huge ape labeled "Texas A&M." In the same issue, the *Days* ran perhaps its largest headlines ever (one and a half inches) celebrating both the first college bowl win and the football team's conference championship. A special article on page two quoted student reactions: "I screamed a lot harder than I ever did at a football game. . . ." "I didn't want people to think that the small Mid-west schools are just emulating the Eastern schools but that we have just as much on the ball in our own right. . . ." And perhaps best of all, from an East Coast student, "Well, at least some people will know how to pronounce 'Ripon' correctly."[10] Two weeks later, the *Days* featured a possibly apocryphal, but nonetheless fitting, anecdote:

A Rippin' Good Cookies truck on its way back from the

East coast was stopped by a man who stepped out of
a manhole and asked if the driver was in any way
connected with the College. After explaining that he
lived in Ripon but was not really connected with the
College itself, the driver was assured by the unknown
workman that "we are all rooting for you."[11]

After the defeat of Texas A&M, 100 students greeted
the team at the Oshkosh airport. And when it was all over,
a caravan of cars carrying several hundred rooters from both
College and community made the trek to Wittman Field. The
Report from Ripon College waxed justifiably eloquent:

Ripon's five appearances. . .had brought the College
tremendous publicity. Twenty million viewers saw
the program each week. Newspapers throughout the
state had articles about the team, they ran editorials,
TV and radio stations carried the news each week, and
finally, WFRV-TV of Green Bay presented a half-hour
special on the team and the College; they belonged to
the state and even to the midwestern region.

The shouts and the cheers have stilled now and the
campus is going about its normal business. To the
casual observer things seem just about the same as
they did before that afternoon of November 3. But
such an observer would be wrong. During five hectic,
thrilling weeks Ripon looked into its heart and liked
what it saw. And the College will never again be the
same.[12]

Nationalization of a different sort came with the
adoption of policies and practices prevalent in the best liberal
arts colleges throughout the country. College Board Aptitude
Tests were required of all entering students; fringe benefits
for faculty and staff were expanded and increased; a sabbatical leave program was adopted, with help from the Ford

Foundation, though not implemented till the spring of 1967; a Parents' Association was formed, and the first Parents' Day was held on November 9, 1957; the composition of the Board of Trustees was broadened both geographically and professionally, as evidenced by the election of Mark Ingraham, Dean of the College of Letters and Science at the University of Wisconsin, and Herbert Stroup, Dean of Students at Brooklyn College; a long-range plan was designed; and a director of development was appointed.

In 1961, the College made one of its most significant faculty appointments: after completing divinity school, former football coach Jerry Thompson became chaplain and assistant professor of religion. Although he taught popular courses and served as a much-valued counselor, his greatest achievement was liberalizing and humanizing a campus that was too conservative, too insulated, and too little concerned with social issues. During the 1964, 1965, and 1966 spring recesses, small groups of students and faculty led by Thompson visited Mississippi. One group worked at the Back Bay Community Center in Biloxi, operated by the United Church of Christ for indigent families of shrimp and oyster fishermen. Another group visited Jackson, Mississippi; three Ripon students were arrested for jaywalking; one student was repeatedly hit by a policeman and was briefly jailed. A later group met with civil rights leaders in Biloxi, attended classes at predominantly black Tougaloo Southern Christian College, and was refused admission to the state legislature in Jackson because the group was integrated. Both short-term and semester student exchanges were arranged between Ripon and Tougaloo.

In the summer of 1965, Ripon College joined 16 other colleges in operating federally funded Upward Bound Programs for promising but culturally disadvantaged students. Only Ripon's had a predominantly American Indian enrollment; it became the model for other Native American programs. The six-week session offered 32 Wisconsin boys age 13 to 15 instruction in reading, writing, mathematics, science, and speech; later programs included girls. Under Thompson's leadership, the Ripon program became one of the most successful in the country. A typically rigid bureaucratic ruling led to the venture's termination in 1976 because Ripon was too far away from the nearest Indian reservation.

A rapid improvement and expansion in facilities began in 1956 with the construction of four new tennis courts and the re-surfacing of the two older ones. In 1958, two men's dormitories, Brockway and Smith (originally known as South and Center) were constructed with low-interest federal funds; the so-called Quads were completed with the building of Mapes (North) in 1961 and Bovay in 1965. In 1962, upperclass women moved into Johnson Hall, dedicated to H. F. Johnson of Johnson Wax in Racine and his wife; Mrs. Johnson served as a trustee from 1953 to 1972. The new dormitories replaced expensive-to-maintain sorority houses like Duffie, Lyle, Parkhurst, and Tracy and enabled male students to move out of West and Middle (then called Smith). West Hall became an office and classroom building for education, English, German, and history; military science continued to occupy the basement and half the first floor, the other half becoming the faculty lounge, previously in the library. The administration, which had been located in East Hall, moved to Middle Hall. Since the Quads had been constructed on the football practice field, a new field was laid out below the old one. Still further below, a baseball diamond was built in 1961 with funds provided by the Sadoff Foundation and named after Howard Sadoff, recently deceased son of Ben Sadoff, a Fond du Lac trustee.

The same year that Mapes was finished saw the completion of the Farr Hall of Science, giving the College, at long last, an up-to-date science facility; the building was constructed largely with funds bequeathed by Shirley Farr, a long-time trustee, and dedicated to her father, also a trustee and benefactor. In 1962, Pickard Commons, named after Sam Pickard, Chairman of the Board of Trustees from 1942 to 1962, replaced the old dining hall in the Harwood

Memorial Union. The change made sense economically since it enabled the College to feed all students at one sitting instead of two, but it was not an unmixed blessing. Soon gone were the "gracious-living" sit-down meals, replaced by cafeteria lines. Also soon gone was Lucille Hawkinson, who, despite the inevitable student complaints, prepared and served perhaps the finest college meals in the country; the national and local chains which replaced her could preserve neither the style nor the quality. The space vacated in the Union became the Great Hall, an all-purpose facility for social events, receptions, parties, small concerts, and public lectures.

Also in 1962, a grant of $100,000 from the Division of Higher Education of the United Church of Christ enabled the College to begin construction of an additional floor of shelves and carrels in Lane Library and to create an endowment for books. Back in 1958, Ripon had decided to renew its historical ties with the Congregational Church and successfully applied for membership in the Council of Congregational Colleges, which included Beloit, Carleton, Grinnell, and Knox. President Pinkham told the trustees that membership would open "opportunities for support (financial and student recruiting)" and would strengthen "the moral and religious phases of college life."[13] In a letter to the *College Days*, he assured the student body that "We are non-sectarian and non-denominational and intend to remain so. . . . [The Council] has no legislature or policy making power and has no authority over the colleges represented."[14] However, this "cake and eat it too" relationship qualified Ripon for the $100,000 grant from the United Church, which included the Congregationalists.

Several building projects—the additions to Scott and Johnson Halls, the Kemper Clinic (named after trustee James Kemper), the Storzer Physical Education Center (named after Coach John Storzer), and a new president's home were planned during President Pinkham's term of office, but completed after he left. The old presidential home has served variously as an honors house for women, a residence for the dean of the College, and finally as Hughes House, headquarters of the Ripon College Society of Scholars, a faculty and staff club.

In March, 1965, the College purchased a huge tract of land west of Union Street. Its 127 acres almost doubled campus acreage and was to become the site of two important campus buildings. It also provides more than enough land for any foreseeable project, such as a football stadium or new tennis courts.

The expansion of facilities enabled the College to make fuller use of the campus during the summer months. Of course, Badger Boys State had for years been holding its week-long program at Ripon. In June, 1957, and for several years thereafter, the College hosted the Wisconsin Open Tennis Tournament. During the same summer and continuing through 1960, grants from the Coe Foundation subsidized an institute for secondary-school teachers of American history. A year later, the National Science Foundation sponsored a summer institute for high-school teachers of science and mathematics; this program continued through 1966. College facilities were also used by educational and religious groups and as overflow housing for the Experimental Aircraft Association Fly-In at Wittman Field in Oshkosh.

After supper on December 8, 1965, President Pinkham called a special meeting of the student body in the Memorial Gymnasium and shocked everyone present by announcing his resignation. Despite the dramatic suddenness of this announcement, the resignation had been in the works for some time, although the sequence of events, as well as the facts and their interpretation, are somewhat confusing and contradictory. In a letter to former Dean Ashley, dated February 29, 1988, Pinkham stated that "a full year before January, 1966," he had written both former Board Chairman Sam Pickard and current Chairman Clark Robertson that he intended to leave Ripon, believing that no college president should serve longer than 10 years. According to

Pinkham, neither one acknowledged his letter or informed the trustees of its contents; "I think they thought I'd change my plans if they ignored them."[15]   None of the trustees received official notification until a December 6, 1965, meeting of the Executive Committee. Board Chairman Paul Rodewald announced that the meeting had been called "to receive a statement from President Pinkham and that because of its importance a number of other trustees who were not members of the committee had been invited to attend." The key section of the minutes read as follows:

> Dr. Pinkham advised the Trustees present that he had accepted a position as Director of the Yardstick Program, a new research project for the scientific evaluation of school systems under the sponsorship of the Martha Holden Jennings Foundation of Cleveland, Ohio.   He stated that he had informed Messrs. Robertson and Pickard over a year ago that it was time for a change. Because of the pending Forward Thrust Campaign and in considering the welfare of the school he had agreed with them to delay any decision until completion of the campaign.[16]

The president then distributed a detailed news release prepared for newspapers and wire services. The next day (December 7), the president announced his resignation at the regularly scheduled faculty meeting and called the special student convocation the same evening. On December 10, the *College Days*, under bold-face headlines, reprinted in its entirety the news release prepared for the Executive Committee. In addition, the issue contained several articles and editorial comments, seven pictures (including one of a standing ovation at the special convocation), and a box headed "Faculty Statement":

> RESOLVED, That the Faculty express its deep regret at the resignation of Dr. Fred O. Pinkham and its

recognition of the fact that Ripon College is in all respects, but especially in those which are the particular concern of the Faculty, an infinitely stronger institution today than it was when he assumed the presidency in April 1955; further that the Faculty record its heartfelt gratitude to President Pinkham for what he has done for them and for the College; and finally that the Faculty wish him the best of luck in his new position.[17]

Both the faculty and the students feted the Pinkhams at special banquets; Student Senate President Byron Sagunski '66 praised Pinkham for the "outstanding service he gave the student body" and presented a silver tray.[18] Ironically, in view of the fact that at least a small number of those present knew of the impending resignation, the trustees at their October 21, 1965, meeting had presented the Pinkhams with a silver double chafing dish "in commendation of the 10th anniversary of Dr. Pinkham's inauguration as President of the College."[19]

One of the more curious aspects of the resignation story is the fact that on April 1, 1965, Pinkham had written a letter to the board proposing the establishment on the newly purchased land west of Union Street of a two-year satellite institution, which would enable Ripon College to remain small and at the same time meet the pressure to expand. The satellite, he said, could offer several types of programs or specialize in a field such as the performing arts. Some satellite students might transfer to Ripon College, replacing freshman and sophomore drop-outs and filling the ranks of the junior and senior years. Although cross enrollment and sharing of facilities would be possible, the new institution would have a separate board of trustees, faculty, philosophy, and admissions office. To explore this idea, Pinkham proposed that he be given a leave of absence for the summer and the fall semester. He went on to say that "granting of this should be conditioned upon my being able to find foundation support to underwrite a temporary replacement for me . . . and also provide the necessary funds for travel, consultation, and other expense. . . ." In Pinkham's view, "it was quite possible that Ripon could move to the forefront in educational leadership" by showing "hundreds of other liberal arts colleges" how to relieve "the pressure upon them to become something different through overexpansion of their present programs and facilities." The president concluded by saying, "For several years now I have been saying that Ripon College needs a 'new idea.' I believe this is it. . . ."[20] Despite the fact that Pinkham had received a financial commitment from a foundation, the trustees took no action on the proposal. According to an undated handwritten note to Ashley, written some time in March, 1988, had the trustees acted affirmatively on his proposal, Pinkham *"might* have stayed, but it was time to move on . . . . My leaving and the Board action or nonaction were not quid pro quo."[21]

Pinkham presided at his final board meeting on February 1, 1966, then "moved on." In another bit of irony, the *Alumnus* back in November of 1965, had summarized Pinkham's achievements in an article entitled "A Decade on the Hill":

Enrollment up from 554 to 931—68%. Students today come from 43 states and 16 foreign countries, meet increasingly higher academic standards.

Faculty members with doctorate up from 23 to 42— 83%. Total full-time members up from 43 to 63— 46%. Average salary up 148%. Retirement and insurance programs added.

Buildings and equipment up from $1.79 million to $9.068 million—406%. **Endowment** up from $.53 million to $1.64 million—209%. **Operating Budget** up from $.85 million to $2.62 million—208%.

Physical Facilities greatly expanded. Farr Hall of Science, Quadrangle Dormitories, Johnson Hall, Pickard Commons constructed.

Long Range Development Program launched. Physical Education Center, Infirmary, new heating facilities construction will begin in 1966. Fine Arts Center will follow.

Guest Professor Program, new school calendar adopted. Curriculum broadened with new studies in Art, Russian and Slavic, Far East countries.

Library Facilities expanded and up-dated. 20,000 new holdings, 129 periodicals added, stacks and reading facilities improved and augmented. Circulation up from 8,900 to 20,000—125%.[22]

Not mentioned was the increase in campus acreage from 30.188 to 245.813—714 percent.[23] The decade was one of the most prosperous and expansive in Ripon College history.

After serving as director of the Yardstick Program (1966-68), Pinkham became vice president and general manager of the Education Division, Western Publishing Company; assistant administrator for Population and Humanitarian Affairs, the Agency for International Development during the Nixon Administration; president and founder, Capital Higher Education Service, in Hartford, Connecticut; and president and chief executive officer, Population Crisis Committee, in Washington, D.C. He served as associate director and senior research associate at the Morrison Institute for Population and Resource Studies at Stanford University from 1987-90 before assuming the position of program officer, population, for the David and Lucile Packard Foundation in Los Altos, California. At the 1990 Commencement, he received an honorary degree.

NOTES TO CHAPTER XIV
FRED O. PINKHAM 1955-1965

[1]"President's Report, 1955-57," *Executive Committee and Trustees' Minutes.*

[2]*Executive Committee and Trustees' Minutes*, Oct. 11 and 21, 1955.

[3]*College Days*, Nov. 8, 1955, 2.

[4]*Ibid.*, Nov. 15, 1955, 2.

[5]*Faculty Minutes*, Oct. 13, 1955.

[6]*College Days*, Nov. 8, 1955, 2.

[7]*Ibid.*, Nov. 15, 1955, 1.

[8]"President's Report," *Trustees' Minutes*, Oct. 18, 1956.

[9]*College Days*, April 7, 1959, 1.

[10]*Ibid.*, Nov. 8, 1963, 1-2.

[11]*Ibid.*, Nov. 22, 1963, 1.

[12]*Report from Ripon College*, Jan., 1964.

[13]*Trustees' Minutes*, April 29, 1958.

[14]*College Days*, Nov. 4, 1958, 1.

[15]See Ripon College Archives.

[16]*Executive Committee Minutes*, Dec. 6, 1965, [1].

[17]*Faculty Minutes*, Dec. 7, 1965, 3.

[18]*College Days*, Jan. 28, 1966, 3.

[19]*Trustees' Minutes*, Oct. 21, 1965, 9.

[20]*Ibid.*, May 10, 1965.

[21]Ripon College Archives.

[22]"A Decade on the Hill," *Alumnus*, Nov., 1965, (corrected by Kenneth Cartier, Vice President for Finance).

[23]Figures supplied by Cartier.

CHAPTER XV

GOLDEN DAYS
STUDENT LIFE 1955-1985

*I liked Ripon students in 1955. I like
them now, and I have liked them in the
years between. Naturally, I don't find
them perfect. But I especially value
their friendliness, their good humor,
their lack of pretense and phoniness.
All in all, I wouldn't swap them for any
other student body I know.*[1]

Robert Ashley

Until the advent of the Viet Nam malaise, extracurricular activities flourished at Ripon as they have never done
since: interest, participation, and quality of achievement
were extremely high.

A 1956 gift of $1,000 from Chairman of the Board
Sam Pickard enabled Howard Hansen, recently appointed
chairman of the Speech Department, to establish a college
radio station. In the related field of forensics, Hansen, Wayne
Mannebach, Bonnie Buzza, and a succession of talented
students sustained the tradition of excellence set earlier by
Bruno Jacob, Allan Michie, and Spencer Tracy, all of whom
were elected to the Famous Fifty Pi Kappa Delta Alumni at the
speech honorary society's Golden Anniversary Convention.
In the 30-year span covered by this chapter, Ripon had so
many talented individuals and teams that it is impossible to
name them all. With apologies to those not mentioned, here
is a sampling. Verne Cronen '63 and Thomas "Duffy"
Farrand '62 were named the outstanding affirmative team at
the Fourth Annual Midwest Debate Tournament in Oshkosh,
losing by a 2-1 vote to the negative team from Northwestern

University but gaining revenge the next academic year (1961-62) by defeating Northwestern in the championship round; in the same academic year, they tied for second among 100 men's teams at the national convention of Pi Kappa Delta at Oklahoma State University and captured the Sweepstakes Trophy at Eau Claire State University. Eau Claire was the site of many Ripon triumphs in addition to those of Cronen and Farrand: in February, 1966, Richard Borchers '68 placed first among 113 participants in group discussion, and the College took permanent possession of the team trophy; a year later, Robert Turner '71 finished at the top in after-dinner speaking. The 1970-71 group earned 81 first-place trophies; Lemoyne Baquet '71 won the National Speech Pentathlon three straight times. Trevor Giles '85 and Christopher Leland '86 were the first Riponites to qualify for the American Forensics National Tournament; a year later, Giles became the first Ripon student to reach the semi-finals.

Unlike forensics, achievement on the stage cannot be precisely measured; still there is no doubt that Ripon College dramatics experienced a 50s-60s golden age. Talented directors like Walter Boughton, Richard Bergstrom, Philip Clarkson, and Edmund Roney drew on a pool of exceptionally able student actors, chief among them Harrison Ford '64 and Frances Lee McCain '66. At Ripon, Ford appeared as the narrator and El Gallo in *The Fantasticks*, Mack the Knife in *The Three-Penny Opera*, and George Antrobus in *The Skin of Our Teeth*. A decade after college, he attracted the attention of George Lucas, played a supporting role in *American Graffiti* and the second male lead in the *Star Wars* series, then graduated to stardom in *Blade Runner*, *Witness* (for which he received an Oscar nomination), *Mosquito Coast*, and the Indiana Jones series. In the third Indiana Jones movie, Ford warmed the cockles of Ripon hearts by mentioning Professor William Tyree of the Philosophy Department.

McCain's Ripon roles included the Queen of the Amazons in Benn Levy's *The Rape of the Belt*, the title role Antigone in Anouilh's adaptation of the Sophocles play, Elise in Molière's *The Miser*, Cathleen in Synge's *Riders to the Sea*, and Rosalind in *As You Like It*.   After graduation, she attended the Central School of Speech and Drama in London and, returning to this country, enjoyed a successful career on stage, screen, and television.   She played the female lead in the prime-time television series *Apple's Way*, toured with Christopher Walken and Charles Durning in Lanford Wilson's *Lemon Sky*, became a fixture in West Coast theatre, and acted feature roles in such films as *Gremlins*, *Back to the Future*, and Agatha Christie's *Murder in Three Acts*. Her ties with Ripon remained close: in the summer of 1986 she received the Distinguished Alumna Award, in the spring of 1987 served as Guest Professor in Drama, and in 1988 gave the commencement address.

On May 16, 1964, the Drama Department lost its home when the Red Barn burned to the ground in a spectacular fire. "Within minutes, flames towered high into the sky, causing a glow visible 20 miles away. Heat was so intense that windows in the Tri-Dorms and Johnson Hall were cracked."[2] In a letter to the trustees, President Pinkham called the fire "certainly the most dramatic of all productions in which the theatre participated. Also, it attracted its largest audience."[3]

Until the construction of the Fine Arts Center, the old Grace Lutheran Church, then situated next to the Congregational Church, became the college theatre. But the new location failed to crimp the Drama Department's style; energized by the constraints and limitations of the new location, the department came through with some of its most ingenious, imaginative, and crowd-pleasing productions: *As You Like It*, *Most Happy Fella*, *The Rivals*, and *Stop the World*. Although the 70s and 80s produced no actors with the national stature of Ford and McCain, nonetheless there were actors and playwrights of considerable talent. Chief among these was Richard Hilger '70. In addition to starring in such plays as Shaw's *The Devil's Disciple* and O'Neill's *Long Day's Journey into Night*, Hilger, while still an undergraduate, wrote a play, *The Day of the Golden Calf*, produced April 2-5, 1970. He received a master of fine arts degree from the University of Minnesota and acted in the famed Guthrie Theatre; a Minneapolis critic said that in the Twin Cities "there is no better actor than he."[4] Another Hilger play, *The Steeple*, was produced at the Chimera Theatre in St. Paul, receiving a Schubert Award. Completely revised, it was performed at Ripon December 6-10, 1978, during one of Hilger's two terms as a sabbatical leave replacement in the Speech and Drama Department.

To complete the summary of dramatic activities, the Ripon College Children's Theatre flourished in the late 60s and early 70s presenting in Ripon and other Wisconsin communities adaptations of *Winnie the Pooh*, *Treasure Island*, and *The Wizard of Oz*. Similarly, the Reader's Theatre, under the leadership of Bonnie Buzza, performed before school and alumni association audiences.

The basement of the new theatre in the old church became the locus of the Brand Rex Coffee House, opened in the spring of 1965 under the leadership of James Bowditch and Seale Doss of the English and Philosophy Departments. The name was derived from huge telephone-cable spools donated by the Brand Rex Division of American Enka Corporation, which served as tables. A non-profit corporation of faculty, students, and even townspeople, Brand Rex served light refreshments and sponsored discussions of college movies and stage productions; musical events, including a "Sing-along with Dino Zei," accordion–playing chairman of the Physics Department; and forums on such topics as "Does the College have the right to interfere in the private lives of students?" and "Is there a sexual revolution going on in America–and if so, does this entail anything for Ripon College?"

For a college of its size, Ripon has provided the world of art and entertainment with a surprising number of stars. In addition to Ford, McCain, and Hilger, Ripon can boast, musically, of Al Jarreau '62 and Gail Dobish '76. Jarreau attended Ripon on the automatic scholarship awarded to governors of Boys State, the annual citizenship conference which brings 1,000 high-school students to the campus every summer. While an undergraduate, along with Peter Bock '61, Thomas Farrand '62, and Anne Hassler '65, he formed the Indigoes; the only vocal group at the Notre Dame Jazz Festival, they won a standing ovation. After graduation, Jarreau became one of the country's most popular jazz singers and winner of many awards including several Grammies. Dobish attended the Juilliard School of Music and subsequently joined the Metropolitan Opera Company, making her debut in 1984 as Fiakermilli in the Richard Strauss opera *Arabella*; her repertory roles at the Met are Adele in *Die Fledermaus* by Johann Strauss, Jr., and Olympia in *Tales of Hoffman* by Jacques Offenbach. Dobish and Jarreau, like McCain, have kept close ties with Ripon. All three received honorary degrees at the 1988 Commencement; Ford was unable to attend because of film commitments.

Another nationally known Ripon graduate is Richard Threlkeld '59, a national correspondent for CBS. He earned a degree in journalism from Northwestern University and for a time served as anchorman on the CBS "Morning News." On several occasions, he has provided voice-narrations for college fund-raising campaigns. In 1977, he was elected an alumnus member of Phi Beta Kappa and in 1989 received an honorary degree and gave the commencement address. Threlkeld also helped design Ripon's first conference on ethics and public policy held in Washington, D.C. in 1989, which focused on television news reporting and advertising during the 1988 presidential election.

Two musical groups spread the name of Ripon beyond the immediate area. During the winter break of 1964-65 the Riponaires, a jazz band led by Ralph Gabriel, gave concerts for servicemen in Korea, Okinawa, and the Phillipines under the joint auspices of the USO and the National Council of Music. Under the direction of Douglas Morris, the Ripon College Singers, a town-gown group later known as the

Choral Union, toured Luxembourg, Great Britain, Switzerland, Germany, and France in May and June of 1979 and subsequently took other European trips.

Dance first appeared on the Ripon campus during the Pinkham administration. This extracurricular activity received a big boost when the Physical Education Department began offering dance courses for academic credit. Variously known as Orchesis or the Ripon College Dance Company, a performing group gave concerts on campus and on tour. As a money-saving move, the P. E. courses were dropped in 1983, but the Dance Company still exists.

In the entirely different arena of military training, Ripon College also achieved distinction. In two consecutive years (1955 and 1956), the Rifle Team, competing against more than 70 colleges and universities, took second place in the National ROTC Intercollegiate Indoor Rifle Match. Earlier, the senior unit had won the Fifth Army title in the 34th Annual William Randolph Hearst National ROTC Intercollegiate Rifle Competition. In February of 1964, the drill team finished first at the University of Wisconsin Invitational Drill Meet; three years later, the women's team took second place in the same meet. The Raiderettes in 1976 did even better, defeating 15 other teams at the University of Illinois. William Kramer '68 was chosen by the Department of the Army from 20,000 senior cadets to represent ROTC at the celebration of India's National Republic Day; in his junior year, he had been named the outstanding student at the Fort Riley summer camp.

The academic year 1967-68 was notable for individual academic achievement. Thomas Reinecke became Ripon's second Rhodes Scholar. Three seniors–Reinecke, Merline Thoma, and John Kristy–won Woodrow Wilson Fellowships (James Reed had been similarly honored in 1967), Patricia Nevers was awarded a Fulbright, and Steve Thompson '69, son of Chaplain Thompson, received the LeClere Midwest Conference Scholar-Athlete Award. In other years, Philip Steans '65 (football), Thomas Wulling '66 (tennis), and

Ludwig Wurtz '78 (basketball) earned NCAA Scholarships for post-graduate study. In 1988, Julie Sikkink became Ripon's second Marshal Scholar; David Schwarz '65 was the first.

During the mid-60s, Dawes Cottage at the corner of Seward and Elm Streets, which had previously housed maintenance and dining hall personnel, became the Dawes Cultural Center. It served as the headquarters of the Women's Interest Organization (successor to the Women's Self-Government Association) and the Ripon Scholastic Honor Society, which organized a cadre of tutors, escorted and entertained guest professors and other campus visitors, organized cultural trips, and sponsored talks and discussions by students, faculty, and campus visitors. The WIO pressed for a women's studies course; their persistence persuaded the faculty to approve The Historical and Social Roles of Women, first offered in the spring semester of 1972-73. Other interest groups sponsored a Blue Grass Festival Concert and a poetry night at which students read original poems as well as those by their favorite poets.

In harmony with national trends during the late 60s and early 70s, Ripon students became more service-oriented and community-conscious. In 1971-72, Students Oriented Toward Narcotics Education, vividly and appropriately acronymmed STONED, received a $19,000 federal grant and was named one of 20 outstanding college-based projects. More than 40 Riponites tutored middle-school students and worked as volunteers for the Cerebral Palsy Rehabilitation Center, the Boy and Girl Scouts, Headstart, and the Big Brothers and Sisters. Mark Conrad '73 made media news by winning election as the city's mayor in his junior year. He was thought to be the youngest mayor in Wisconsin history and the only one to be elected while still in college.

In the early spring of 1965, the campus erupted in a controversy over a proposed trip to Selma, Alabama, to support voting rights demonstrations and protest marches. At a special emergency evening session on March 15, the Student Senate had voted 13-9 to provide a $400 fund, and in the absence of President Pinkham, Dean Ashley had granted permission for Chaplain Thompson, three other faculty members, and six students to make the trip. During a midnight broadcast over WRPN, Richard Singer '67 had called for a demonstration to protest the Senate's action. The next morning, protesters gathered on Seward Street near the Harwood Union, where cars were loading for the trip; estimates of the crowd size varied from 175 to 400. Supporters of the trip carried signs reading "Selma Yes" and sang both the "Alma Mater" and "We Shall Overcome." Just as the dispute was reaching a crisis, Singer, who was leading the protesters, relented and waved the cars on.

The only 60s controversy to rival that over Selma arose when some students in Madison asked whether Ripon would like to have Gus Hall, Secretary of the American Communist Party, speak at Ripon. On May 9, 1962, the Student Senate unanimously passed a resolution that an invitation be extended, not to Hall, but to party leader Fred Blair, noting that "American standards of freedom of speech and freedom of assembly must be unreservedly honored in American institutions devoted to freedom of learning and freedom of study." The Senate also urged that an exchange program be initiated to "bring in a student raised under communism." The *Days* front-paged a cartoon labeled "Ultra-Conservative View of Exchange Program." The cartoon featured a seductively clad lady communist standing on the steps of an airplane and holding a placard "Sign Here to be a Card Carrying *Communist*"; on the tarmac stood three Ripon males, one with arms longingly extended toward the commie siren. In a reasoned and sensible editorial, the *Days* described the invitation "as an educational opportunity, one which will both broaden the student's point of view and improve his intellectual opportunity." Additionally, the editorial suggested that "specific ground rules of conduct" such as prohibiting the solicitation of funds and the distribution of pamphlets would minimize "the chance for undesirable consequences."[5]

President Pinkham supported the exchange plan, but felt that making college facilities available to a communist speaker was an issue for the trustees to consider. In a statement to the board, he outlined clearly the two conflicting principles involved:

> On the one side is the fact that–if such a controversial person and a known Communist is provided facilities for rendering such an address, the College is in effect lending its facilities in support of a person who admittedly is actively advocating the overthrow of the United States Government. . . . On the other side of the argument is that–if such a person is not permitted to speak on College property, the College is in effect taking a stand which is contrary to the broad concept of academic freedom.[6]

The trustees, unsurprisingly, believed the first principle to be overriding and passed the following resolution by a 16-5 vote:

> That speakers of a controversial nature should not, in general, be prohibited from expressing their views within the confines of the campus; but that no one known to advocate the overthrow of the United States government by force or who is closely identified with an organized conspiracy to overthrow the United States government by force should be permitted to use College facilities in the dissemination of his or her views.[7]

But the issue refused to die. Both the Student Senate and the *College Days* kept it alive. In the meantime, the Board of Trustees was already considering a revision of their previous policy and almost a year after its adoption unanimously passed a new resolution recommended by the faculty's Educational Policy Committee and their own Education Committee. Its key paragraph read:

> Invitations to outside speakers must always represent the desire of a recognized campus group, not the will of an external organization, must be approved by the faculty adviser of the organization, or, if there is no faculty adviser, by the Dean of the College and must be registered in the offices of the Dean and the President prior to issuance of an invitation. Invitations to persons under indictment or judicial review are to be avoided. When there is question as to the suitability of a speaker, a screening committee consisting of a Trustee, the President, the Dean, a senior member of the Faculty Educational Policy Committee, and the President of the Student Senate shall consider and decide the matter. This committee also may hear appeals from student organizations whose proposed invitation to an outside speaker has been vetoed by a faculty adviser, by the Dean, or by the President.[8]

Except for the committee machinery, the new statement wasn't much of an improvement over the old, though most of the college community seemed to think it was. Not the *College Days*, which expressed outrage, claiming that the statement was stupid, capricious, contradictory, hypocritical, insulting to the students, and suited to a sixth-grade mentality. Furthermore, the "indictment or judicial review" section violated a cardinal tenet of American justice that a man was innocent till proved guilty. The pot boiled for a while: two letters from trustees (one pro, one con), a faculty letter (pro), a letter from a parent (con), and even one (con) from a Lieutentant Donald Dotson of Attack Squadron 125 at the Naval Air Station in Livermore, California, appeared in the *Trustees' Minutes*, the *Alumnus*, and the *Days*. Dotson, a 1960 graduate of the University of North Carolina in Chapel Hill, had no Ripon connection whatsoever, but he had read a letter from Trustee Robert Gibson in a copy of the *Alumnus*, which he found in his squad reading room, and felt urged to comment.[9] Eventually, the campus calmed down.

At President Kuebler's urging, nationalization of fraternities and sororities had been approved by the trustees as early as 1952; the first national fraternities were Sigma Nu (Hall) and Theta Chi (Bartlett) in 1954. Sigma Chi (Smith) followed in 1955, Sigma Alpha Epsilon (Smith) in 1958, Delta Upsilon (Barker) in 1959, and Phi Delta Theta (West) in 1960. For sororities, Alpha Xi Delta (Parkhurst) was chartered in 1958, Alpha Chi Omega (Lyle) and Alpha Phi (Duffie) in 1959, Alpha Delta Pi (Tracy) and Kappa Delta (Harwood) in 1960. This process left Merriman as the only local Greek organization and, after the construction of the Quads and Johnson Hall, the only one with its own separate chapter house. In a report to President Pinkham, David L. Harris, Dean of Men, defended nationalization.

> Ripon College already had most of the so-called "evils" of Greek-letter groups–i.e., development of cliques within the student body, the pressures and disappointments, the inconvenience and embarrassment of initiation hazing . . . without securing for itself any of the attendant advantages . . . [such as] the enhanced prestige of national groups, additional control over the activities of the chapters, opportunity to break out of the provincialism that necessarily accompanies local groups, assistance in securing larger numbers of applicants for admission. . . .[10]

But some members of the college community felt that nationalization accentuated rather than mitigated the weaknesses of Greek-letter groups and in one significant area presented a new "evil": the charters of several nationals contained explicit exclusionary clauses. This problem came to a head towards the end of the Pinkham administration. In January of 1963, the Education Committee of the Board of Trustees passed the following resolution:

> Resolved, That the Board of Trustees, recognizing the conflict between the purposes of Ripon College, as stated in its charter, and the membership selection practices of certain national fraternities and sororities, declares that it will endorse and support the action of its local chapters to select new members regardless of race, nationality, or religion.[11]

The resolution was adopted by the full board later the same day. However, the faculty felt that the resolution was a bit of a weasel and on December 8 accepted with near unanimity a recommendation from the local chapter of the AAUP:

> 1.   That it [the faculty] stands opposed to any fraternity or sorority which contains in its charter, or its National Charter, an explicit or implicit exclusion clause; 2.   That the administration will actively support any living group that chooses to challenge, on principle or with a test case, the National Exclusion Clause and will guarantee the right of that living group to remain on campus; 3.   That within two years of this date no living group with an explicit or implicit exclusion clause in its local or National Charter be allowed to remain on the Ripon Campus.[12]

Two months later the trustees, despite objections from Deans Harris and van Hengel that the time limit might be impossible for some nationals to meet, gave the Greek societies a date of September, 1967, by which to comply. As it turned out, Ripon's fraternities and sororities had little difficulty conforming to the new policy. All local chapters except one sorority either received assurance that the national organizations had no exclusionary clauses or received a waiver from those that did. The one dissenting sorority, Kappa Delta, withdrew from the campus; the Ripon chapter had virtually decided to go local anyway.

As disillusionment with the Viet Nam War increased, so did student disenchantment with both frivolous and serious extracurricular campus activities. On February 14, 1967, the Student Senate abolished hazing by a 12-10 vote. Out the window went all the perhaps silly, but nonetheless nostalgically remembered, business of beanies, buttoning, sophomore hellers, and other remnants of the old interclass rivalries. Many of the Greek-letter groups began to live a somewhat precarious existence, a few disappearing altogether, others teetering back and forth between independence and national affiliation. Precise statistics do not exist, but at their peak in the late 50s and early 60s, the Greeks enrolled a very high percentage of the student body, possibly 80 or 90 percent. By 1970, the percentage had dropped to 65 and by 1978 to 55 for fraternities and 40 for sororities. In 1966, there were five sororities (all national) and eight fraternities (five national and three local) for a total of 13. By the end of the Adams administration (1985), the number had dropped to 10 (three national sororities, six fraternities split evenly between nationals and locals, and one local coed society). Among sororities, Alpha Phi and Kappa Delta had disappeared, leaving Alpha Chi Omega, Alpha Delta Pi, and Alpha Xi Delta; among national fraternities, Sigma Alpha Epsilon, Delta Upsilon, and Sigma Nu were gone, with Phi Delta Theta, Sigma Chi, and Theta Chi remaining.

A similar malaise hit many extracurricular activities. The *College Days* provides a typical example. During the Pinkham and part of the Adams administrations, it had been a lively and literate weekly, often running to 12 pages, full of pictures, cartoons, and discussions of controversial issues; as such it was a fairly reliable source of information for this history. Nowadays, it rarely exceeds four pages (even with considerable padding), appears irregularly, and often contains outdated news. Student attendance at lectures, concerts, plays, and athletic events is spotty at best. Gone are the Brand Rex Coffee House, the Dawes Cultural Center, and the Black Cultural Center (to be discussed later), with little to replace them. One might have expected that waning concern for social and political problems might have rekindled interest in traditional extracurricular activities, but this has not happened. Explanations for this phenomenon are many and varied. In the past, students were required to earn "convocation points" by attending cultural events; failure to do so meant a notation of "Convocation Probation" on transcripts. Thus, large crowds were somewhat artificially induced. It may be that students are simply otherwise occupied. The tremendous increase in intercollegiate sports, especially for women, the prosperity of intramurals, and the large number of joggers, weight lifters, and iron-pumpers suggest that more people are participating rather than watching. There are more musical organizations, the magazine *Politico* is new, and certain organizations like the International Club, the Romance Languages Club, and the Multicultural Committee are flourishing. Idealists may say that students are studying harder, but this is a very dubious proposition.

Over the years, the *in loco parentis* concept was whittled away and finally died on the vine, partly because of pressure from the admissions counselors, who felt that prospective students, if not their parents, were turned off by Ripon's restrictive social policies. The academic year 1970-71 seems to have been a watershed time for the relaxation of such policies: Sit down meals and the dress code as well as "hours" for women were eliminated, although doors to the Tri-Dorms and Johnson Hall are still locked at midnight and their residents given keycards for late entrance. The first

coed dorm was established when 19 women moved into the
center section of the second floor of North Hall (now Mapes);
eventually a second upperclass coeducational dorm was
opened, and freshman women began living in New Scott Hall.
At one time, freshmen and students receiving financial aid
were not allowed to have automobiles. Beginning in the
spring of 1972, all car regulations were abolished, except that
vehicles had to be registered and were not allowed in the
Quad area. Permission to live off campus, once granted only
in special circumstances, has become virtually automatic.

     Alcoholic beverages were a knottier problem. At the
request of the Student Senate, the Executive Committee of
the trustees on December 5, 1968, authorized the sale of
beer at certain social events on campus under the supervision of the Student Union Board; the Pub in the Student
Union first served beer on September 9, 1970. Drinking in
the dorms for students 18 or older (a large majority) became
permissible somewhat later. But a Wisconsin law, passed in
the mid-80s, prohibited the consumption of alcohol by
persons who did not become 19 by September 1, 1986, and
thereafter by persons under 21. This law created enormous
complexities, which have yet to be satisfactorily resolved.

     For many years, the hottest campus issue was "visi-
tation" privileges. Until the mid-60s, the question hardly
arose: everyone simply assumed that the sexes never legally
mingled in the residence halls except in the lounges. Then,
the students began to crusade for visitation in individual
rooms; the problems posed by this crusade were exceedingly
complicated and occasionally comical. Should doors be
closed or open? If open, by how much? By the length or width
of a book? How about a book of matches? Annoyed by the
occasional silliness of the discussion at one meeting, Dean
Ashley suggested an ice cube, which, because of the heat
generated in the room, would quickly melt. Should visitation
be restricted to weekends or allowed at all times? All night
or for how many hours? What if one roommate wanted
visitation privileges and the other did not?   In what

dormitories–upperclass men's, upperclass women's, freshman men's, freshman women's? Would visitation violate
state laws on cohabitation? What would happen to Ripon's
image? How would alumni, parents, and donors react?
Would open dorms attract or repel prospective students?

Inching forward slowly, the College took a decade to
reach a solution reasonably acceptable to all parties. The
students obviously wanted visitation privileges, but even
they had difficulty reaching agreement on details. In a poll
taken in January of 1967, 545 of 657 opposed closed doors;
286 favored weekend visitation only, with 320 preferring an
all-week arrangement. A Student Senate policy, drafted by
the men's living groups and recommending a "12-inch" requirement rather than closed doors, received strong faculty
support (44-15) in February, 1968. As might have been
expected, the trustees were much harder to convince; quite
naturally they were concerned about Ripon's image, financial
implications (i.e., fund raising and enrollment), and possible
violations of state law. After they had rejected 24-hour visitation, President Adams told the *Days* that even though
visitation in and of itself would not violate Wisconsin stat-
utes, it "would, however, be construed by the general public
as tacitly condoning living arrangements under which violations of the law would take place."[13] However, in December,
1973, Adams was able to announce that the board had
approved an 18-hour policy. Finally, in late April, 1977, the
board, by a 15-7 vote, accepted the 24-hour arrangement,
with certain provisos: freshman dorms were excluded, upperclass living groups must approve visitation by a two-
thirds written ballot at the beginning of each semester, one
roommate could veto the privilege even if the other desired it,
and cohabitation was prohibited. This is pretty much the
policy which now prevails, though somewhat liberalized.[14]
Thus ended what the *Days* had called "the great neander-
thal."[15] In terms of the real world, Ripon College simply
bowed to the inevitable. The sexes have always "visited" each
other, and generations of Ripon students had devised ingen-

ious ways, such as putting ties on doors, to make "visiting" possible.

Ripon College survived the Viet Nam era virtually unscathed. Not that the great issue of the late 60s and early 70s was ignored; it wasn't. But none of the violence, sit-ins, blockades, and other destructive actions which disrupted the educational process at other institutions occurred at Ripon. That this was so could be credited to the entire administration, especially President Adams, to the faculty, to the students themselves, and to the close and generally positive relationship which existed among all three groups. But the greatest share of the credit should probably go to Chaplain Thompson. Although he was the most vocal anti-Viet Nam spokesman on the campus, he was also a man of peace, unalterably opposed to any form of violence, who personified orderly, peaceful, and non-violent forms of protest.

Serious concern about the Viet Nam War began on the campus during the 1966-67 academic year. The *Days* was full of editorials, columnist comments, and letters to the editor. Ripon's only "incident" occurred April 14, 1967, on Upper Sadoff Field during the annual federal inspection of ROTC. Generally, what happened is not in dispute, but the precise details and the assessment of blame became the subject of considerable controversy. Two cadets in fatigues seized and destroyed signs carried by three demonstrators on the gravel road above the field and behind Bovay Hall. The two cadets said they acted under orders from Major Herman Lukow, who was taking pictures at the time; one cadet told the *Days*, "I am reasonably sure he gave me an order"; one demonstrator claimed to have heard Lukow say, "Get that one." Lukow denied this, though he admitted, "I should have stopped it . . . but . . . I was preoccupied with the camera."[16]

Colonel Leo Eberhardt, Professor of Military Science,

supported Lukow and wrote President Adams, "Instructions were given that if the demonstration interfered with the inspection appropriate action would be taken" but that the "destruction of the picket signs was in direct violation of instructions." In a letter printed in the *Days*, Adams stated that "the demonstrators' right to free expression and to orderly demonstration was obstructed, directly by the actions of several cadets and indirectly by the failure of an officer to instruct the cadets to desist." He also mentioned that a student carrying a fourth poster, "Kill for Peace," was "attacked with noticeably greater force and this sign too was destroyed."[17]

A second letter from the president informed the *Days* that the two cadets who destroyed signs were not in formation because they did not own dress uniforms, hence did not hear the instructions given to their fellow students. Consequently, he concluded that "we should declare the cadets essentially cleared of the charges implied in my first statement." The *Days* praised Major Lukow for voluntarily accepting blame and admitting neglect, but still criticized him because, whether he issued an order or not, "he still neglected to stop the destruction of the signs even though he was in the midst of the entire affair." The *Days* felt that a major portion of the blame should be shouldered by Colonel Eberhardt "for not issuing clear orders, for not accepting responsibility and not issuing a proper apology." Toward the two cadets, the *Days* expressed its sympathy. They were not to be considered guilty because they were "understandably bewildered by the entire course of action . . . for even if they had acted on their own, which is very much in doubt, they still could have been stopped by their superiors."[18] Since the college paper was probably pro-student and anti-military, it may have been too critical of the ROTC officers; it's hard to determine the truth in matters of this kind.

About the same time as the incident just described, a minor storm was brewing over an imminent speech by General Maxwell Taylor, who had been superintendent of the

Military Academy, chairman of the Joint Chiefs of Staff, and also, unfortunately, ambassador to Viet Nam. In a March 31 editorial, the *Days* wondered whether Taylor was worth his $2,500 fee. The Ripon Public Relations Office sent a copy of the editorial to Taylor's agent, who became very indignant and told Dean Ashley over the phone that the general might cancel his engagement. Ashley said the general had every right to do so if he wished, but the agent was not about to surrender his fee and Taylor showed up on the appointed day, May 3. As he entered the Memorial Gymnasium, sign-carrying town-gown picketers marched up and down the student union sidewalk across the street in an orderly and peaceful fashion and a group of students lining both sides of the walk into the gym turned their backs as he passed through. Taylor later commented that it was the most effective demonstration he had ever seen. A packed house, including all the demonstrators, was courteous and attentive.

A somewhat more serious controversy arose in the fall of 1970 when the External Affairs Committee of the Student Senate scheduled a speech by attorney William Kunstler, who had won nationwide fame by defending the Chicago Seven, the Catonsville Nine (including Father Daniel Berrigan, who later spoke at Ripon), Stoakley Carmichael, Rap Brown, Adam Clayton Powell, and other anti-establishment figures. After hearing of the invitation to Kunstler, three parents wrote the trustees suggesting that President Adams compose a letter to all parents explaining the College's position; a telegram from Northfield, Illinois, also requested a letter "so that parents who share our deep seated concern can take whatever action they deem necessary in view of Ripon College's refusal to act." The result was a statement signed by both Adams and Chairman of the Board Robert Abendroth defending the right of "free speech, free inquiry, and free advocacy so central to the democratic, and especially, the academic tradition" as well as the students' right "to hear speakers of their own choosing." The letter also expressed the opinion that "although 98% of the student body will disagree strongly with Mr. Kunstler's views, there is a virtual unanimity that he should be heard." Finally, Adams and Abendroth promised that the trustees "will definitely review the Kunstler experience and determine whether or not some kind of administrative review of the speaker program should be instituted."[19]

Fortunately or unfortunately, depending on one's attitude, there wasn't much to review. On September 29, 1970, Kunstler addressed without incident a crowd of 1,700 in the Memorial Gymnasium. But President Adams had to re-enact the old speaker-ban-free-speech-student-rights drama featuring much correspondence and innumerable meetings of faculty and trustees, so that the whole affair began to sound like a broken record left over from the Pinkham administration. Only this time, Ripon had impressive external authority to bolster its position. As Adams pointed out in still another letter (to 98 parents, 49 supporting the College, 41 favoring restraints, and the other eight apparently not taking a strong position either way), the trustees had adopted the *Joint Statement on the Rights and Freedoms of Students* endorsed by the Association of American Colleges, the American Association of University Professors, the National Association of Student Personnel Administrators, the National Student Association, and other prestigious groups. In summary, said the letter, "There is no question, then, that violent or disruptive *actions* will not be tolerated by Ripon although complete freedom of expression certainly will be."[20]

At the time of the Kunstler speech, the *Days* distributed a lengthy questionnaire to 600 students (almost two-thirds of the student body); 464 replied. The results were somewhat startling and suggest that Ripon's students were perhaps less conservative, in thought if not in action, than was usually assumed.

In summary, 63 percent agreed "basically" with Kunstler (remember that President Adams' first letter to the parents assured them that 98 percent of the students would not support Kunstler); 90 percent believed that Kunstler-type speakers should be sponsored; 77 percent said that the trustees should not investigate Ripon's speaker program; seven percent identified themselves as radical left, 44 percent as liberal, 29 percent as middleroaders, 19 percent as conservative; 51 percent would "support direct, militant, but peaceful confrontation of the 'establishment'"; 49 percent would "support such confrontation even with the risk of violent reaction for a cause [they] believe in; 89 percent would not "support violence on the campus by students who had no direct provocation"; 22 percent would "support Palestinian Arab guerrilla attempts to regain their homeland," though 42 percent would not; 47 percent "believe that there is an 'armed conspiracy' attempting to destroy the Black Panthers, Weathermen, etc."; 75 percent would want their congressmen to support "withdrawal of all troops by the end of 1971."[22]

The Viet Nam War had a noticeable effect on the Ripon curriculum; this will be considered in the next chapter.

During the Pinkham and Adams administrations, Ripon enjoyed an athletic renaissance, especially in football, basketball, and tennis. In the fall of 1956, Jerry Thompson succeeded Carl Doehling as football coach. Thompson had played football and baseball at both St. Olaf and Wisconsin and then coached at Augustana (South Dakota) and Upsala Colleges and Neenah High School. Before resigning to attend divinity school, Thompson compiled a two-year record of 12-3-1, despite squads numbering only 19 and 24; his 1957 team won the conference title. It is difficult today, when Ripon has become accustomed to championships, to understand the excitement generated by the 1957 team's accomplishments. For perhaps the first time in Ripon history, athletic achievement was recognized by an all-college convocation. On the Sunday following the final game, students, faculty, staff, and townspeople gathered in the Red Barn to hear celebratory speeches by the president, the dean, Th-

ompson, and others. One member of the team, end Pete
Kasson '59, won Little All-American honors; another, running back Dave Smith '59, played for Houston in the American Football League. Thompson's successor, John Storzer,
coached football at Ripon longer than anyone except Doehling.
His 16-year record was 88-40-4, including four consecutive
championships between 1963 and 1966 and a fifth in 1968.
In 1964, quarterback Jack Ankerson '64 set an NCAA eight-
game scoring record of 145 points.

On October 31, 1966, a *Sports Illustrated* article gave
Ripon football some unexpected publicity. Thirty-three fans
in Rochester, Pennsylvania, none of whom attended Ripon or
had even heard of it previously and all of whom no doubt
mispronounced the College's name, included the 1963 Ri-
pon-Coe game in a football pool as a gag. When Ripon won,
they founded the Pennsylvania Subway Alumni Club of
Ripon.

> They wear Ripon sweat shirts, wave Ripon pennants,
> paste Ripon decals on their windshields and Ripon
> stickers on their bumpers, and cover their books with
> Ripon book covers. Each week during the football
> season they send Coach John Storzer an inspirational
> telegram, and the club has held the Ripon Munch-On
> (a Girl Scout cooky raffle), the Ripon Chip-On (a golf
> tournament) and the Ripon Bowl-On (a bowling tour-
> nament) to raise funds for all the sweat shirts, pen-
> nants, decals, etc. The club president is Joe Mundo,
> and before this year's Ripon-Coe game the member-
> ship talked him into driving the 650 miles to Ripon to
> see it in person. Mundo arrived unannounced, but
> his fame had preceded him. No sooner had he hit town
> than the cry was raised: "Where's Joe Mundo?" He
> must have been found, for he was the guest of honor
> at the Ripon Alumni Association reception, he got five
> guided tours of the Ripon campus and he met every-

one from the Ripon president, Dr. Bernard S. Adams, down to Mrs. Aleen Bruce of the Ripon College Bookstore–the source of the sweat shirts, pennants, decals, etc. Mundo sat on the Ripon bench during the game (Ripon won again 42-0) and returned to Rochester with snapshots of the Ripon campus and two game films, which were shown at the next meeting of the Pennsylvania Subway Alumni Club.[23]

After Storzer's sudden death two weeks before the end of the 1973 season, Ripon waited four years for Bob Giesey's two championships in 1977 and 1978. Larry Terry won another in 1982; his team was ranked 14th nationally in Division III. Center Dick Rehbein '75, end Art Peters '80, and offensive lineman Bob Wallner '83 won Little All-American honors; linebacker Jeff Gabrielson '80 played in the Canadian and United States Football Leagues. Rehbein has been an assistant coach for the Green Bay Packers, the Los Angeles Express (USFL), and the Minnesota Vikings. Then, as suddenly as its rebirth occurred under Thompson, the football program collapsed; Ripon has not had a winning season since 1982 (as of fall 1989).

Ripon's winning ways in basketball were reestablished by Coach Kermit "Doc" Weiske '50, whose undergraduate scoring record of 1,188 points held up until broken by Lud Wurtz '78. Between 1958 and 1966, Weiske won three titles: 1962-63 (tie), 1963-64, and 1964-65 (triple tie). After a six-year interim under John Weinert, whose 1971-72 team tied for the championship, Weiske returned for another eight-year stint. In this second tenure, Weiske added titles in 1977-78 and 1979-80; his total record was 203-148. Weiske's successor, Bob Gillespie, by 1986-87 had won 100 games and lost 60, capturing conference crowns in 1985-86 and 1986-87; his 1985-86 team reached the regional finals before losing to seventh-ranked Illinois Wesleyan on Wesleyan's home court. Forward Ashley Cooper '82 led the NCAA, Division III, in scoring in 1981-82.

Dean Ashley founded Ripon's tennis dynasty. After a disastrous 0-8 record in 1956, his teams never had a losing season; the 1964 group won Ripon's first conference tennis championship. Two years later, Chuck Larson '65, a member of the 1964 team, returned from graduate school to become the most successful tennis coach in Ripon's history, winning titles in 1971, 1979, 1980, 1981, 1985, 1986, 1987, 1988, and 1989; the '86, '87, and '88 teams earned national rankings of 13, 20, and 18, respectively. In the fall of 1987, Larson took over the women's team and in the following year won the Midwest Conference Championship and had an undefeated season, both firsts in the history of women's tennis at Ripon; another championship followed in 1989. Besides tennis, Larson also coached swimming and won conference titles in 1970-71 and 1971-72. Since 1978, he has been director of athletics and chairman of the Physical Education Department.

Following a lapse of 35 years, baseball, which had been one of Ripon's first intercollegiate sports, was reintroduced in 1956 by Doehling. As Doehling's successor, Storzer duplicated his success in football, winning five championships between 1963 and 1967. Not until 1989 did Ripon win another undisputed baseball crown; the coach was Bob Gillespie.

Ripon has not distinguished itself in cross country, golf, soccer, track and field, or wrestling. In track, Ripon last won a crown in 1923-24, but has placed second twice; Todd Cieslelcyk '87 won All-American Division III honors in shot-put outdoors (1986), shot-put indoors (1987), shot-put and discuss outdoors (1987). The cross country team has never finished higher in the conference than fourth (1973); the wrestling team, third (1974-75). However, in 1974 Mike Van Boxel '76 won the NCAA Division III Championship at 167 pounds and in 1983 Kurt Searvogel '85 placed seventh at 177 pounds; both were named All-American. In golf, Ripon has not won a conference crown since 1936. Founded in 1963 as a club sport, soccer went varsity in 1972; the 1974 team tied for second in the Midwest Conference. Because of declining interest, cross country was discontinued in 1976, but was revived as a club in 1986 and as a varsity sport in 1987 for both men and women. Other club sports for men are ice hockey, indoor soccer, lacrosse, and rugby.

With the appointment of Elaine Coll as part-time coach and assistant professor of physical education in 1973, the College initiated a full-scale intercollegiate program for women. At first, Ripon competed in the Wisconsin Independent Colleges Women's Athletic Conference, consisting of 15 women's and co-educational institutions. In this conference, Ripon won four titles in track (1977, 1981, 1982, 1983), four in volleyball (1976, 1981, 1982, 1983), two in basketball (1978, 1985), one in softball (1983), and one, a tie with Lawrence, in tennis (1977); Coll, who became full time in 1979, coached the first three sports. For one year, the College belonged to both the state league and the Midwest Conference, but, beginning in the fall of 1985, only to the latter, where the competition is much tougher. Nonetheless, the basketball team ranked fifth nationally on defense in 1985-86 and seventh in 1986-87. After being a club sport briefly, women's soccer went varsity in 1985. With the resumption of cross country in 1987, women began competing in that sport also.

Ripon's top female athlete is undoubtedly Dewi Oleson '82, who in 1982 finished fifth nationally at the 1500 meters and seventh at the 800 meters. The first qualified her as a Little All-American; her time of 4.34 is likely to remain a Ripon record for many years. The College's other lady All-American is Tracie Kinard '90, who earned the honor as a soccer player in 1986 and 1987. In the summer of 1988, Linda Secor '78, a three-sport athlete, became the first woman to be elected to the Ripon College Athletic Hall of Fame. Lori Stich '92 became Ripon's first conference champion in cross country in 1989 and also the first to qualify for the national meet.

With swimming recently added, the women have

eight varsity teams compared to 10 for men; this is close to parity. In an interview for the *Ripon Commonwealth Press*, Coach Coll commented, "We get along and share in our department. I know a lot of those schools [in the Midwest Conference] get by with lip service to their women."[24] Rugby and lacrosse are club sports for women; downhill skiing, fencing, and judo are available to both men and women.

No discussion of student life would be complete without a tribute to David Harris, whose tenure as dean of men corresponds almost exactly with the scope of this chapter. In the spring of 1981, the National Association of Student Personnel Administrators gave him the Scott Goodnight Award for "outstanding performance as a Dean"; it was a first for a college of Ripon's size as well as a first for a Wisconsin institution. President Adams said, "I have never known anybody who knows more students and alumni and is known by more students and alumni."[25] His sudden death in 1981 deeply saddened the campus.

NOTES TO CHAPTER XV
STUDENT LIFE 1955-1985

[1]"Looking Backwards: Ashley Reflects," *College Days*, Nov. 19, 1979, 1, 6, and 8.   A somewhat longer version appeared in the *Days*, April 23, 1976, 3ff.

[2]*Report from Ripon College*, June, 1964.

[3]*Trustees' Minutes*, May 17, 1964.

[4]*Ripon College Magazine*, Spring Issue, 1979, 4-5.

[5]*College Days*, May 11, 1962, 1-2 and 4.

[6]*Trustees' Minutes*, May 22, 1962, 5.

[7]*Ibid.*

[8]*Ibid.*, May 23, 1963.

[9]*Alumnus*, Nov., 1963; *College Days*, Jan. 17, 1964, 5.

[10]*Trustees' Minutes*, Aug. 8, 1958.

[11]*Education Committee Minutes*, Jan. 24, 1963.

[12]*Faculty Minutes*, Dec. 8, 1964, 2.

[13]*College Days*, Oct. 27, 1972, 5.

[14]See *Ripon College Student Handbook, 1987-88*, 26.

[15]*College Days*, Nov. 5, 1976, 2.

[16]*College Days*, April 21, 1967, 9.

[17]*Ibid.*, April 28, 1967, 3.

[18]*Ibid.*, May 8, 1967, 4 and 7.

[19]*College Days*, Oct. 2, 1970, 13.

[20]*Ibid.*, 1.

[21]*Faculty Minutes*, Sept. 30, 1969.

[22]*College Days*, Oct. 2, 1970, 7.

[23]*Ripon College Magazine*, Feb., 1967.

[24]*Commonwealth Press*, Feb. 12, 1987.

[25]*College Days*, April 10, 1981, 3.

CHAPTER XVI

UPS AND DOWNS: I
BERNARD S. ADAMS
1966-1985

*Every college today, and particularly
every liberal arts college, has got to be
a changing kind of institution. If an
institution does not change, it doesn't
stand still–it slips backwards.*

Bernard Adams

Following the resignation of Fred Pinkham, the trustees began a search for his successor. The result was the election of Bernard S. Adams as Ripon's ninth president. He assumed office in October, 1966, and presided over his first faculty meeting on the 11th of that month. His undergraduate work was done at Princeton, where he had been senior class president and captain of the basketball team. Subsequently, he earned a master's degree from Yale and a doctorate from Pittsburgh, both degrees being in English literature. Between Yale and Pittsburgh, he served as an officer in the Air Force during the Korean War. He worked in admissions at Princeton and at Pittsburgh, where he also became special assistant to the chancellor. At the time of his appointment to Ripon's presidency, he was Oberlin's dean of students.

In interviews with the *College Days*, a speech to the Alumni Association, and his inaugural address, the new president enunciated his educational philosophy and his hopes for the future.

The traditional role of the liberal arts college has been

to guide younger generations toward the acquisition of judgment and the cultivation of mind and spirit. Such colleges have sought to develop in young people knowledge and understanding of themselves and of their social and physical environment, to the end that they may achieve maximum personal fulfillment and contribute to the welfare of others and to the strength and harmony of a free society.[1]

The chief responsibility of a college president is "to embody and make articulate an educational philosophy."[2] Adams expressed a hope that Ripon would become more heterogeneous "in personality types, in socioeconomic backgrounds, and geographical origins"[3] and emphasized the need for change and innovation: "Every college today, and particularly every liberal arts college, has got to be a changing kind of institution. If an institution does not change, it doesn't stand still–it slips backwards."[4]   From the students, he expected "a more complete commitment to the life of the mind" and from the faculty, more interest in scholarly research "because research is essential to good teaching."[5] Specifically, he looked forward to the construction of a fine arts complex, the addition of anthropology and sociology to the curriculum, and an increase in enrollment to 1,000 or 1,500 students. Most of his ambitions were realized; some were not.

For several years, Ripon's growth and prosperity continued, and the new president profited from the momentum generated by his predecessor, especially in the expansion of facilities, many of which had been anticipated and even partially planned. When Adams arrived, Bovay, the Johnson and Scott additions, the Kemper Clinic, and a new president's home had been completed or were well underway. The J. M. Storzer Physical Education Center opened in 1967. It contained a basketball court and a tartan area, both of which could be used for badminton, tennis, and volleyball; a competition-sized swimming pool; handball, racquetball, and squash courts; a dance studio; a weight room; a small classroom; and offices. The priority given to physical education and athletics did not meet with universal approval. The fine arts people would have preferred a building to meet their desperate desires; other faculty would have liked an addition to the library; the admissions staff might have opted for refurbished dormitories. Even the students got into the act: the *Days* printed a cartoon which showed a basketball player leaning against a collapsing Ingram Hall and a new gym looming in the background. "One can easily do without paddle-tennis, but we can't do without Plato,"[6] said the editor. A fine arts complex, a library addition, a new classroom building, and refurbished dorms were legitimate needs, soon to be met, but the campus structure most inadequate for its purposes was certainly the Memorial Gymnasium. The College could not satisfactorily run an expanding intercollegiate program for both men and women, accommodate intramurals, and teach physical education in one huge room built in 1910.

The other much needed facilities came in due course. In the late spring of 1968, the east end of Ingram Hall was torn down to make room for a new building. One morning, the campus and the city woke up to find the fire wall facing Ransom Street decorated with graffiti: "Rev. Thompson uses Brylcreme [he's bald]," "Playtex girdles make hippies disappear," "Due to loss of interest tomorrow will be cancelled," "Studying causes cancer," "Sex stops tension fast," "Betsy Ross had an average build," and "King Kong died of smog!" A year later, the rest of Ingram was demolished and the new classroom building, named after Milwaukee industrialist Todd Wehr, completed. A few alumni bemoaned Ingram's demise, but the old building had always been a white elephant and an eyesore; it bisected the campus at the wrong angle, and its ugly red bricks clashed with the color of all other structures on the upper campus. Graduates and older faculty still tell stories of sand and other building materials falling on their heads from the ceiling above.

Next to come was the C. J. Rodman Center for the Arts, named after Clarence J. Rodman '13. At long last, the "poor relations" of the faculty, after years of being kicked from pillar to post, had found a permanent home and offices in the new building. The Speech and Drama Department moved out of the old Grace Lutheran Church and into Benstead Theatre. Unfortunately, the later razing of the church dispossessed Raphael the Ghost, who had turned lights on and off, locked students out in the cold, and rung bells in the Congregational Church; he is also said to have played the role of the invisible rabbit in *Harvey*. In revenge for his displacement, he allegedly caused the roofing problems in Rodman.

The Music Department, which had at various times occupied the top floor of East Hall, part of Bartlett, and a house on Thorne Street and had given its concerts all over the campus, now had Demmer Recital Hall for its exclusive use. Several years later, a "custom-built mechanical action . . . three-manual, eighteen-stop organ," made possible in part by a gift from Mildred Thiel '25, formerly an instructor in music and administrative assistant to the dean of the College, was installed in Demmer.[7] Only the Art Department was shortchanged; lack of funds prevented the completion of an "art wing," with the result that some studio courses continued to be held on the upper campus.

In 1974, the capacity of Lane Library was more than doubled by the construction of the Wehr Learning Resources Center. Unlike earlier construction during the Pinkham and Adams administrations, which were federally financed, the three most recent buildings were funded by foundations and capital campaigns. Over the years through sale or destruction, the College gradually got rid of several surplus, expensive-to-maintain structures such as the Grace Lutheran Church and a number of sorority houses. For many years, maintenance of the residence halls was a constant source of concern. The admissions staff continually complained that both the architecture and the condition of the dormitories adversely affected both recruitment and retention of students; it also limited the rental of dormitory space during the summer. In a report to the trustees, Vice President for Finance Kenneth Cartier stated that the residence halls had "received only minimal maintenance and no real renovation, except in a cosmetic sense"; he estimated that "renovation of the entire system would require something like $1 million" but that a few hundred thousand dollars would do much.[8] According to President Adams, maintenance had been deferred because of emphasis on salary improvement. Eventually, the trustees in April of 1983 allotted $225,000 for a Quad renovation project. The Tri-Dorms had to wait longer. On February 2, 1985, Adams recommended that Tri-Dorms renovation be given number one priority; their "condition," he said, "appears far beyond the cosmetic repairs/improvements that we generally address."[9] A complete overhaul was accomplished during the Stott administration.

Another, but different, problem was the Kemper Clinic. Since 1966, the clinic had provided free space for two doctors, who used it for their private practice in return for a salary of $11,025 and an hour per day of service to students. The vice president for finance estimated the value of the space to the physicians as $54,000, and the question arose whether the College was getting its money's worth, especially since the undergraduates were constantly complaining about the quality of the service, particularly with diagnoses, the priority given to private patients, and the inconvenience of the allotted hour, which conflicted with both lunch and the heavily scheduled 11:15 class time. A committee, consisting of the dean of students and physicians on the Board of Trustees, concluded that the health service, provided at no charge to the students, was too costly and "not central to the overall mission of the College"; however, the clinic's "bonding agreements stipulate[d] that the building will be a health service and will be run as such until the bonds are retired."[10] Therefore, the clinic could not be closed, although the physicians could be and were dismissed. But the building remained open with a gradually reduced staff of nurses. When the bonds matured, the clinic became the computer center, and a new infirmary, staffed by one nurse, was opened in Bartlett Hall.

In the meantime, the needs of the faculty were not being ignored. In 1980, the interior of East Hall was virtually rebuilt to provide offices for the Anthropology-Sociology, History, Politics and Government, and Philosophy Departments. About the same time, West Hall, home of the Education, English, and German Departments, was refurbished.

Another bit of unfinished business left over from the Pinkham administration was the sabbatical leave program, which had been first discussed way back in 1960. A Ford Foundation grant of $50,000 to get the program started was received in 1965; the first four leaves were granted in the spring of 1967.

Although Fred Pinkham had repeatedly sought "new ideas," President Adams played a more active role in curricular innovation than any of his predecessors. When he arrived on campus, consideration of the four-four curriculum was nearing its end; the new president gave his enthusiastic support. Basically, four-four meant that all students would elect four four-credit courses each semester, with provision made for a certain number of half-courses carrying two credits (departmental teaching methods courses, for instance) and quarter-courses carrying one credit but not counted in semester or cumulative averages (mostly freshman-sophomore courses in military science and activities courses in physical education and the fine arts). Instructors, teaching courses previously worth three credits, were encouraged to use the fourth hour in new and different ways; also, the fourth class could be cancelled and the students put to work on independent projects. The prime purpose was to encourage study in depth and to prevent students spreading themselves too thinly (five three-credit courses versus four four-credit

courses).   The number of final examinations would be
reduced; many faculty members would have one fewer course
to prepare and probably fewer students.   Obviously, the
disadvantages of four-four were 1) its rigidity (some courses
and even some disciplines might not be ideally suited to four
credits), and 2) loss of breadth and variety: students would
have fewer electives and thus be exposed to fewer fields of
study. Fundamentally, the choice was between depth and
breadth; eventually, the faculty opted for depth, but only
after two years of grueling and exhausting study.

The four-four probably received more thorough ex-
amination by all segments of the college community than any
proposal in Ripon's history. It was discussed at Parents' Day;
at administration-faculty-student meetings in Racine, site of
the Johnson Foundation's Wingspread Conference Center;
at several campus forums, including one in the Brand Rex
Coffee House. The Student Senate appointed a special ad hoc
committee. Reporters, editorialists, and columnists filled the
pages of the *Days*. The *Days* sent two staff members to
Cornell College, where a four-four curriculum already existed; their report appeared in two issues of the paper. Even
the cartoonists got into the act; one of them, labeled "Touchdown?", showed Dean Ashley, the prime mover behind four-
four and for many people the chief villain, wearing the
number "4-4," carrying a football, and heading toward three
faculty tacklers waiting with outstretched arms.[11]

Of course, the heaviest burden was borne by the
faculty and its Curriculum Committee. By a vote of 47-22-
2, the faculty approved four-four in principle on October 22,
1965. What consumed so much time thereafter was that
every academic department, whether it wanted to or not, had
to revise its offerings completely, submit them to the committee, and then get final approval by the entire faculty; after
that was accomplished, the four-four had to be fitted into a
new set of graduation requirements. This process required
almost weekly meetings of both the committee and the
faculty; in fact, between February 14 and May 1, 1966, the

faculty met not only in the afternoon, but also at night. The last department to revise its courses was Economics, which had been four-four's most articulate critic. The entire package was adopted on February 14, 1967, by a 50-34 vote. The overall structure and a new set of graduation requirements had been approved in the fall, and some departments were already operating within a four-four framework. The changes in graduation requirements were minor: Modern European History was dropped as a specific requirement, history was included in the two-course history and social sciences requirement, and students were allowed to substitute participation in activities or the summer art and architecture tour for course work in the fine arts.

Because of his interest in curricular reform, the new president was pleased with the faculty's action and told the trustees that "academically, the year 1966-67 was one of the most significant in the history of Ripon College."[12] But it had been an exhausting, divisive, and sometimes bitter year and a half, from which the faculty did not recover quickly, and it can be seriously questioned whether it was worth the effort. Conversion from four-four to four-one-four, the "one" representing an interim three-week term between the two semesters, during which students would study one subject intensively, was rejected by the faculty in January, 1971, despite, or perhaps because of, strong support from the dean and the president. The *Days* reacted in a typically virulent editorial:

> The faculty . . . demonstrated once and for all its total impotence as an organ for constructive change . . . . The meeting was a Ph.D. temper tantrum against the powers that be . . . . An even greater case for despair was the mishandling of the 4-1-4 plan by the administration. . . . The faculty seems to dote on downing administration proposals and the administration seems to dote on walking into any and all traps the faculty lays.[13]

In the following fall the faculty, by a 51-12 vote, junked four-four as an all-embracing structure, granting individual departments the right to assign credit value to their courses in any way they wished. But several departments, including, ironically, some which had resisted most vigorously, still retain the basic four-four structure, proving its essential soundness for some disciplines. A year later (1972), the faculty made further minor alterations in graduation requirements: physical education was reduced from four to two semesters, and the fine arts requirement increased from one to two; the philosophy requirement was dropped, and philosophy became an option in the two-semester humanities requirement as did history when a new division of behavioral and social sciences was created; and academic credit for one-hour courses was restored, although most of them continued to be graded pass-fail.

As could have been expected, the Viet Nam War caused considerable soul searching about ROTC. Throughout its history, a small, but vocal, minority of faculty members had opposed military science on the ground that, since it inculcated obedience, it violated the very essence of liberal education. Naturally, Viet Nam increased both the number and the virulence of the protesters; no one doubted their sincerity or denied that their views contained a certain logic. On the other hand, the case for retaining ROTC at Ripon was extremely strong. First, was the unit's national reputation; only forensics, Harley Barber's physicists, and to a lesser extent the Economics Department's reputation with graduate schools of business came even close. Second, through both scholarships and subsistence allowances, ROTC brought a hefty sum of money to Ripon: students in the junior-senior courses received $100 per month; in addition, scholarships covered tuition, fees, and books; loss of this source of money would seriously strain Ripon's financial aid budget. Third, the country needed ROTC to provide officers; furthermore, the availability of liberally educated men was a decided plus for the Army. The solution that would satisfy most adherents to either side of the controversy was to make ROTC voluntary rather than required of all men. But that raised another vexing question: could ROTC survive at Ripon; in other words, would the program produce enough officers to convince the Army not to withdraw from the campus? If the answer to this question was affirmative, then the Military Science Department itself would benefit because ROTC classes would consist only of students who wanted to be there rather than largely of students who would prefer to be someplace else. As for recruitment of students, Director of Admissions Kent Davies stated in a memo to Dean Ashley, "A number of students definitely come to Ripon because of the ROTC requirement. A larger number do not come because of it. Those who are interested . . . do not care, of course, whether the program is mandatory or voluntary."[14] At any rate, volunteerism was the position the College eventually adopted, although it took a few years to get there.

In the meantime, the issue obsessed the campus. As was to be expected, the opposition was led by Chaplain Thompson, but also, as was to be expected, he made certain that the opposition was orderly and peaceful, in fact, what is often termed "a loyal opposition." Its most visible symbol was an alternative to Military Science 111-12. In the fall of 1969, approximately 50 freshman men boycotted the class, "marched" across the campus from the Farr Hall Auditorium to the Great Hall, where the chaplain conducted "counter-class activities." But, as has been mentioned in the previous chapter, Ripon suffered only one disruptive disturbance.

In 1967, military science had been reduced from four required semesters to two, then to one in 1969, and finally made voluntary in 1970. At the same time, the freshman-sophomore non-graded, non-credit quarter courses became two-credit graded courses, the drill period was replaced by a course in military history and defense department policies, and women were admitted to the program; Denise Nicholls '77 became the first woman to receive a commission. Overall, the lady cadets distinguished themselves. During the 1980 summer at Fort Lewis, Washington, Ripon's contingent ranked seventh nationally among 65 institutions and first among the eight midwest states comprising the Second Region. Of the nine cadets, four were women. Donna Leslie '81 and Tammy Thomas Osborn '86 became Ripon cadet commanders. Jeanne Feldman '79 served as a company training officer at the Fort Lewis summer camp; her commanding officer wrote President Adams that he had never known in 20 years of service a junior officer who performed better. As it turned out, the program probably could not have survived without women.

For several years, voluntary ROTC lived a precarious existence, and at one point Ripon's worst fear, loss of the program, was on the verge of becoming a reality: the College was not commissioning the stipulated number of officers. In the spring of 1974, Ripon was one of 147 institutions to receive a "letter of concern," placing it in "evaluation status." The immediate solution was the Wisconsin Central Group Plan, under which Oshkosh, Ripon, and St. Norbert were placed in a "control group" headquartered in Oshkosh under a single professor of military science, who was expected to spend at least one day per week at each school. The departments at the individual schools were reduced by a single officer, but still controlled their own programs. All three were soon removed from evaluation status. As Ripon enters the 1990s, concern over the number of officers commissioned continues. The potential exists that the College could lose its "host school" status and become merely a part of the ROTC program at Oshkosh.

The foreign language requirement vexed the faculty for several years, partly because the admissions staff was convinced that it drove away prospective students. Several options were considered: eliminating the requirement entirely, reducing it from two years to one, and introducing literature and civilization courses in English as the whole or part of the requirement. On April 16, 1974, by a 36-35 vote, with the president breaking the tie, the faculty accepted the first alternative, but a week later voted 48-22 to refer the problem back to the Curriculum Committee. The eventual solution was a one-year requirement.

An even more vexing question was whether to introduce business courses. Once again, the initiative came from the admissions counselors, who believed that such courses would attract students. Dean of Admissions Christopher Small had told the trustees in the summer of 1979 that Ripon was losing students to both public and private institutions within the state offering business courses and that only Ripon and Lawrence drew a complete blank on business as a major area of study in a high-school counselors' notebook prepared annually by the Wisconsin Association of Independent Colleges and Universities. A few months later, President Adams informed the trustees that Ripon had just admitted the smallest freshman class in 20 years. Ripon's enrollment had reached a peak of 1,065 during the 1969-70 academic year, dropped to 1,049 and 1,027 the next two years, climbed back to 1,060 in 1973-74, declined to 1,006 in 1973-74 and to 933 in 1974-75, and remained in the nine hundreds for several years before collapsing to 870 (the lowest figure since 1964) in 1983.[15] Consequently, enrollment was a legitimate concern for the entire college, especially the administration and the trustees, both of whom were responsible for the financial well-being of the institution. The Economics Department unanimously and vigorously opposed the introduction of business courses, believing that more or less pure economics was the best preparation for graduate schools of business or immediate entrance into the business world; in defense of this position, they could cite the impressive record of their majors in business schools and business careers. The economists were supported by faculty who, despite the presence of business courses in the curricula of several sister colleges in the ACM, felt that such courses violated the liberal arts ideal. Many teachers complained that the admissions office was determining the curriculum; they were soon to level the same charge against the trustees.

During the 1973-74 academic year, the faculty adopted an interdisciplinary Pre-Management Program (i.e., not a major); participating departments included computer science, economics, mathematics, psychology, and speech. In 1977-78, the Economics Department, now expanded to five teachers, designed four new courses preparing students for direct entry into business. Then on January 20, 1980, the faculty accepted, by a 45-23-3 vote, the Curriculum Committee's recommendation of a Business Management Major ("management" was apparently a more acceptable term than "administration"). But the trustees were not satisfied. They accepted the new major "with appreciation," but "believing some modification is necessary if the new major is to encourage enrollment," they referred the proposal to the Executive Committee "to take such final action as it deems necessary." The board did not instruct the committee "whether or not it should consult further with the Faculty," but did suggest that it confer with the president and the dean.[16] Chairman of the Board Robert Abendroth told the faculty representatives at the board's winter meeting that "curricular matters are delegated to the faculty," but that the specific delegation of this power, according to the By-Laws of the College, in no way limited or affected "the final authority of the Board" and that "it was clearly the responsibility of the Board to see to the financial viability of the College."[17] President Adams had not supported the motion to refer the matter to the Executive Committee and later told the faculty he would do everything in his power to prevent that committee's taking final action. At a special meeting on February 12, the faculty adopted a resolution urging the Board of Trustees and the Executive Committee "to observe its historic policy of exercising authority in academic matters through the faculty, and to present for the faculty's consideration and action any adjustments they propose in Ripon's curricular program."[18] Fortunately, the Executive Committee honored this request and for-

warded to the faculty a recommendation that three courses—
Marketing, Business Policy, and an additional semester of
Accounting be added to the new major. The faculty approved
only the first two, but the trustee committee accepted the
compromise "with thanks"; the full board subsequently voted
their unanimous approval. Thus, a potentially damaging
confrontation was avoided.[19] In October, 1980, Dean Small
estimated that "there probably are thirty freshmen in this
fall's class who would not have been here had Ripon not
added the Business Management Major."[20] The new major
grew by leaps and bounds and eventually surpassed economics as the most popular program on the campus.

Ripon purchased its first computer in the late 1960s
and offered a one-semester course, Beginning Programming,
in 1968-69. Initially, one man, Robert Taylor, handled all
computer services for the entire College in addition to teaching computer courses. But the load very shortly became too
heavy for one person, and members of the Mathematics and
Science Departments took over the academic work. During
the 1978-79 academic year, all computer courses were absorbed by a new Mathematics and Computer Science Department and shortly thereafter the faculty approved a combined
major, which would enable students to enroll in a graduate
school of computer science or enter the field directly. Eventually, the department developed a separate major. On
January 25 and 26, 1984, Carl Henry, Director of Computing Activities at Carleton, visited the campus to evaluate
Ripon's computer services. In his report, he stated that
Ripon had once been a leader in the field among ACM
colleges, but now the system was so swamped that Ripon's
students were able to use terminal time only half as much as
Carleton's and two thirds as much as Lawrence's. He
recommended the appointment of a coordinator of academic
computing, improved salaries and working conditions to
reduce turnover, and expansion of space. When the com-

puter center moved into the former clinic in 1988-89, all of Henry's recommendations had been followed.

Perhaps the most innovative program ever introduced into the Ripon curriculum was a minor in Leadership Studies. Certainly, the various service academies and possibly some universities offer courses in leadership as does the Military Science Department here, but it is doubtful that any other small liberal arts college supports a full program. The idea was first conceived in the fall of 1975 by Seale Doss of the Philosophy Department, who as a reserve brigadier general, had a natural interest in the subject. After being studied by ad hoc faculty committees, the concept was approved by the trustees in the spring of 1976, by the Curriculum Committee in the fall, and by the faculty at a special meeting in March, 1977. Because of the widespread concern over failures of presidential leadership in Washington, the subject was obviously current and relevant. The faculty had requested the administration to seek external support for developing and initiating a Program for the Study of Organizations and Organizational Leadership and authorized the Curriculum Committee to study and develop such a program, to review it annually, and to report on its development throughout a trial period of four years. The necessary external funding was received from the Johnson Foundation in Racine, and Jack Christ was appointed director of the program. Christ had been a member of the English Department for several years, had served as associate director of College Relations, had taught courses in journalism, and had been one of the guiding spirits behind the Ten O'Clock Scholars (to be mentioned later). The program developed gradually and incrementally until the faculty voted unanimously to add Leadership and Organizational Values (acronymmed RIPLOV) to the curriculum; at this point RIPLOV consisted of three courses: 1) Leadership, Organization, and Values, 2) Groups, Organizations, and Institutions: Evolution and Revolution, and 3) Biographical Studies (Christ's doctoral dissertation at Pennsylvania had been on autobiography). After the addition of Departmental Studies and a Seminar in Leadership Studies, the faculty, in the spring of 1982, approved a minor called Leadership Studies. (A program of minors had been approved in 1974-75. Currently, the College offers 19 minors, most of them affiliated with a single department, but some, like Law and Society and Women's Studies, interdepartmental.) Leadership Studies proved to be a popular minor, graduating about five students per year; an equal number expanded the minor into a self-designed major. When funding by the Johnson Foundation expired, both faculty and trustees agreed that the College should support the program with its own money; a grant from the DeFrees Foundation helped in the transition.

The list of curricular changes, additions, and especially innovations during the Adams administration is impressive, perhaps more impressive than that of any other administration in Ripon's history. President Adams proposed several of these during an off-campus conference of trustees, students, faculty, and administrators at Camp Lucerne in Neshkoro in the late 60s; the College had been holding such conferences, usually during the Thanksgiving break, either at Camp Lucerne or Wingspread, the headquarters of the Johnson Foundation in Racine. Specifically, the president proposed a three-year degree, a self-designed major, and self-designed off-campus study. The first reduced the credits but increased the grade point required for graduation and stipulated that all courses must be taken at Ripon. The second allowed students to design their own majors, combining independent study with courses from various academic departments. The third provided an opportunity for a student to earn up to 16 credits on a special project undertaken off campus. All three probably enhance the College's image, but only the self-designed major proved very popular.

In the mid-60s, Dean Ashley attempted an experiment with residential seminars, the purpose being to discover whether living and learning in the same place was in any way more effective than living in one place (a residence hall) and taking classes in another (a classroom building). Incoming freshmen were invited to reside and take the same three courses (plus an elective) in Harwood (for women) and a section of Scott Hall (for men). It was hoped that the common experience of the groups would cause continued discussion of course material after a particular class ended. But the results were mixed, inconclusive, and almost impossible to measure, so the program was cancelled after two years. The *Days* theorized that "social pressure from friends and a fear of the 'academic stigma'" plus a "vague fear of isolation and loss of contact with present 'in-groups'" militated against the success of the experiment.[21]

Over a period of 10 years, Ripon made some changes in its grading system. Mention has already been made of pass-fail grades for certain courses in the fine arts, military science, and physical education in which students receive credits but not honor points. In 1967-68 a satisfactory-unsatisfactory grade option was introduced, its purpose being to encourage students to take courses in which they had a strong interest but were fearful of doing poorly. Juniors, seniors, and eventually sophomores were allowed to elect one course per semester but no more than a total of four on an S-U basis. Instructors submit the usual grades, which are then changed to S (A through C-) or U (D+ through F); however, students can now request conversion to regular grades, an option not available when the plan was first adopted. In the initial year of the option, 44 S-U grades were submitted (nine As, 17 Bs, 15 Cs, two Ds, and one F). In the following year, the faculty introduced another option, allowing students to drop a course with permission and to receive a grade of W; 395 Ws were recorded in 1969-70. The dates before which this option can be exercised have varied over the years. Finally, in 1978 the College converted from a five-point to a 12-point grading system by using pluses and minuses, a much fairer method.

In the mid-70s, Karl Beres '66 of the Mathematics Department conceived the idea of an on-going series of

Saturday morning programs to be called the Ten O'Clock Scholars. The first featured the Presidential Election of 1976, under the direction of George Miller of the History Department. Among the most interesting of subsequent programs were two which featured film adaptations and discussions of classic American short stories.   Jointly sponsored by the College and the Ripon Public Library and funded by the Wisconsin Humanities Committee, the two series were organized by William Schang of the English Department.

Beginning in 1972, the College sponsored an annual philosophy conference; the founding father was Robert Hannaford. A year later, Vance Kasten and William Woolley of the Philosophy and History Departments organized the yearly Liberal Arts Symposium.

The students themselves sometimes took the initiative. In the late 60s, they organized RAP (Ripon and Personality), a week-long program examining the total educational scene at the College. This led to a "Free University," which offered non-credit courses suggested by students and taught by both student and faculty volunteers. Content varied from occasional bull sessions to significant informal or experimental activity. Although short-lived, it was considered "a very real success" by President Adams.[22]

Anthropology first entered the curriculum in 1967-68; sociology was re-introduced shortly thereafter. The combined Anthropology-Sociology Department offers a major in anthropology and in sociology-anthropology as well as minors in anthropology and sociology. These additions were offset by the elimination of majors in classics, religion, and Russian upon the retirement of Sidney Goodrich, John Radomsky, and Chaplain Thompson; instruction in all three subjects was continued for a while on a part-time basis. Then in 1987 and 1988, endowed chairs were funded in religion and in classical studies and filled by Brian Smith and Eddie Lowry, Jr. A major in religion was re-established; classical studies were absorbed by a new Department of Romance and Classical Languages; Russian remains absent.

Beginning in 1971, the English Department and its required eight-hour course in Literature and Composition came under attack. In that year, a motion to suspend this course was defeated. But, when enrollment began to decline, the English Department, being the largest in the College, was a prime candidate for a staff reduction. However, reduction was not possible as long as the freshman English requirement remained. Before the consolidation of freshman literature and sophomore composition into one eight-hour freshman course in 1967, the English staff consisted of seven teachers. When reduced to six, the department still had continuing help from Dean Ashley and occasional help from Deans Harris and Tuttle. Even so, the freshman sections were too large for a course requiring lots of writing. The obvious solution was to spread the burden of teaching composition among several disciplines. This is exactly what the Educational Policy Committee recommended, using as its guideline a memorandum from Dean of Faculty Douglas Northrop. The committee defended its recommendation in a five-part rationale:

1) "Some existing positions, now used almost exclusively to teach writing in the English Department, can be transferred to other departments. In those other departments, the positions can be used both to maintain the strength of the major as well as to satisfy the writing requirement." 2) Courses in these departments, especially the humanities and social sciences, are already writing courses. 3) Veteran teachers of writing in other departments can teach writing as well as rookie English teachers fresh out of graduate school. 4) Teachers in these departments would become "less willing to accept trashy writing in upperclass student papers." 5) The proposal does not violate the intent of the present requirement, which teaches literature in order to give students something to write about; the change would simply give them something else to write about.[23]

A minority report complained that the "proposal restricts its definition of what counts as important language

skills to the production of logical arguments and exposition"
and "views aesthetic, figurative use of language—and therefore the aesthetic experience—[as] at best optional, but not
essential." Furthermore, the proposal "assumes that anyone
who has learned to write for academe is competent . . . to
teach good writing. This assumption is quite questionable."
The Student Senate agreed with the minority and forwarded
to the Educational Policy Committee its conviction "that the
faculty in other departments could not teach writing skills as
successfully as the faculty in the English Department. It is
also believed that the present English requirement is necessary in a liberal education. . . ."[24] Certain safeguards were
included in the proposal: faculty members who wished to
include composition in their courses had to submit evidence
of competence to do so, such as completion of a graduate-
level course in writing or submission of a "sampling of papers
which show the kind of feedback the instructor has provided
when helping students in prior courses."[25] Also, regularly
scheduled workshops were conducted by the English Department, although attendance was not required.

The new program was approved for the 1984-85
academic year; the English Department was reduced as was
the number of freshman English sections. Several departments, including some surprises such as art, biology, chemistry, military science, physical education, and physics,
offered "writing intensive" courses. Most students, however,
preferred to meet the writing requirement, partially at least,
through freshman English courses, but the department was
unable to accommodate all those that wished to do so. One
unfortunate consequence of the new policy was that, for the
first time in Ripon's history, students could graduate without
ever having studied literature at the college level. After the
lapse of a mandated two-year trial period, the faculty plugged
this gap by requiring all freshmen to take English 110 either
in the first or second semester before electing the "writing
intensive" courses in other departments. This new course
with the old title Literature and Composition emphasized

"reading and analyzing imaginative literature . . . integrated with the study of the writing process,"[26] thus meeting the minority report's objection. The English Department also achieved its long-cherished objective of limiting enrollment in freshman sections to the manageable number of 20.

One of the most remarkable features of the Ripon curriculum was the continued success of the humanities at a time when they were considered irrelevant to the modern world and were dying on the vine all over the country. For example, in 1978-79 there were 57 history majors, 43 English majors, and 26 philosophy majors in the pipeline.

In 1969-70, the ACM formed a "periodical bank" in Chicago. Each member college was asked to sell $50,000 worth of periodicals (Ripon succeeded in selling only $32,000) and contribute the money to the bank. The bank, in turn, used the money to assemble a collection of magazines on microfilm and microfiche, pages of which could be duplicated and sent upon request to individual students and faculty. Thus, each campus had relatively easy and quick access to more periodicals than were available in the separate libraries. But the bank lasted only three years because various state interlibrary loan systems had much larger collections and could provide materials at considerably less cost. Consequently, Ripon in 1972 joined the Wisconsin Interlibrary Services and somewhat later the Fox Valley Library Council.

Concern over the inadequacy of the library has been a constant in Ripon's history, the College comparing unfavorably in this area to most other ACM schools, especially those with larger general endowments as well as specific library endowments. Although well aware of this deficiency, no one—library staff, administration, trustees—had moved aggressively enough to remedy it. Dissatisfaction peaked in the spring of 1978. Two students appeared before the board at its April meeting, and a group accosted the trustees in the Rodman lobby to protest low budget priorities for the library. At the same time, President Adams reported that Lane

Library was definitely the College's "single most serious problem" and that $200,000 were needed immediately for acquisitions as well as a $500,000 endowment "to keep up from year to year."[27] Dean Northrop secured the services of two consultants, who visited the campus in November, 1978, and April, 1979. Their report recommended less professional staff time on clerical chores, more effective use of student assistants, installation of computer terminals and of a security system to reduce theft of books, an increase from $45 to $65-70 per student for acquisitions, relocation of the reference and periodicals collections to make them more accessible, conversion from the Dewey to the Library of Congress classification system, and use of the Ohio Conference Library Center's computerized cataloging service, the latter two recommendations being designed to reduce an enormous backlog of uncataloged books. With the help of a hefty increase in the library budget and grants from the Demmer Foundation and the National Endowment for the Humanities, most of the reforms were accomplished, although some, like the conversion to Library of Congress cataloging, are long-term projects.

The fine arts continued to flourish. In 1976, two original portraits by Sir Anthony Van Dyke were deeded to the College by Lillian Beckman, previously the wife of Marc Rojtman, President of the J. I. Case Company of Racine. They hang in the lobby of the Rodman Center, making Ripon, according to President Adams, "among the few small colleges in the country to hold and have on display works by one of the world's great artists."[28] Beginning in 1972, a chamber music series, the brainchild of Raymond Stahura of the Music Department, brought professional musicians to the campus and still does; this series provides a different kind of entertainment and enrichment from that offered by the larger scale programs of the Fine Arts Series. Another member of the Music Department, Douglas Morris, went half time in 1980 and founded the Green Lake Festival of Music, which brings summer concerts to Ripon, Green Lake, Oshkosh,

Appleton, Beaver Dam, and other Wisconsin communities.

With funds provided by the Rockefeller Foundation and the federal government, the College in 1968 established a Transitional Year Program to help promising but disadvantaged students bridge the gap between high school and college. Most, but not all, were blacks. They were housed in freshman dorms, participated in freshman athletics, and took courses in English, mathematics, and study skills. Directed by Chaplain Thompson and James Bowditch of the English Department, the program lasted for three years and was remarkably successful in placing its participants as regular freshmen in Ripon and other ACM colleges. There were several spin-offs: courses in Black Literature and in Afro-American History and Culture; the Black Experience, a lecture series funded by the Sperry and Hutchison Foundation; a mostly black group called Student Organization for Understanding and Love (acronymmed SOUL), which sponsored, among other activities, a gospel choir. In 1970, the College purchased the Ihland house on Woodside Avenue next to the former Duffie House site; it became the Black Cultural, Research, and Educational Center.

Chaplain Thompson was also instrumental in establishing the Educational Development Program, which provides free academic assistance, counseling, and tutoring for low-income students; funds originally came from the federal government via the ACM office in Chicago. Thompson ran the program for several years until it was taken over by Betty Christ in 1985; an application for funds designed by Christ had tied for first among 800 institutions in 1984.

In 1976, the Ripon College Press, another brainchild of Doss, was founded. Among other works, it has published the proceedings of the Philosophy Conference and of the Liberal Arts Symposium as well as a college text, *Elementary Logic for Philosophy Students*, by Doss. It also serves as publisher of this history.

Whatever evaluation is made of the Adams admini-

stration must take into account that no other period in
Ripon's history saw so much enrichment, expansion, and
innovation in the curriculum and in co-curricular programs.

NOTES TO CHAPTER XVI
BERNARD S. ADAMS 1966-1985

[1]*Alumnus*, Aug., 1967, 6.

[2]*Ibid.*, Feb., 1967.

[3]*Ibid.*

[4]*College Days*, Oct. 14, 1966, 3.

[5]*Alumnus*, Feb., 1967.

[6]*College Days*, Sept. 8, 1966, 5 and Sept. 30, 1966, 6.

[7]*Ripon College Magazine*, Spring, 1980, 8.

[8]*Trustees' Minutes*, Oct. 6, 1982, 13.

[9]*Ibid.*, Feb. 2, 1985, Attachment E.

[10]*Ibid.*, July 31, 1982, 17-18.

[11]*College Days*, Feb. 25, 1966, 4; see also issues for Nov. 5, 12, and 19, 1965.

[12]*President's Report 1966-67*, 10.

[13]*College Days*, Jan. 22, 1971, 2.

[14]*Faculty Minutes*, Jan. 20, 1970.

[15]Enrollment figures vary according to methods of counting and the source consulted. The figures cited here are taken from the President's Annual Reports.

[16]*Faculty Minutes*, Feb. 5, 1980, 4.

[17]*Ibid.*, 12 and 13.

[18]*Ibid.*, Feb. 12, 1980, 1.

[19]*Ibid.*, March 4, 1980, 2.

[20]*Trustees' Minutes*, Oct. 11, 1980, 4.

[21]*College Days*, Nov. 18, 1966, 1.

[22]*President's Report 1969-70*, 3-4.

[23]*Faculty Minutes*, Dec. 6, 1983, "Rationale."

[24]*Ibid.*, "Minority Report."

[25]*Ibid.*, "Rationale."

[26]*1986-87 Catalog*, 54-55.

[27]*Trustees' Minutes*, April 29, 1978, 11.

[28]*Ripon College Magazine*, March, 1977, 1.

CHAPTER XVII

UPS AND DOWNS: II
BERNARD S. ADAMS
1966-1985

*As I leave, I want all of you to know that
I always will be intensely interested in
and committed to the college that I
have come to love as if she were my
own alma mater. I shall "keep the
faith" and I urge all of you to do the
same. And so, for Natalie and myself,
this is "hail and farewell"; but farewell,
I remind you, is not good-bye.*

Bernard Adams

In 1974, halfway through the Adams administration,
Robert Ashley resigned as dean, having held the position
since 1955. He had become disenchanted with the rising tide
of "collegiality," which was swamping the intercollegiate
shores. Collegiality meant government by committees rather
than by individuals. It meant that everyone had to get into
the act, that nothing could be done without the approval of
all segments of the college community—administrators,
faculty, students, trustees, sometimes even alumni. Theoretically at least, collegiality made sense, and it also made
lots of people feel important. But the decisions reached were
not necessarily the wisest ones. There is a lot of truth in the
old joke that a camel is a horse designed by a committee. And
it was a tremendously time-consuming way of doing business; decisions that a president and a dean could make in five
minutes now consumed five months.

A case in point is the selection of a commencement theme and of honorary degree recipients. In what Ashley came to consider the good old days, he would suggest a theme, the president would say, "Okay, whom shall we invite?" and that was it. Under collegiality, the senior class would be asked to suggest themes, not a bad idea actually, since it was their Commencement. After a faculty committee had approved one of these themes, everyone was invited to nominate honoraries. These were evaluated by the faculty committee, and a suggested list, together with the theme, would be forwarded to the trustee Committee on Instruction and Appointments. They, in turn, would make a recommendation to the full board. Sometimes, the committee or the board would disapprove the theme; more often they would strike certain candidates from the list, usually because of their political philosophies. Either way, the whole matter could be referred back to the faculty committee for reconsideration. In one instance, the faculty slightly altered the wording of the theme and sent it to the trustees once more; this time it was accepted.

Anyhow, Ashley resigned in the spring of 1974 and became a full-time member of the English Department. He was replaced as dean by Henry F. Pommer after an extensive search by a combined administration-alumni-faculty-student-trustee committee. Pommer was a graduate of Pennsylvania, with both advanced degrees from Yale. He had taught at Swarthmore, Cornell (New York), and Allegheny and had served as dean of the faculty at Cedar Crest College in Allentown, Pennsylvania. Although his degrees were all in English and he taught literature at Ripon, he did not join the English Department but was given the title professor at large. He did not remain as dean long enough to make much of a mark, being hospitalized in the spring of 1977 with a serious heart illness. When released, he wished to continue as dean, but President Adams thought the job too strenuous for a recovered heart patient and Pommer reluctantly resigned.

Then ensued a game of musical chairs. Douglas A. Northrop, a product of Wesleyan (Connecticut) and Chicago, who had taught at Ripon since 1960 and was slated to become chairman of the English Department, assumed the deanship; Pommer took his spot in English; and Ashley, who had pinch-hit in the administration during Pommer's illness, became department chairman. The selection of a dean by presidential appointment rather than by a search committee caused some faculty grumbling, but Adams did not wish to appoint an acting dean during a prolonged search for a permanent one. However, Adams promised the faculty that the usual procedure would be followed in the future; he did not ask for a formal endorsement, but received assurance that his choice was fully acceptable.

Backtracking to the early years of the Adams administration, the narrative of "collegiality" began in 1967-68, when two students were added as voting members to seven faculty committees, except for those which considered personnel action or matters that affect the faculty alone. A year later, three students began serving as voting members of the faculty; similar status was awarded to two faculty and two students on the trustees' Committee on Student Life as well as the Committee on Instruction and Appointments; two voting faculty members were given similar privileges on the board's Finance Committee; furthermore, the president was authorized to invite one or more faculty and students to attend and speak at board meetings on issues of direct concern to faculty and students. Still another year later, students elected to the Student Senate and to faculty committees were welcomed to faculty meetings without the privilege of voting. In October, 1971, the trustees agreed to allow a Special Graduate Trustee, elected by the student body from a list of graduating seniors nominated by the Senate, to attend board meetings for one year with full voting rights and responsibilities.

However, all did not go smoothly with these arrangements. On February 23, 1971, the faculty had defeated a motion to allow a group of students 10 minutes to express their views and to attend the meeting as observers. A much more serious and atypical confrontation occurred when approximately 30 students other than the authorized representative of the *College Days* and the three voting student members showed up for the March 9 faculty meeting; they wished to discuss a new class attendance policy being considered by a faculty committee. After the faculty voted to deny admission, President Adams asked the students to leave. They did so, but shortly afterwards filed through the upper doors of Farr Hall Auditorium and "calmly . . . settled back in their chairs."[1] The president once again asked them to leave. When they did not, the faculty adjourned.

Next came a flurry of recommendations from the faculty's Committee on Committees: 1) "If the Faculty is prevented from conducting its business at its scheduled faculty meetings, the power to conduct such business is delegated to the duly elected or appointed faculty committees." 2) Student members of faculty committees allowed to attend faculty meetings concerning committee business may talk but not vote. 3) Certain committee meetings can be declared open to all faculty and students, again with a "talking but not vote" restriction. 4) "The Faculty invites all duly elected members of the Student Senate and all student members of faculty committees to attend faculty meetings as non-voting participants."[2] The faculty passed the entire package 42-22; no further problems arose.

About this time, the faculty began agitating for the right to choose its own presiding officer in lieu of the president of the College. Specifically, they wished to elect from their tenured colleagues a chairman of the faculty to serve for two years because of "a conflict of interest between the demands of the chair and the needs of the administration to pursue administrative proposals or take positions on other proposals being considered by the faculty."[3] A month later, President Adams informed the faculty that, to his surprise, the trustees had declined to act on the faculty's request largely because they considered the chairmanship "symbolic." Said Adams, "They want to think of the President as both representative of the Board of Trustees to the Faculty *and* the representative of the Faculty to the Board of Trustees."[4] Some faculty thought the board's rationale flimsy and wanted to proceed to an election anyhow; a motion to do so was referred to the Committee on Committees. Two months later, the committee simply recommended that the proposal be resubmitted; the faculty agreed.

Despite a request from the president that the trustees accommodate the faculty in order "to avoid a confrontation over something . . . comparatively unimportant," the board agreed only to a compromise: "The Faculty may elect from among its members, at times to be determined by the Faculty, a 'Deputy Chairman' who, at the discretion of the President, shall preside over faculty meetings or portions thereof." Their reasoning was threefold: 1) reluctance to change the By-Laws, 2) concern for "accountability," and 3) fear of "dividing the College and the leadership of the College into two groups."[5] The faculty rejected the compromise.

Early in 1974, another appeal from the faculty to the board met a similar fate. At a February 28 meeting closed to students, the faculty forwarded to the trustees a petition, drawn up by John Livingston of the Economics Department and signed by 83 teachers, requesting the addition of two voting faculty to the Board of Trustees, a proposal similar to one designed by Dean Tenney back in the Kuebler administration. This, too, was rejected by the board as "a confusion of roles and not the best way to bring about communication."[6] Collegiality apparently had its limits.

Even the students enjoyed a minor brouhaha with the trustees, though it seemed largely to have been based on misunderstandings. At the April, 1978, board meeting, President Adams reported the receipt of two letters from three students complaining that communication between students and trustees was minimal. The first letter, dated March

27 and signed by a single student, stated that "the student body's view of the Board of Trustees [is] absolutely negative" because "the Trustees have created the impression that they don't care about the students *at all.*"[7] Only three trustees had accepted invitations to eat with students on Saturday evening during the winter meeting. Adams replied that two students had met with the Instruction and Appointments Committee on Friday evening. Furthermore, by Saturday evening, most of the trustees had left the campus. Adams pointed out that the seniors had been granted the privilege of electing the Special Graduate Trustee, that four students were serving on trustee committees, and that the president and president-elect of the Senate as well as the Special Graduate Trustee-Elect had been invited to attend the spring meeting. In fact, he said, "There is more student-trustee communication at Ripon than at any other college of which I am aware. . . . I was . . . much surprised by the vitriolic tone and the obvious inaccuracies."[8]

After the merger of Congregational Churches with Evangelical and Reformed Denominations to create the United Church of Christ, the General Synod of that body issued a "Statement on Meaning, Purpose, and Standards of the Relationship among Colleges, Academies and the United Church of Christ," which attempted to define the relationship between the UCC and the 30 colleges and four academies belonging to the UCC's Council for Higher Education. President Adams asked the faculty to investigate whether the "Statement" contained "implications" for curricular policy or for faculty and general institutional "prerogatives" and to reaffirm the relationship between the College and the church. This was a very touchy subject, since it impinged on the whole question of academic freedom. A resolution proposing "reaffirmation with at least tacit endorsement of the 'Statement'" lost by a large margin. Another resolution to dissolve the relationship entirely was barely defeated. Finally, in a very close vote, the faculty adopted a fourfold resolution issued by the Educational Policy Committee: 1) The "Statement" is "a highly 'liberal' document," which does not "constrain" the faculty in developing the curriculum or limit "the autonomy or authority of the Board"; 2) nevertheless, the "Statement" should not be "adopted, endorsed, or acknowledged in any formal fashion" since it "sets forth a particular world view" and "a liberal arts college ought to remain open to *all* avenues to truth"; 3) still, neither the committee nor the faculty objects to the "continuing relation" between college and church re-established back in 1958 and reaffirmed in 1969; 4) finally, although college publications would still publicize this relationship, they should also stress Ripon's "willingness to enter into other similar relationships." With one dissenting vote, the trustees accepted the faculty's recommendations. This was entirely acceptable to the United Church, which had not asked for adoption of the "Statement," which is considered merely "a kind of 'explanation' as to what the relationship means."[9] Carleton, Grinnell, Beloit, and Franklin and Marshall took the same position as Ripon; 25 colleges approved full endorsement.

Meanwhile, Ripon's administrative structure was being reorganized. In 1979, Dean Northrop became dean of faculty instead of dean of the College. Two years later, a fourth vice presidency was created with Professor of Psychology Robert H. Young becoming Dean of Students, the deans of men and women now reporting to him rather than to Dean Northrop. This move, which had been recommended by a Long-Range Planning Committee in 1977 and even earlier than that by Dean Ashley, was accompanied by some controversy, not over Young's qualifications, which were unquestionable, but over the circumstances and timing of the appointment. In the first place, it roughly coincided with and was perhaps precipitated by the resignation of Stephen

Gould, Associate Dean of Students.   Gould had told the
College Days:

> I don't want to work anymore in an administrative
> structured environment where you have to answer to
> a number of people. The administration needs to take
> the initiative in more cases instead of sitting back and
> waiting for a crisis to arrive or a group of people to get
> upset or disturbed. . . .   In many ways the concerns
> of the student personnel area appear not to be a high
> priority to the administration.[10]

As a matter of fact, the appointment of Young was
designed to address the problems mentioned by Gould.
Among its purposes were to take the president out of the
appeals route from decisions made by the deans of men and
women, to get quicker action, and eventually to eliminate
their positions. Although Dean Northrop stated that "Young's
appointment in no way reflects upon the job that Harris and
Tuttle have done or are doing,"[11] that is how it was perceived
by many members of the college community and privately by
Harris and Tuttle themselves. Dean Tuttle told the *Days* that
she knew as little about the matter as anyone else. President
Adams admitted that the two deans had "minimal" input, but
that both were informed, thought the idea "splendid," and
had reservations only about appointing a dean of students
without a degree in student personnel administration. President Adams stated that there had been no need for a
nationwide talent search since Young's academic discipline
(psychology) was "pretty ideal for this kind of job."[12] Ironically, the same issue of the *College Days* which announced
the appointment of Dean Young also informed its readers
that Dean Harris had received the Scott Goodnight Award
"for outstanding performance as a Dean."[13] (See Chapter
XV.)

During a Senate meeting called at Adams' request on

April 13, 1981, the president admitted that he had not solicited any student input on the position or the individual appointed, but he recalled that there had been a great deal of community input in 1977, when the idea was first broached. The Senate voted its disapproval of the manner of the search by a 19-2-5 vote. A *Days* editorial summed it all up as follows:

> In conclusion, there are really few reasons for anyone to be against the position of Vice President and Dean of Students or the appointment to that position. However, there are a number of reasons backing disappointment of the swift and silent manner in which this position and appointment came to be.[14]

Harris and Tuttle continued shortly as deans of men and women. With Harris' sudden death in 1984, both positions were abolished and Tuttle became dean of student campus life.

In the fall of 1980, the faculty finally came round to former Dean Ashley's conviction that the College was "over-committeed." The Faculty Development Committee was instructed to "reduce significantly the number of faculty committees and the amount of time faculty members spend on committee work."[15] As a result, five major committees were established: 1) Educational Policy, 2) Academic Standards, 3) Faculty Appointments (later changed to Promotion and Tenure), 4) Faculty Development, and 5) Faculty Advisory Council, consisting of a representative from each of the previous four committees and an at-large member. The Administrative Council, composed of the president, the four vice presidents, and the director of admissions was retained. The two councils, plus five undergraduates representing student organizations, constituted the Community Council. Greater authority was given to the committees and to administrators so that faculty meetings were less cluttered with trivia. For instance, minor curricular changes could be made by the dean of faculty and reported to the Educational Policy Committee. Major changes were forwarded to the committee and later listed as either information or action items on the faculty agenda; if it wished, the faculty could overrule information actions, but rarely chose to do so. The admission of new students and the dismissal of students with poor academic records, previously the prerogative of the Committee on Admissions and Academic Standards, were turned over to the Admissions Office and the dean of students, respectively. Faculty meetings, previously held at least once a month, were greatly reduced in number.

Before proceeding to the resignation of President Adams, a few odds and ends need to be cleared from the board. During the 1965-85 double decade, the College undertook several fund-raising campaigns, some general and others designed for specific purposes such as construction and renovation of buildings; most met their goals, although none succeeded in creating an endowment suitable for an institution of Ripon's size and quality. The generally accepted rule of thumb was that endowment ought to be two-and-a-half-times a college's annual budget. In 1981-82, when Ripon's endowment was $6.56 million, it should have been approximately $24 million; two years later, it was only $8,413,282; when Adams resigned it was $9,353,733, next to last in the ACM. Annual gifts, both restricted and unrestricted, totaled $2,576,502 in 1984-85. Ripon's small number of graduates and their relative lack of wealth severely limited the alumni fund. However, the percentage of donors was remarkable, frequently the highest in the ACM; the national average was about 22 percent, but Ripon's was often twice that. When one considers the College's monetary handicaps, its financial stability seems all the more surprising. The explanation lies in the fact that Ripon has always operated with extraordinary efficiency, especially under such astute business managers as Wilbur Hannon and Kenneth Cartier. In 1973-74, the College recorded its 18th consecutive year in the black. Then came two years in the red, followed by six in the black, and then in 1983-84, by another in the red. The balanced budgets were, of course, accomplished by building gift income into the operating budget; if that had not been necessary, Ripon's endowment would have grown much more swiftly.

The academic year 1974-75 marked a turning point in the fortunes of the Adams administration; at that time, as previously stated, enrollment dipped below 1,000, never to attain that figure again. At one time, President Adams had confidently predicted an institution of 1,200-1,500. When it became apparent that this was a pipe dream, everyone was shocked and surprised; they became even more so as enrollment dropped more or less steadily to the low 800s in the next 10 years. Of course, demographers had predicted a decrease in the college-age population. But few had foreseen the rise in both the quality and popularity of public institutions. Because of their low fees, the state schools had always posed a threat, especially for those wishing to become teachers. To use one example, Oshkosh Normal School did not offer much of a challenge to Ripon. But when Oshkosh Normal changed to Oshkosh State Teachers College to Oshkosh State College to Oshkosh State University to the University of Wisconsin-Oshkosh, the competition became critical. The same phenomenon occurred out of state, especially in the East, where the private liberal arts colleges and private universities had reigned supreme for centuries and the states put their money into agricultural schools. If a student could not get into a prestigious private eastern college, he would much prefer to become a Ripon Redman than a Mass Aggie or a Connecticut Aggie; he did not feel the same way about attending the University of Massachusetts or the University of Connecticut. And these universities compounded the problem by

opening branches all over their respective states. Furthermore, there occurred both a quantitative and qualitative
ripple effect: with the diminishing college-age population,
students who came to Ripon because they could not get into
Carleton or Grinnell, Amherst or Williams, discovered they
could now secure admission to these schools. With endowments ranging from $50 to $75 million, the Carletons and the
Amhersts could offer more scholarships and superior facilities. And when state governments began offering financial
aid, some limited it to students attending institutions within
the state.

So, Ripon suddenly found itself in a new ball game.
Competition for limited funds became fierce: do you spend
it on faculty salaries, larger scholarships and grants-in-aid,
more admissions counselors, renovation of facilities? One
solution is to raise tuition and fees, but this often had the
effect of driving students away. Another is to eliminate
departments, as was done with classics, religion, and Russian, or reduce the size of departments—in fact, the faculty
declined from a high of 82 in both 1970-71 and 1971-72 to
a low of 64 in 1984-85. But this emasculated some departments and greatly reduced the overall variety of course offerings.

During periods of rising enrollments in the 1960s
under both Pinkham and Adams, the faculty had become
accustomed to very generous raises, and Ripon had occasionally ranked quite high on both ACM and national AAUP
rating scales. In May, 1967, the Associated Colleges reported
that Ripon ranked second to Carleton in average base
salaries; during the same month, AAUP ranked Ripon second
only to the University of Wisconsin-Madison within the state.
However, when Ripon's minimal fringe benefits were included, the picture was much less rosy. Ultimately, in 1969,
the president was forced to confess that "for the last two years
salary improvement has been a low-priority item. . . . We
have 'coasted' on the achievements of 1964-65 through
1966-67 when Ripon salaries reached levels comparable to

those at the best colleges in the country."[16] Responding to President Nixon's request for a nationwide freeze, the trustees froze salaries in 1970-71, 1971-72, and 1972-73. In all three instances, however, the freezes were eventually lifted. A more serious crisis arose in 1974 when it became clear to everyone that the faculty's standard of living was being seriously eroded by inflation due largely to the Arab oil embargo and resultant steep increases in fuel prices. The trustees directed the administration "to prepare immediately a proposal for adjustments in salaries and wages . . . to respond to . . . the massive increase in the cost of living."[17] Money to finance these adjustments would come from reserves "built up partly as a result of the faculty and staff salaries not having kept pace with increases in the Consumer Price Index"; this would be a way of "expressing gratitude to the faculty and staff for allowing the College to accumulate the reserves."[18]

These reserves were a particularly sore point with faculty members. Year after year, the College would "cry wolf," predict difficulty in balancing the budget, and use this difficulty as a justification for extreme conservatism in raising salaries. But year after year, Ripon would accumulate a surplus and plow it back into the reserve fund instead of applying it to salaries. With considerable justification, faculty members felt that they were being "used" to create surpluses. In 1973-74, however, the board did withdraw a hefty sum from the reserves and distribute it in across-the-board raises.

In his 1977-78 *President's Report*, Adams noted with pride that Ripon's average salary exceeded Lawrence's, but went on to say:

We are still trying to catch up. . . . It is discouraging to know that the priority given to faculty salaries in recent years (to the detriment of other expenditures areas also essential to a high quality educational program) has resulted only in more ground being lost. We are doing better than many of our peers . . . but that fact is of little comfort when it becomes time to pay the family bills.[19]

It is clear that President Adams was not insensitive to the faculty's plight, and he tried to ease the burden. He introduced an early retirement plan, designed by Livingston of the Economics Department, whereby teachers could retire at age 62 with pension benefits equal to those received by faculty who served until normal retirement time; money to make this possible came from hiring replacements at lower rank and salary. Rules regulating sabbatical leaves were eased so that professors could remain on campus instead of incurring the additional expense of studying elsewhere. Fringe benefits were increased, though they still were minimal. Hughes House became the headquarters of the Ripon College Society of Scholars under generous rental terms. But the president faced insuperable obstacles, not the least of which was a Board of Trustees even more financially conservative than he.

Meanwhile, the Faculty Advisory Council was becoming increasingly militant. In a 1981 report to the faculty, the council stated:

When needed for administrative purposes, money is available. . . . *Conclusion: Your Declining Real Income is Policy, Not Necessity.* It seems a reasonable conclusion that the continuing impoverishment of the faculty is not a budgetary or financial necessity. Rather it is college policy formulated and adopted by the President, Vice Presidents, and Trustees.[20]

For the next few years, the same story kept repeating itself. The faculty would request raises sometimes as high as 10 percent, the president would support the percentage or diminish it slightly, and the board would agree on an even lower figure. The teaching staff became increasingly frustrated, pessimistic, even bitter, and certainly resentful over what they perceived as "a trustee attitude." After the board's midwinter 1982 meeting, Seth Singleton, who had attended along with Librarian Sarah McGowan, told the faculty he had "left the meeting dismayed," convinced that faculty compensation is to be "minimalized." The faculty "is viewed as a labor force. . . . Any hope for improvement in the foreseeable future is . . . 'pie in the sky.'"[21] The Faculty Advisory Council estimated the loss of faculty purchasing power over the past decade to be 20 percent. Despite occasional dramatic improvements in Ripon's salary scale, the College remained generally in the bottom third of the ACM. President Adams' views on the foreign language requirement and the adoption of business courses had created considerable ill will although these views were shared by many administrators and faculty. Further, the faculty generally began to believe that the president had presented their case to the trustees with considerably less than the enthusiasm it deserved. At any rate, matters reached a crisis during the 1983-84 academic year.

President Adams announced his resignation to the Board of Trustees on April 28, 1984. Typically, Ripon's official records are vague about presidential resignations: details are hard to come by and often seem contradictory. Furthermore, in this instance, many actions, particularly those taken by the faculty, are veiled in a secrecy that would incite the envy of the CIA. According to the Executive Committee minutes for June 28, 1984, Adams had requested at the April 28 meeting "that the Trustees undertake planning for presidential succession";[22] apparently, Adams made his request in executive session, since the minutes contain no mention of it. However, both trustee and faculty records clearly indicate that the long-simmering disagreements among the faculty, the president, and the trustees over salaries climaxed and exploded in the winter of 1983-84.

On December 6, 1983, the faculty, with no dissenting votes and one abstention, approved a unanimous recommendation from its Advisory Council for a 10 percent increase in average compensation per annum over a five-year period, which would move Ripon from next to last to the middle of the ACM salary scale. This resolution later received the unanimous backing of both the Community Council (composed of administrators, faculty, and students) and the Administrative Council (composed of the president and the five senior administrators). Data supporting the resolution were mailed to the Finance and Executive Committees of the board, drawing a rebuke from Adams, who quoted a statement in the By-Laws of the College that "All matters originating with the faculty which require Board consideration or review shall be first presented to the president."[23] Although the faculty believed that Adams intended to support the 10 percent increase, he, in fact, recommended only eight percent to the trustee Finance Committee; this committee on January 23, 1984, accepted his recommendation by a 6-3 vote. At the full board meeting on February 4, Chairman Abendroth distributed a mimeographed alternative, which he said had the approval of the president and several trustees, proposing a five percent increase. Exercising his prerogative as chairman, Abendroth explained that the Finance Committee report would be placed on the floor and then the alternative motion introduced as an amendment, thus assuring that the latter would be considered first; he also suggested that neither motion be amended, although discussion would be encouraged. During the ensuing debate, Dean Northrop expressed his support for the higher figure. When the tally was finally taken, the five percent amendment lost by an 11-12 vote, with the president voting in its favor; this left the eight-percent Finance Committee motion on the floor. It too lost, by a 10-12-1 count; the president did not support the committee despite the fact that its members were following his own recommendation. Obviously, the trustees had reached an impasse, so the chairman announced that the administration would undertake further study and report to the Executive Committee at an early date. The faculty ultimately received an average raise of six percent, but it is doubtful that any percentage less than eight or 10 would have satisfied the teaching staff. Clearly, President Adams was in an untenable position and, having lost the trust of the teaching staff, could no longer effectively lead the College.

As is usual in such circumstances, public pronouncements skirted the substantive issues. In the *President's Report for 1983-84*, Adams said he had told the trustees that his tenure at Ripon had been three times longer than the national average, that he "wanted to move on to new challenges and a new environment and that some time before July of 1985 seemed best, as regards timing, both for me and the College." He also stated that the coming years were "a most propitious time for a presidential search because the year just past . . . has seen Ripon reach a record level of strength as regards both its educational effectiveness and its financial condition."[24] On December 6, the *Days* quoted the president, "'I plain want to do something else'" and commented, "He is admittedly tired of administration, and in the future hopes to be able to get a job involving a combination of teaching of English . . . and some administrative responsibilities at an institution larger than Ripon."[25]

At a June 28 meeting, the Executive Committee considered three statements passed by the faculty on May 1. The first of these, "Faculty Statement on Presidential Leadership," expressed the faculty's "appreciation to the Board of Trustees in anticipation of the Board's decision to seek new leadership in the presidency," assured the board of its "continuing loyalty," offered "assistance in establishing criteria and procedures to be used in searching for and selecting a new president," and described the qualities desired in its next leader.[26] The second document, "Faculty Statement on Presidential Search and Selection," asserted the availability of the Faculty Council "for appointment to a joint committee on the role of the president at Ripon College and to a joint search committee."[27] A third document, "Faculty Concerns Regarding Presidential Selection Procedures," urged "progressive openness as the field of candidates narrows" and expressed the hope that, although the candidates' credential files should be available only to the Search Committee, summaries should be circulated to the entire college community. In its concluding paragraph, this document became quite specific about "the final stages of the search": each candidate should be brought to the campus for at least three or four days and "should make a presentation of educational views and philosophy to the College Community." Additionally, "General discussion sessions of approximately two hours' duration should be scheduled . . . with faculty from each of the major academic areas" (fine arts, humanities, natural sciences, and social sciences, plus the library) as well as with students, administrators, and staff.[28]

Predictably, the Executive Committee, with the concurrence of other trustees present, rejected by unanimous vote the "Faculty Statement on Presidential Leadership," "particularly noting disapproval of the implication in the statement that it was the Board's decision to seek new leadership." The chairman was asked to remind "the College community that the Board neither requested nor sought the President's resignation and that the request that the Board undertake planning for his successor was the President's alone."[29] A previously appointed *ad hoc* committee on the role of the president was disbanded, and Chairman Abendroth was "authorized to appoint a search and screening committee composed of four trustees, four faculty members, a senior administrator, a student, a representative of the Alumni Association, and a public member,"[30] who turned out to be Wesley Hotchkiss, a former trustee; the faculty members were to be selected by the Faculty Council on Presidential Search and Selection or its chairman from the members of that council. The Search and Screening Committee was directed to prepare an unranked list of three to five candidates, from which list a committee of five trustees would recommend one candidate to the full board.

At the trustees' winter meeting of 1985, Adams announced his appointment as president of Fort Lewis College, a public four-year liberal arts college in Durango, Colorado, effective March 15. He attributed his appointment, in part, to Ripon's stature and reputation. The trustees' minutes summarized Adams' concluding remarks as follows:

> Fort Lewis aspires to be the premier public liberal arts institution in the Southwest and quite consciously sought a president whose experience at a similar institution would help that college realize its potential. . . . He went on to say that over half of Ripon's living alumni had graduated since his first commencement in 1967 and that it was contributing to the growth of these splendid young people that "made it all worthwhile. . . ." Finally, he said that the Adamses always would feel a part of "all things Ripon" and he thanked the trustees for helping to make his 18 years "so very special."[31]

In response, Abendroth proposed a resolution reaffirming "the esteem, respect, and affection it holds for Bernard S. Adams and publicly acknowledges its deep gratitude for the distinguished contributions he has made to Ripon College during his eighteen and a half years as president."[32] A second, by acclamation, and a standing ovation followed. Some months earlier, the chairman of the board had written in the *Ripon College Magazine* that "Dr. Adams' leadership not only has strengthened Ripon's educational program and financial operations but has resulted in a reputation for quality and effectiveness recognized throughout the Middle West."[33]

Back on the campus, the faculty emeriti still living in Ripon feted the Adamses at a banquet in February and presented them with a portrait of the president's home painted by Professor Erwin Breithaupt. On the seventh day of the same month, the Student Senate passed a resolution to present the president and his wife with "a plaque and scrapbook of newspaper articles and photos over the years."[34] The plaque read as follows:

> We, the students of Ripon College deeply appreciate more than 18 years of faithful, devoted and valuable service (1966-1985) given by Dr. Bernard S. Adams as president of the college and wish him and his wife, Natalie, the very best for the future.[35]

At the request of the seniors, Adams returned for the 1985 Commencement to present their diplomas. His portrait, painted by George Rapp from photographs, was unveiled during the intermission of a concert by the Jazz Ensemble on the evening of the previous day. Rapp had also done the portrait of President Hughes, father of Rapp's wife, Eleanor. In the 1984-85 annual report, Dean Northrop added his words of praise:

> Mr. Adams' eighteen plus years as president at Ripon College were marked by significant diversification in the academic program, increased opportunities in student services, and major growth in both the endowment and the level of annual giving. Mr. Adams' open and flexible style served the College particularly well during the decade of student unrest. His willingness to meet with students, his ability to find non-confrontational solutions, and his reasonableness helped to diffuse many potentially disruptive situations.[36]

Particularly in view of all they had gone through, the Adamses made a gracious and dignified exit. The president's valedictory, entitled "Hail and Farewell" and printed in the March, 1985, issue of the *Magazine*, read in part:

This is a *great* college, fully deserving of all the good things that have come her way in the past and of all the good things that will come in the future.

I know of no college president anywhere who could have been happier in his student and alumni relationships. . . .

As I leave, I want all of you to know that I always will be intensely interested in and committed to the college that I have come to love as if she were my own *alma mater*. I shall "keep the faith" and I urge all of you to do the same. And so, for Natalie and myself, this is "hail and farewell"; but farewell, I remind you, is not good-bye.[37]

In the same issue, the *Magazine* asked the Adamses how they would remember Ripon College.   Mrs. Adams replied, "As eighteen of the best years of our lives! . . .   Ripon is quite a place."[38] On May 28, Mrs. Adams wrote her two children a letter in which she said: "There are hurts along with the joys, but . . . one would quickly, even eagerly, say 'yes' to the opportunity to serve Ripon all over again. May God bless this College and all who are a part of her fibre in the years ahead as in the past. . . ."[39]

Bernard Adams presided over his last faculty meeting on February 26, 1985. His tenure at Fort Lewis was a short one; he resigned on November 19, 1986, effective June 30, 1987, after unearthing financial problems which had existed previous to his administration. Although he had not created any of these problems, they were discovered "on his watch" and he felt compelled to resign. Since August 29, 1988, he has been serving as vice president for resources at Goodwill Industries in Colorado Springs.

Despite its sad ending, the Adams administration was one of solid achievement. Average faculty salaries increased from $11,009, to $26,555; endowment, from $2,716,615 to $9,853,733; combined endowment and plant values, from $16,702,833 to $31,884,384.[40] The campus building program was virtually completed so that Ripon now has practically all the facilities it needs. But Adams' chief legacy was a greatly expanded, diversified, and enriched curriculum.

NOTES TO CHAPTER XVII
BERNARD S. ADAMS 1966-1985

[1]*College Days*, March 12, 1971, [1].

[2]*Faculty Minutes*, March 16, 1971, 1-5.

[3]*Ibid.*, Sept. 19, 1972, 3.

[4]*Ibid.*, Oct. 17, 1972, 2-3.

[5]*Trustees' Minutes*, Jan. 6, 1973, 14-18.

[6]*Ibid.*, Oct. 11, 1974, 11.

[7]*Trustees' Minutes*, April 29, 1978, "Attachment A," April 17, 1978, 2.

[8]*Ibid.*, 3.

[9]*Ibid.*, Feb. 6, 1982, "Attachment H"; see also *Trustees' Minutes*, July, 1981, Oct. 23, 1981, July 31, 1982, 5-6, as well as *Faculty Minutes*, Sept. 1, 1981, 7-14 and Dec. 1, 1981, 2.

[10]*College Days*, April 10, 1981, [1].

[11]*Ibid.*, 4-5.

[12]*Ibid.*, 3.

[13]*Ibid.*

[14]*Ibid.*, April 17, 1981, 2.

[15]*Faculty Minutes*, Nov. 4, 1980, [1], 5-7.

[16]*Trustees' Minutes*, Feb. 7, 1969, "Attachment D."

[17]*Ibid.*, Oct. 11, 1974, 8.

[18]*Ibid.*

[19]*President's Report 1977-78*, 3-4.

[20]*Faculty Minutes*, Dec. 1, 1981, 3, "Advisory Council Report."

[21]*Ibid.*, Feb. 2, 1982, 7, 8.

[22]*Executive Committee Minutes*, July 28, 1984, 1.

[23]*Faculty Minutes*, Feb. 7, 1984, attachment entitled "Faculty Salary Considerations," [1].

[24]*President's Report 1983-84*.

[25]*College Days*, Dec. 6, 1984, 9.

[26]*Executive Committee Minutes*, June 28, 1984, "Attachment A."

[27]*Ibid.*, "Attachment B."

[28]*Ibid.*, "Attachment C," 2.

[29]*Ibid.*, 3.

[30]*Ibid.*, 2.

[31]*Trustees' Minutes*, Feb. 2, 1985, 4.

[32]*Ibid.*, 11.

[33]*Ripon College Magazine*, June, 1984, 3.

[34]*College Days*, Feb. 15, 1985, 3.

[35]*Ibid.*, April 5, 1985, 4.

[36]*Annual Report of the College*, 1984-85, 1.

[37]*Ripon College Magazine*, March, 1985, 1.

[38]*Ibid.*, 7.

[39]*Ibid.*, 8.

[40]Figures supplied by Kenneth Cartier, Vice President for Finance.

CHAPTER XVIII

COMMENCEMENT
WILLIAM R. STOTT, JR.

The Board of Trustees selected William R. Stott, Jr., as Ripon's 10th president on March 15, 1985; ironically, Bernard Adams officially began his incumbency at Fort Lewis College on the very same date. A graduate of Georgetown University, with a master's degree from Columbia, Stott had served for nine years as vice president and dean of students at Georgetown; he left this position in the summer of 1985, took office at Ripon on July 1, and was inaugurated in October. He has an unusual combination of scholarly interests—ornithology and English literature, especially Shakespeare—and he is the only Ripon president in more than half a century to teach regular courses in the curriculum. He is also the first Roman Catholic ever to assume the presidency, a fact all the more remarkable since as recently as the late 1950s there had been concern over appointing a Catholic basketball coach; paradoxically, all basketball coaches since then have been Catholics, as is the director of athletics.

The new president moved quickly and vigorously to become acquainted with the entire campus community, to understand the problems he faced, and to outline goals for the future. Over the summer, he interviewed every member of the faculty and administration, asked each senior administrator "to walk the campus with a clipboard, a pencil, and a constructively critical eye,"[1] held a two-day retreat of the Administrative Council, and directed all academic departments "to consider their needs and to provide for the Dean of Faculty an analysis of . . . personnel, equipment or facilities . . . necessary for the improvement of their program." Later, the entire student body was polled "in order to determine their perceived needs." Recent reports of consultants were reviewed and new consultants "were engaged to formulate a master plan for landscaping, a survey of college-owned property, and the wage policy."[2] The result of all this activity was "A Case Statement" defining the mission and assessing the needs of the College; the Case Statement formed the basis "for a comprehensive and continuing long-range plan," which Stott identified as the "initial task . . . fundamental and crucial to Ripon College's future."[3]

President Stott has been the most able fund-raiser in Ripon College history. The three-year $13 million capital campaign has been a resounding success; endowment has increased from $9,853,733 in 1984-85 to $17,281,698 in 1988-89 and to $18 million before 1990. Over the same time span, Ripon's rank in the ACM salary scale has improved from 11th to ninth. All external debt has been retired.

The long-deferred rehabilitation of the Tri-Dorms finally has been accomplished. Bartlett Hall has been transformed from a dormitory to a student services center with a connecting link to the Harwood Union. The Union itself is currently undergoing renovation. When this is completed, attention will turn to the Memorial Gymnasium, the intent being to create a three-building student union, "a model of its kind"; a grant of $1.5 million from the Bradley Foundation has helped make this project possible.[4] The conversion of the Kemper Clinic to a computer center has already been mentioned.

Two chairs endowed by trustees have enabled the College to re-establish the major in religion and reintroduce classical studies: the Charles and Joan Van Zoeren Chair in Religion, Ethics, and Values and the Marie Zarwell Uihlein Chair in Classical Studies. Religion is a separate department, but classical studies are offered by a new combined Department of Romance and Classical Languages; most courses in classics are offered in English, but there are also basic language courses in Greek and Latin. A third trustee-endowed position—the Barbara Baldwin DeFrees Professorship in the Performing Arts—has underwritten a permanent position in the arts.

All of these efforts and successes, however, have not yet solved the enrollment problem. Improved retention has moderated the effect of small freshman classes, but the opening enrollment of 827 in 1987 was the smallest since 1964.

In the fall of 1988, Robert Abendroth resigned as chairman of the board, but remained a trustee. He had served on the board since 1965 and as chairman since 1969 and had guided the College through some of its most difficult years as well as years of considerable success and prosperity. His replacement is Robert Lambert '52, Senior Executive Vice President, Aviation, of Ryder System in Dallas, Texas, and a trustee since 1975.

Certainly, Ripon continues to face many of the problems that have provided challenges throughout the College's history. But, as President Stott has said,

> It is a good time to be at Ripon College. . . . My confidence in Ripon's ability to fulfill the dream inherent in its life to date is greater than ever. I have no doubt we are as well positioned as we could be in terms of fiscal prudence, institutional commitment, and belief in the future.[5]

NOTES TO CHAPTER XVIII
WILLIAM R. STOTT, JR.

[1]*President's Report 1985-86*, 3.

[2]*Ibid.*, 3.

[3]*Ibid.*, 1.

[4]*President's Report 1986-87*, 6.

[5]*Ibid.*, 7.

WORKS CITED

Baldwin, Theron. "Historical Sketch of the Society," *Proceedings at the Quarter-Century Anniversary of the Society for the Promotion of Collegiate and Theological Education at the West, Marietta, Ohio, November 7-10, 1868.* New York, The Trow and Smith Book Manufacturing Company, 1868.

Boody, H. Phillips. "Spencer Tracy at Ripon," *The Forensic of Pi Kappa Delta*, Jan., 1936, 38-39.

Catalogue. Catalogs of Ripon College, College Archives.

Clapp, H. L. "Reminiscences of Way Back When," *Way Back When.* Ripon, The Ripon Press, [1929], in College Archives.

College Charter. Acts and Resolves Passed by the Legislature of Wisconsin, 1851, Ch. 24.

College Days. Ripon student newspaper, College Archives.

Commonwealth-Press. Ripon weekly newspaper, Ripon Public Library.

Davis, Calvin O. *History of the North Central Association of Colleges and Secondary Schools, 1895-1945.* Ann Arbor, NCACSS, 1945.

Dictionary of Wisconsin Biography. Madison, The State Historical Society of Wisconsin, 1960.

Dopp, Pearl. *From the Top of a Secret Tree.* Chicago, Adams Press, 1979.

Evans Papers, College Archives.

Faculty Minutes, College Archives and office of the Vice President and Dean of Faculty.

Hofstadter, Richard, and Wilson Smith, eds. *American Higher Education: A Documentary History.* 2 vols. Chicago, The University of Chicago Press, 1961.

Hopkins, C. Howard, *John R. Mott, 1865-1955: A Biography.* Grand Rapids, Mich., Eerdmans, 1979.

Kuebler Papers, College Archives.

Mapes, David P. *History of the City of Ripon, and of Its Founder, David P. Mapes with His Opinion of Men and Manners of the Day.* Milwaukee, Cramer, Aikens and Cramer, 1873.

Merrell, Ada Clark. *Life and Poems of Clarissa Tucker Tracy.* Chicago, R. R. Donnelly and Sons, 1908.

Merrell, Edward H. "Ripon College," *Columbian History of Education in Wisconsin,* J. W. Stearns, ed. Milwaukee, The Evening Wisconsin Company, 1893, 154-88. Also printed separately as a pamphlet under the title *Ripon College: A Historical Sketch.* Ripon, *Ripon Free Press,* 1893. Page references are to the original.

Pedrick, Samuel M., and George H. Miller. *A History of Ripon, Wisconsin.* Ripon, Ripon Historical Society, 1964.

Pedrick Genealogies: "Biographical and statistical information relating to many families that have lived in Ripon and vicinity. Compiled by Samuel M. Pedrick from miscellaneous sources," College Archives.

Pickard, Dorothea Wilgus. *"Call Me Sam": A Biography of Samuel Nelson Pickard.* Madison, Wisconsin House, 1972.

President's Reports," College Archives.

Report from Ripon College, College Archives.

Ripon Alumnus, College Archives.

Ripon College Magazine, College Archives.

Ripon Herald. Weekly newspaper, Ripon Public Library.

Spencer, Jenny. "Bartlett Hall: Her Life and History." Independent study paper, Ripon College, 1983, College Archives.

Student Handbook., College Archives.

Swindell, Larry. *Spencer Tracy: A Biography.* New York, World Publishing Company, [1969].

Thompson, Paul J. "Silas Evans as a Student," *Ripon Alumnus,* XVII (June 1943), 11-13.

Tracy, Spencer. "Professor Boody Pointed My Nose Toward the Stage," *The Forensic of Pi Kappa Delta,* Jan., 1936, 37, 39.

Trustees' Minutes. Minutes of the Board of Trustees of Brockway College and Ripon College including miscellaneous committee and departmental reports College Archives and Office of the President.

Winnebago Convention Minutes. Winnebago District Convention of Presbyterian and Congregational Churches, 1851-68, Archives, State Historical Society of Wisconsin, Madison.

THE AUTHORS

The two collaborators on *Ripon College: A History* are accustomed to being "paired." For many years they team-taught the History Department's interdisciplinary course the American Civil War. On the occasion of the inauguration of President William R. Stott, Jr., in October, 1985, they both received honorary doctorates in humane letters.

George Miller was the first to arrive at Ripon. He had done his undergraduate work at the University of Michigan and, after a four-year hiatus for military service during World War II, earned graduate degrees in history at Michigan and Harvard. He taught for three years at Michigan before coming to Ripon in 1954. Among his published works are *A History of Ripon, Wisconsin,* with Samuel M. Pedrick, and *Railroads and the Granger Laws*. He has been a member of the Board of Curators of the State Historical Society of Wisconsin since 1980 and is currently serving as the society's president. He was the first recipient of the Ralph Hale Ruppert Distinguished Professorship of American History, Principles, and Traditions, which he held from 1976 until his retirement in 1981.

Robert Ashley came to Ripon a year later, having accepted appointment as dean of the College, professor of English, and coach of tennis. A graduate of Bowdoin College with advanced degrees from Harvard, he had previously taught at Harvard, Washington and Jefferson College, and the United States Military Academy. He retired as tennis coach in 1964 after winning a conference championship, as dean in 1974, and as an English professor in 1982. He was appointed the William Harley Barber Distinguished Professor in 1974 and served the first four-year term in that position. His off-campus activities include six years as commissioner of the Midwest Collegiate Athletic Conference, two years as secretary of the Wisconsin Association of Independent Colleges and Universities, and one year as chairman of the Wisconsin State Commission for Higher Educational Aids and chairman of the National Summer

Conference of Academic Deans. His publications include a biography of Wilkie Collins, author of the 19th-century British mystery classic *The Moonstone;* two civil war historical novels for teenagers; two high-school English texts (*Understanding the Novel*, with his daughter Dianne Ashley Per-Lee '64, and *The Bible as Literature*, with Ripon Chaplain Jerry Thompson), and several anthologies.

INDEX